Mongolia

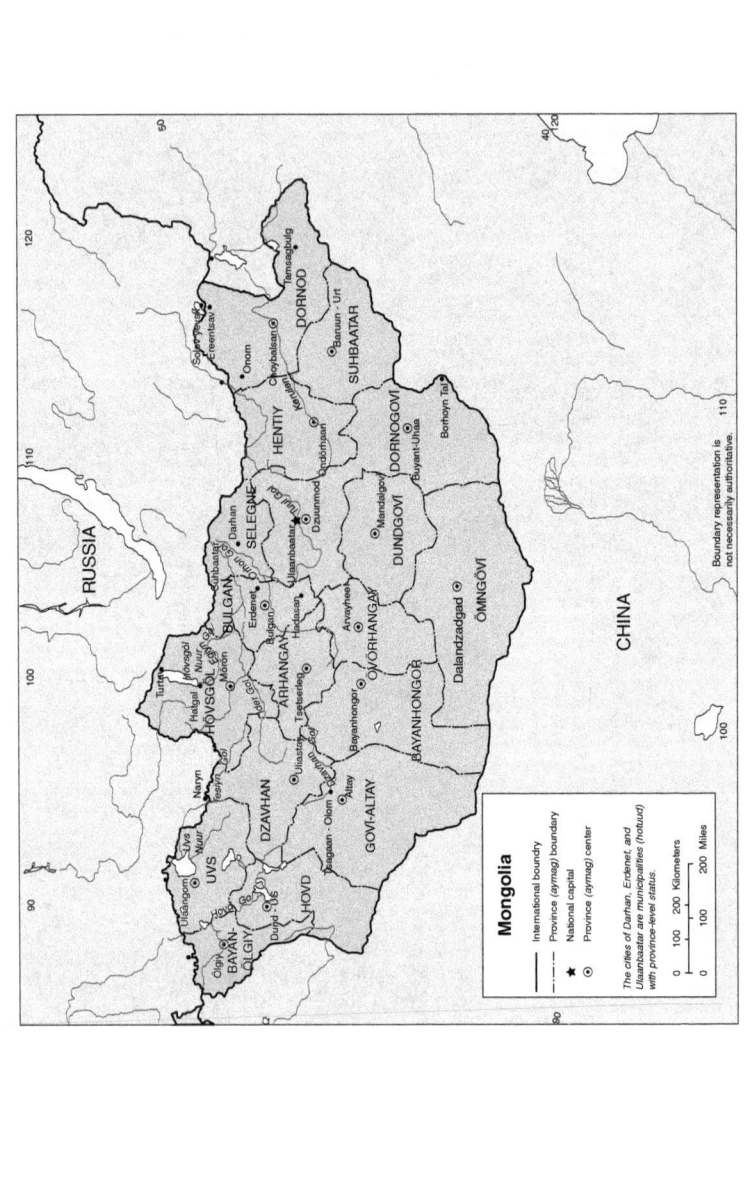

Mongolia

A Political History of the Land and Its People

Michael Dillon

I.B.TAURIS
LONDON • NEW YORK • OXFORD • NEW DELHI • SYDNEY

I.B. TAURIS
Bloomsbury Publishing Plc
50 Bedford Square, London, WC1B 3DP, UK
1385 Broadway, New York, NY 10018, USA

BLOOMSBURY, I.B. TAURIS and the I.B. Tauris logo are trademarks of
Bloomsbury Publishing Plc

First published in Great Britain 2020

Copyright © Michael Dillon, 2020

Michael Dillon has asserted his right under the Copyright, Designs
and Patents Act, 1988, to be identified as Author of this work.

Cover design by Adriana Brioso
Cover image © Joel Santos

All rights reserved. No part of this publication may be reproduced or
transmitted in any form or by any means, electronic or mechanical,
including photocopying, recording, or any information storage or retrieval
system, without prior permission in writing from the publishers.

Bloomsbury Publishing Plc does not have any control over, or responsibility for,
any third-party websites referred to or in this book. All internet addresses given
in this book were correct at the time of going to press. The author and publisher
regret any inconvenience caused if addresses have changed or sites have ceased
to exist, but can accept no responsibility for any such changes.

A catalogue record for this book is available from the British Library.

A catalog record for this book is available from the Library of Congress.

ISBN: HB: 978-1-7845-3549-0
PB: 978-1-8386-0670-1
ePDF: 978-1-7883-1695-8
eBook: 978-1-7883-1696-5

Typeset by Newgen KnowledgeWorks Pvt. Ltd., Chennai, India

To find out more about our authors and books visit www.bloomsbury.com
and sign up for our newsletters

Contents

Preface and Acknowledgements — vi

Introduction — 1
1. Mongolia and the Mongols: Land, people and traditions — 9
2. Revolutionary Mongolia in the early twentieth century — 43
3. Establishing the Mongolian People's Republic: Sükhbaatar and Choibalsan (1921–4) — 57
4. Mongolian People's Revolutionary Party in power: The Choibalsan years (1924–52) — 73
5. Post-War Mongolia: The Tsedenbal (1952–84) and Batmönkh (1984–90) years — 103
6. Democratic Revolution: Mongolia after the collapse of Soviet power (1991–2019) — 121
7. Collapse and recovery of the Mongolian economy — 139
8. Mongolia and the new East Asian order — 151
9. The Mongols and China: Inner Mongolia and Ulaanbaatar's relations with Beijing — 161
10. Looking back to the future: Mongolia's search for identity and the contemporary cult of Chinggis Khan — 175

Notes — 195
Bibliography — 209
Index — 215

Preface and Acknowledgements

In the course of just over a hundred years Mongolia has experienced the revolutions of 1911 and 1921; seventy years as a dependent state of the Soviet Union; and almost thirty years as a fully independent country. Despite the colossal changes that have taken place domestically and in the international context, one constant factor has been the need of its leadership to balance geopolitical pressures that have remained fundamentally unchanged. As far as I am aware no other book has attempted to cover this extended period.

Mongolia's experience is important as a case study of social and political revolution in an underdeveloped Asian society and, moreover, a society in which the predominant means of subsistence has been pastoral nomadism rather than settled agriculture. It was the prototype 'satellite' of the infant Soviet Union and, as a small nation sandwiched between the Russian bear and the Chinese dragon, the history of its struggle for nationhood and independence as it negotiated with its two powerful neighbours illustrates many of the pressures and compromises imposed by geopolitics.

I owe my original interest in Mongolia to lectures on Chinese history given by Owen Lattimore (1900–89) to undergraduates who followed the course in Chinese Studies that he established at the University of Leeds in 1963. Lattimore had moved to the United Kingdom after his contract at Johns Hopkins University was revoked as a result of the McCarthy hearings, one of the darkest periods in modern American history. As the pre-eminent Western Mongolist of his generation and the author of the seminal *Inner Asian Frontiers of China*, he naturally developed the study of Mongolia and the Mongol language in Leeds, and the relationship between China and Mongolia featured prominently in his teaching on China. Owen Lattimore's writings on Mongolia are classic texts, combining a profound knowledge of the country and its language and culture with sympathy for its people. He rejected the simplistic anti-Communism of the times but maintained a sceptical approach to the politics of Mongolia, and the Soviet Union to which it was so closely bound. While research and greater access to Mongolia since his death require some revision of his analysis, his approach remains of great value.[1] Another of my teachers of Chinese at Leeds was his colleague, Urgunge Onon, a Mongol from Manchuria, who had served as bodyguard to Prince Demchukdongrob and later became an eminent writer on Mongol matters and a translator of the *Secret History of the Mongols*.

As primarily a China specialist, my research interests and fieldwork have focused on the non-Han people of northern and north-western China, primarily the Hui Muslims of Ningxia and Gansu and the Uyghurs of Xinjiang, but also the Mongols of Inner Mongolia.

I first visited Mongolia in October 1990, as the authority of the Communist parties in the Soviet Union and its client states in Eastern Europe was collapsing, and Mongolia's drive to build a modern democracy and a developed economy was just beginning. During that visit I was privileged to attend the inaugural meeting of the Mongolian Association of Sinologists and to stay in the State Guest House across the Tuul River to the south of Ulaanbaatar. After academic exchanges and meetings with political leaders and government officials, the conference delegates, most of them from China, toured the grasslands. For the invitation and organization of this visit, hospitality at the Ikh Tengger State Guest House and discussions on relations between Mongolia and China, I am grateful to H. Ayurzana and his colleagues in the Ministry of Foreign Affairs and the Mongolian Association of Sinologists. From the government, there was support from the then First Deputy Prime Minister Ganbold who attended the conference and Deputy Prime Minister Purevdorj. There were no other Western participants at the conference and I was adopted as an honorary member of the Chinese delegation. This gave me an unusual opportunity to observe Chinese attitudes towards Mongolia and relations between Chinese and Mongols.

My most recent visit to Mongolia in September 2016 enabled me to familiarize myself with current developments and to collect recent publications on the history of Mongolia. In Ulaanbaatar, I am grateful to the staff of the Choijin Lama Museum, the Winter Palace of the Bogd Khan and the National Museum of Mongolia for their assistance.

During the 1990s I also carried out research among the Mongol population in neighbouring China, both in Inner Mongolia which is home to far more Mongols than live in Mongolia and in the Ili region of the Xinjiang Uyghur Autonomous Region – Xinjiang has a designated Mongol prefecture, although the proportion of ethnic Mongols has been drastically reduced by Chinese migration. I am grateful to Ma Ping of the Ningxia Academy of Social Sciences in Yinchuan for assistance with my research in Inner Mongolia and for facilitating an expedition to the Alxa (Alashan) region.

I have previously written about Mongolia and its relations with China in *China: A Modern History* and on the Mongols of Inner Mongolia in *Religious Minorities in China*; 'Unrest in Inner Mongolia May 2011', a briefing paper for the European External Action Service; and *Lesser Dragons*, a book on the minorities of China.

I am fortunate to have been able to draw on papers on contemporary and historical Mongolian culture presented by Mongolian scholars at a conference arranged by the Niedersächsiche Staats-und Universitätsbibliothek Göttingen in 2015, organized by the librarian Dr Johannes Reckel, himself a considerable scholar of matters Mongolian. I have drawn on the work of many Mongolian Studies specialists; in addition to the books by Owen Lattimore that have been referred to, the writings of Fujiko Isono, Tom Ewing, Charles Bawden, Morris Rossabi and Alan Sanders have been particularly valuable.

At I.B. Tauris I am very grateful for the support and assistance of Tomasz Hoskins and Nayiri Kendir. I have also benefited greatly from the detailed and constructive comments of anonymous readers, whose observations and suggestions I have incorporated where possible.

Sherwood Forest
August 2019

Introduction

Contemporary Mongolia rarely features in the Western media, or even in the consciousness of most Westerners, although there is a persistent folk memory in Europe of the threat posed by what are invariably referred to as Mongol 'hordes' to mediaeval Christendom. The name of Chinggis Khan is often invoked – even if normally in his Persian or Turkic guise as Genghis – as the epitome of a violent and reactionary ruler. In many works on the history and culture of Asia written in the last few decades, the Mongols appear as an exotic and ancient people, with little indication that they might be in any way connected with the population of present-day Mongolia. For example, *The Mongols*, written by the classicist E. D. Phillips and a useful summary of the period under Chinggis Khan and his successors, was published in 1969. It was included in a series under the rubric *Ancient Peoples and Places* and even the epilogue, which endeavours to bring the story up to date, does not hint at anything beyond the fall of the Chinese Empire after the collapse of the Qing dynasty in 1911. Even David Morgan's otherwise excellent book, *The Mongols*, published in 1986 and rightly admired for the use of Persian chronicles, devotes only a chapter of only eight pages on 'What Became of the Mongols?': only the last page and a half covers the twentieth century.[1]

Outside Mongolia, the authentic history of the Mongols is no more familiar than the present-day reality, but that history, and the changing way in which it is remembered, has had a profound effect on contemporary social, economic and political developments in Mongolia and on the way in which Mongolia is perceived by the outside world. J. Boldbaatar of Ulaanbaatar University has reflected on the changes in the approach of Mongolians to their history in a short essay for the International Institute for Asian Studies in 2015. He argues that before 1990 Mongolian historians had been constrained by a version of the crude Marxist periodization that was the approved academic standard in the USSR. In recent years, after the collapse of Soviet power, they were able to adopt a more judicious approach and began to move towards a schema similar to that used in the West. In this newer representation, the immense span of time from the earliest known human settlement through to the twelfth century CE is characterized as the ancient and early mediaeval period. The subsequent mediaeval and post-mediaeval period includes the emergence of a distinctive Mongolian state and its downfall. This is usually divided into the imperial period of the thirteenth and fourteenth centuries; the dissolution of the Chinggisid Empire from the end of the fourteenth to the beginning of the seventeenth century; and the Qing period when the Mongols were formally a vassal people subservient to the empire of the Manchus who also ruled China. Modern Mongolian history does not begin until the twentieth century. This contemporary attempt at a more generally acceptable periodization has been sketched with a broad brush and, in their determination to abandon the old Soviet ways, some historical babies have been jettisoned with the bathwater of Stalinist historiography. Mongolian historians still struggle to find satisfactory explanations for historical changes, notably the underlying cause of the revolutionary period of 1911–1924; the emergence of an authoritarian and often brutal regime in the 1930s; and its eventual collapse of 1990.[2] The construction of a new and independent narrative of this history has played an important part in the transformation of the country from the Mongolian People's Republic (MPR) into simply Mongolia.

When Mongolia is mentioned at all in the West, it is generally dismissed as a small and insignificant country, dominated by its powerful neighbours, China and Russia. It is undeniably small, but only in terms of its population and that population is growing rapidly. In 2019 there were just over 3.24 million Mongolian citizens, of whom 1.4 million lived in the capital, Ulaanbaatar, almost half the total population of the country. Mongolia was traditionally a rural country but today, largely because of that concentration in the capital, over 70 per cent of the population live in urban areas.[3] The population passed the 3 million mark in 2015, and a girl born on 24 January in Ömnogövi Province in the south of Mongolia was identified as the three millionth Mongolian. At the request of her parents, the then President, Elbegdorj, conferred on her the name Mongoljin and presented her, and 181 children born on the same day, with money and other gifts. Special postage stamps were issued on 28 January to mark the occasion. Mongoljin is a name with a long historical pedigree; it appears at the very beginning of the *Secret History of the Mongols* in the genealogy of Chinggis Khan. Mongoljin ('the fairest of the Mongols' in Urgungge Onon's translation of the book that he calls *The Golden History of the Mongols*) was the wife of Borjigidai-mergen, one of Chinggis Khan's ancestors and the name has also been translated as 'Mongolian lady' and 'Mongolian queen'. Unlike its southern neighbour, China, which for decades implemented the controversial one-child policy to restrict population growth, an increase in the number of its citizens is a high priority for the government of Mongolia.[4]

Between Russia and China

The current population of Mongolia might be small, but it occupies an immense tract of land. The dramatic scenery of the Mongolian countryside, with its expanses of grassland, mountains, desert and semi-desert, impresses visitors by its vastness and its emptiness. Mongolia is only slightly smaller than Iran and appreciably larger than either Turkey or France. It is however the country's strategic location rather than its size, that largely determines its role in the modern world.

Mongolia is entirely landlocked so it is inevitable that its history has been linked with, if not determined by, the histories of the only two countries with which it has international borders – China and Russia (Imperial Russia until 1917, the Soviet Union between 1922 and 1991 and thereafter the Russian Federation). Although these two great powers have overshadowed Mongolia for centuries, its role in Asia has not been insignificant. For many centuries the destiny of the Mongol people depended almost entirely on the relationship of their leaders with successive Chinese dynasties. By the nineteenth century Mongolia also had to contend with the eastward expansion of Tsarist Russia: maintaining a state of equilibrium under pressure from both China and Russia became a high priority. In the early twentieth century the westward expansion of the Japanese Empire further complicated this relationship. When that expansion ended in 1945, with the defeat of the militarist Japanese government at the end of the Second World War, the Soviet Union emerged as the dominant power in Asia, although diminished by the ravages of war; it fulfilled a similar role to that played by the Tsarist Russian Empire prior to 1917. Soon there was countervailing pressure from the People's Republic of China (PRC) which was inaugurated in 1949 after the armies of the Chinese Communist Party defeated the Chinese Nationalists, the Guomindang, in a civil war. During the 1950s Mongolia sought to maintain good relations with China; initially both Communist governments were tied economically and politically to the Soviet Union. Mongolia's relations with Beijing soured in the late 1950s as Mao Zedong steered the PRC away from Soviet-style planning and launched the radical and ultimately disastrous experiments of the Great Leap Forward and the Cultural Revolution.

Mongolia's interactions with Russia and China have never been on an equal basis and they have been complicated by the presence within both those countries of significant communities of ethnic Mongols – notably in Russia's Buryatia and China's Inner Mongolia. Traditionally, China was regarded as the greater threat to Mongol autonomy and Russia as the weaker but useful countervailing power. The balance changed in the twentieth century as the

Soviet Union established itself as one of the two major world powers, in an antagonistic relationship with the United States. In that period Mongolia's political history was marked by conflicts between ideologies and internal factions over the creation of a nominally independent modern state, the fate of which seemed inextricably and eternally linked to that of the USSR.

After the collapse of the Soviet Union in 1991 this bond was severed abruptly and new links had to be forged with the successor states of the USSR and other neighbouring countries. Although the Russian Federation that emerged from this collapse gradually became stronger economically, it has not so far caught up with China. Beijing became a crucial source of financial support for Mongolia but was also treated warily: not only was it the new and undisputed regional superpower, it also had long-standing and unresolved territorial claims on Mongol lands. Political relations between Mongolia and China gradually recovered, but Ulaanbaatar had to accept the reality of its newly powerful neighbour deploying economic might and political influence vastly greater than that of the newly emerging Russian state. Mongolia also had to negotiate new diplomatic and commercial relationships with its near neighbours – Japan and North and South Korea. In the face of such conflicting pressures from these diverse neighbours, the political history of Mongolia since the collapse of the USSR has inevitably been dominated by its struggle to retain and assert its own identity.

From nomads and commissars to regional power brokers

After the revolution of 1921 and the proclamation of the Mongolian People's Republic (MPR) in 1924, Mongolia's independence of China was ensured and it experienced remarkable and sometimes bewildering economic, political and social changes. Owen Lattimore, who had travelled through Inner Mongolia and Manchuria on camel and by car during the 1930s and knew the Mongols of those regions and their language well, made his first extended visit to the MPR in 1961. He had spent three days in Ulaanbaatar in 1944 when he had accompanied the American vice president, Henry A. Wallace, on a wartime mission, but as he pointed out, 'three days does not add up to a claim to first-hand knowledge'. It did give him the opportunity to meet the prime minister, Choibalsan, briefly – and greet him in Mongol – in a pavilion-sized Mongol *ger* where the delegation was received and housed.[5] Mongolia was by then a well-established one-party state, controlled by the Mongolian People's Revolutionary Party (MPRP), and had just been admitted to the United Nations, in spite of the rigorous opposition of the Nationalist Chinese Guomindang regime in Taiwan which still considered Mongolia to be part of

China. In Lattimore's important study, *Nomads and Commissars: Mongolia Revisited*, which resulted from this visit, he compared the pastoral and nomadic society that he had known when he had crossed the Gobi desert in the 1930s with the changes that followed the intervention of the MPRP and its commissars, leading to what he described as Mongolia's 'satellite' relationship with the USSR; this was probably the first use of that term.[6]

That altered society, with some changes of personnel and internal reforms that reflected the shifting political culture of the Soviet Union during and after the Stalin era, persisted until 1991. After the collapse of the Soviet Union, the MPRP which had been almost entirely dependent on the support of Moscow lost its monopoly of political power in an upheaval now called the democratic revolution, but effectively a counter-revolution as it overturned the state structure established in the 1920s. In the 1990s, Mongolia endured a period of uncertainty and instability, during which a large proportion of the population suffered from desperate poverty and deprivation. Gradually there emerged a viable if flawed economy, a flourishing but chaotic parliamentary structure and electoral system, and a deeply divided society.

The government has never been able to extricate the economy completely from the crisis of the early 1990s. As recently as 2015, the minister of foreign affairs, Purevsuren Lundeg, speaking at the foreign affairs think tank Chatham House in London, conceded that, despite its recent economic boom, Mongolia was facing serious economic and financial challenges. He set out the government's efforts to overcome these difficulties, arguing that Mongolia was and would remain an attractive country for investors. He also emphasized that the Ulaanbaatar government intended to pursue an active and long-term role in international affairs and insisted that its only appropriate stance was one of permanent neutrality. Mongolia, he argued, would consequently be in a strong position to use its soft power to broker relations between the countries of East Asia.[7]

Searching for a modern Mongolian identity

A modern economy and society are emerging in Mongolia and it is increasingly aiming to play an important but still largely untested role as a pivot, or intermediary, in its home region of north-eastern Asia. At the same time, it is determined to preserve, or recover, essential features of its traditional Mongol identity. In Ulaanbaatar and many other cities, hundreds of the traditional *ger* tents of the nomadic tradition continue to exist alongside modern high-rise buildings. On one level this reflects the poverty of many Mongols, often members of nomad families displaced from the rural areas who live on the margins of the cities in communities of *ger*, homes and the lack of resources available to house them. However, in Ulaanbaatar and other large cities, many modern buildings make provision for a *ger* on a roof or in an annexe, a symbol of continuity and respect for Mongol tradition. For many years the State Guest House proudly displayed a *ger* on a flat roof.

Countless buildings remain from the era of greatest Soviet influence (the 1960s to the late 1980s). Many are architecturally undistinguished but others have stood the test of time. The public and the government are ambivalent towards this period of Mongolian history; it is undeniably modern but, equally undeniably, it represents an expression of modernity that is of Soviet, or occasionally pre-Soviet Russian, inspiration rather than Mongolian. For many Mongolian politicians, retrieving or recreating a Mongol form of modernity has been a high priority. Some streets in Ulaanbaatar that were named after revolutionary heroes, or too obviously reflected Mongolia's close links with the Soviet Union, have been renamed, reflecting new alignments and a rejection of the Communist past. As is common in these cases, the older names remain in use by the general public and it is not certain for how long the new names will persist. Natsagdorj Street, which was named after the leading officially approved writer of the Socialist period, became Seoul Street, indicating the low-key but growing influence of South Korean businesses in Mongolia. The most striking example of this attempt to reclaim the pre-Soviet past is the renaming of the main square in Ulaanbaatar. It was built as Sükhbaatar Square to honour the hero of the 1921 revolution but renamed Chinggis Khan Square after the 1991 revolution. In 2016 it reverted to its original name – which most people in the capital had continued to use anyway.

The struggle to establish a modern Mongolian identity coexists with a rising commercialization that has dramatically increased inequality. This is immediately apparent in the capital where children from prosperous families, attending international schools and wearing British-style school uniforms, share the pavements with poorly dressed street kids, beggars, hawkers and pickpockets, although admittedly there are fewer of these than there were ten or twenty years ago. There is a very marked social division in housing: luxurious city-centre developments cater for the wealthy professional class and executives of foreign firms while, as has been noted, the expanding *ger* communities on the outskirts of the city, which were expected to be a temporary phenomenon, provide the only accommodation that the poorer section of the population can afford; this includes many public sector employees working for modest incomes.

Modern Mongolia is a work in progress and a balancing act. Mongolians are determined to be part of the modern world. They reject much of what now appears as an outmoded Soviet culture that was imposed on them, although they are inclined to retain selected aspects of that culture, such as ballet and opera, albeit in a modified national form where possible. They are willing to experiment with economic and social models borrowed from the West, but are determined to retain and strengthen their traditional cultural heritage by exploring and reinventing areas of their history that have been hidden or understated for decades.

1

Mongolia and the Mongols: Land, people and traditions

Mongolia and the Mongolian people

What is Mongolia and who are the Mongols? The answers to these questions are not as simple or as obvious as it might seem. Many different communities identify themselves as Mongol; most are in or close to present-day Mongolia, but some are long settled in lands far beyond the present-day borders of Mongolia, primarily in Russia and China.

Mongolia today (*Mongol Uls* in modern Mongolian) is the successor to the former Mongolian People's Republic (MPR, *Bügd Nairamdag Mongol Ard Uls*), which lasted from 1924 to 1992. Before the revolution of 1921 it was a semi-autonomous region of China, known as Outer Mongolia on account of its great distance from Beijing. Most of the remaining Mongol territories are in Inner Mongolia, which is much closer to Beijing and is today part of the People's Republic of China (PRC); the greater part of traditional Inner Mongolia is officially known as the Inner Mongolian Autonomous Region, other parts having been hived off into neighbouring provinces. This region is home to a considerable population of Mongols, 4.2 million at the time of the Chinese 2010 census. This is greater than the population of independent Mongolia, which did not reach the figure of 3 million until 2015. Although Inner Mongolia is therefore home to far more Mongolians than Mongolia, they are in a minority as they constitute less than 20 per cent of the total population which is dominated by 20 million Han Chinese. By contrast the 3 million inhabitants of Mongolia consider themselves to be overwhelmingly Mongolian, although many families are the result of mixed marriages with Buryat Mongols, Russians or Chinese.

There are also substantial communities of ethnic Mongols living in other parts of China, in the north of the Xinjiang Uyghur Autonomous Region and the province of Qinghai, and there is a smaller population in Gansu and in north-eastern China, the region formerly known as Manchuria.

Buryatia is a republic within the Russian Federation and lies to the north of Mongolia. Although the great majority of the population of that republic is

Russian, Buryat Mongols constitute about 30 per cent and both the present-day Russian Federation and its predecessor in the USSR, the Buryat Mongol Autonomous Soviet Socialist Republic, were named after them. Although the language of the Buryats belongs to the Mongolian language family, and some of its dialects are close to the Khalkh Mongol of Mongolia, they are often treated as a distinct group and not always accepted as 'pure' Mongol.[1] These distinctions are significant as Buryats played a crucial and controversial role in links with Russia during the Mongolian revolution in the 1920s and in the development of the MPR.

In the 1960s Owen Lattimore commented on the strained relations between Buryat Mongols and the Mongols of Mongolia who mainly belong to the Khalkh sub-group. He concluded that the migration of Buryats into Siberia and their closer relations with Russians had made them, as far as the Mongols of Mongolia were concerned, 'less Mongol'. The original name Buryat Mongol Republic was replaced by Buryat Republic for this reason:

> When Buryats use the term 'Mongol', it means for them 'the larger family of which we are an offshoot'; but the Mongols of Mongolia, if they grant the name 'Mongol' to the Buryats at all, do so a little doubtfully, and this has been true for some centuries. For them the name 'Buryat' means very definitely 'people who are different from us Mongols'.[2]

Mongolians, Mongols and Mongolia

Even the names 'Mongolian' and 'Mongol' are problematic. Mongolians refer to themselves as *Mongol* and their language as *Mongol xel* in the standard Khalkh Mongolian of Mongolia, but that term is complicated by the fact that in the West, for at least a century, 'Mongol' and 'Mongolism' were used as descriptions of the genetic anomaly that is now almost universally known as Down's or Down syndrome. That usage originated in the middle of the nineteenth century and reflected not only an insensitive approach to those people with the syndrome, but also the crude classification of ethnic groups that was in vogue at that time. Most of the population of eastern Asia were aggregated under the undifferentiated category of 'Mongolian' or 'Mongoloid'. It was thought in the West that people with Down's syndrome had a facial resemblance to eastern Asians so the name was applied to them.

By the 1960s it had been realized that the use of these terms was offensive, both to people with Down's syndrome and to Mongolians, who did not exhibit this syndrome and considered it to be a racial slur. The embarrassment grew with the increasing participation of Asian professionals in international organizations, and correspondents to medical journals proposed that an alternative designation be adopted. Following its admission to the United Nations on 27 October 1961, the MPR became a member of the World Health Organization (WHO): in 1965 its government wrote formally to the director-general of the WHO requesting that such an offensive term should no longer be used. The usage was eliminated from WHO documents forthwith and disappeared from professional communications during the 1970s, although it persisted in common use in the English-speaking world well into the 1980s and has not entirely disappeared in casual usage.[3]

'Mongolian' and 'Mongol' can be used interchangeably but it is convenient to restrict the use of 'Mongolian' to the citizens of the independent state of Mongolia; 'Mongol' can be used to describe more generally those who speak Mongolian (*Mongol xel*) or one of the related Mongolic languages, or identify themselves as Mongols. The Mongolian plural, *Mongolchuud*, 'Mongols', is also sometimes used in a more general sense to mean 'the Mongols', including all those who possess 'Mongolness'.

Historic Mongol lands

During their long and often turbulent history, and as a consequence of their nomadic lifestyle, proficiency on horseback and their military prowess, different groups of Mongols have been able to inhabit or control various widely separated tracts of territory across the whole of Eurasia from Manchuria to the basin of the Volga River in south-western Russia. This does not mean that they controlled the entire area over which their search for pasture and power took them and indeed in pre-modern times there was really no such thing as a Mongol state. As the eminent British Mongolist, Charles Bawden, pointed out, 'at the most generous estimate it would be anachronistic to speak of a Mongol state, in the modern sense of the word, as existing before the end of 1911.'[4]

The primary focus of this book is on the contemporary successor of that state which was created in 1911, the present-day territory of Mongolia, which is the former MPR and is often still referred to as Outer Mongolia. As the only state controlled entirely by Mongols it has a strong case to be considered as the centre of Mongolian culture, especially political culture, both historically as the home of the ancient capital Karakorum and in the present day. Mongolia is a small country with a population at the beginning of 2019 estimated to be 3,200,000: this number is growing at a rate of 1.44 per cent per annum. Almost 95 per cent of the population are ethnic Mongols, who are mostly professed Lama Buddhists in the Tibetan tradition. However, shamanism, the complex belief system of the Mongols and other north-east Asian peoples that long preceded the introduction of Buddhism, has played and continues to play a central role in Mongol culture, complementing and often influencing the variety of Tibetan Buddhism practised in Mongolia. Although the overwhelming majority of Mongols are Buddhists by tradition, if not always by practice, there is a small Muslim community in the west of Mongolia, most of whom are ethnic Kazakhs, although some identify as Mongols.

Two other Mongol regions that have also been mentioned will be covered in less detail. Four million Mongols live in neighbouring Inner Mongolia, which since 1947 has been the Inner Mongolian Autonomous Region of the PRC. There are, as has been noted, more Mongols in Inner Mongolia than in independent Mongolia, although in the autonomous region they only constitute about 20 per cent of a total regional population of nearly 25 million. The vast majority of the population of Inner Mongolia are Han Chinese and the minority status of Mongols in the region formally designated as their homeland has given rise to concerns that Mongol language, culture and their traditional pastoral way of life, are under threat. In Mongolia itself, where the population is almost entirely Mongolian, there is no such threat, especially since the demise of the Soviet Union which had introduced into the MPR many facets of Russian language and culture. The state that is now called simply Mongolia can legitimately present itself as a champion of modern Mongol culture. The other significant Mongol community is settled in the Republic of Buryatia, currently an autonomous republic within the Russian Federation and with its capital at Ulan Ude (*Ulaan Üüde*, Red Gate). This Buryat republic lies to the north of Mongolia and borders the eastern and northern shores of Lake Baikal: its population today is approximately 30 per cent Mongol and 70 per cent Russian.

Mongols and their languages

The people who live in Mongolia and the other Mongol regions and are referred to simply as Mongols or Mongolians belong in reality to a multitude of different tribal confederations: the principal ones are the Khalkh, Oirats, Buryats and Kalmyks, Barga, and the Chahar (together with other southern Mongols). The Khalkh (or Khalkha) Mongols are the majority in Mongolia and their language, Khalkh Mongolian, has been adopted as the national standard in that country. Other varieties of Mongolian are treated as dialects although some, like Buryat, Oirat and Kalmuk, claim the status of separate languages. In Inner Mongolia, which is part of China, the official standard language is known as Southern Mongolian. This is based on a group of

Southern Mongolian dialects that include Chahar, Ordos, Baarin, Khorchin, Kharchin and Alasha. There is, as might be expected, a continuum of comprehensibility between these different spoken forms of Mongolian and the Inner Mongolian standard pronunciation is based on a southern dialect that, conveniently, is not too different from the speech of Ulaanbaatar.

The differences between the languages of Mongolia and Inner Mongolia are accentuated by the different scripts that are used, neither of which has any connection or any similarity to the Chinese script. The Mongols of Inner Mongolia, who live in a predominantly Chinese language environment and for practical purposes need to be bilingual, retain the traditional vertical script which dates back to the thirteenth century and slightly resembles Arabic turned through ninety degrees. This offers a clue to its distant origins in the ancient Syriac script that was used in the Middle East to write one of the Semitic languages, Aramaic. Mongolia on the other hand uses the Cyrillic alphabet that was introduced by the Russians during the country's long association with the Soviet Union. Since 1991 there has been a formal commitment to restore the traditional script in Mongolia but, although it has been reintroduced to the school curriculum, it is rarely used other than as ornamentation.[5]

From world conquerors to marginalized nomadic tribes

All Mongols are acutely aware of, and most are proud to recognize, the continuing influence of the legacy of Chinggis Khan, the 'world-conqueror' who is better known in the West by the Persian or Turkish version of his name – Genghis. He began the expansion of the Mongol world in the thirteenth century, when he succeeded in unifying the disparate and warring Mongol tribes and laid the foundations for the creation of an empire that stretched westwards as far as Europe. While the brutality and slaughter that resulted from this enterprise are acknowledged in Mongolia today, there is a sense that, behind the state's modernizing and developmental projects, it is necessary to recover at least some of the former greatness of the Chinggis Khan era.

Mongol pride in the military and diplomatic achievements of Chinggis Khan and his successors was not necessarily shared by those who were the objects of the conquering armies. The Mongol Empire was extended under his heirs, notably his successor as Great Khan, Ögödei Khan; Tolui Khan who controlled the original native territory of the Mongols; Chagatai Khan who ruled Central Asia and parts of what is now Iran and whose name lives on in the Turkic Chagatai language that was the lingua franca of the steppes until the nineteenth century; and the *khans* Batu and Orda whose territory brought the Mongol Empire to its furthest western extent on the frontiers of Europe. Relatively small numbers of Mongols took part in the military conquest of these regions so the victors were obliged to administer their new territories by recruiting officials from the local elites. As a result, the Mongolian language was never as important in those far-flung parts as the local languages of their subordinate administrators. Persian was the language not only of the territory that we know today as Persia or Iran but of much of Central Asia and was also used in the north of India and Afghanistan where a local version of Persian survives as Dari. It was the single most important of the written languages of the region and Persian-language sources afford invaluable insights into the rule of the Mongols; there are few comparable extant documents in the Mongolian language. As their name suggests, the Mughal emperors of the Indian subcontinent were of Mongol origin; they were the descendants of the Mongol emperor, Timur.[6]

Almost all Asia was affected to a greater or lesser degree by the Mongols. Their conquest of the continent was brutal and pitiless and the loss of life colossal. Traditional ways of life, especially those of cultured urban societies, were devastated, or in some cases eradicated. The best known example of the devastation wrought by the conquering Mongols was the sacking by the armies of Hulegu in 1258, and again by Timur in 1401, of the city of Baghdad. Being the capital of the Abbasid Caliphate, it was also the symbolic centre of Muslim culture and its destruction by the Mongols was a bitter blow to the authority of Islam in its heartland. The architectural heritage of the city was obliterated; the great library known as the House of Wisdom was destroyed and its contents cast into the River Tigris.

The Mongols were nomads and warriors and appeared to have no interest in preserving or rebuilding the urban civilizations that they sacked. The best architects and builders from the subjugated lands were, however, transported back to the Mongol heartlands where they were enslaved and obliged to build new cities for their conquerors. In spite of the destruction during the conquests, enough of the previously existing Islamic urban culture survived; the khanates that were imposed by the victors after the invasion were not replicas of the steppe society of the original Mongols but hybrid cultures that blended traditional Central Asian and Muslim elements.[7]

In China the Yuan dynasty was the official ruling house from 1271 to 1368. It was founded by the Mongol Khubilai Khan from his palace in Shangdu (Xanadu) which was close to the site of the modern town of Duolun in the Xilingol League of Inner Mongolia. Khubilai Khan re-established his capital at Khanbalig (Dadu in Chinese), on the site of modern Beijing, from where – as Great Khan – he claimed to exercise sovereignty over the whole of the Mongol Empire, although what would become a prolonged process of fragmentation had already begun. Although they proclaimed themselves to be a Chinese dynasty, and in spite of multifarious commercial and other contacts with the Chinese, the Mongol ruling elite were never fully Sinicized. They kept their distance from the native Chinese population and relied for administration, architecture and many other services on imported Central Asian officials, most of whom were Muslims. Chinese people tend to have a negative view of the Yuan dynasty, which they regard as a 'barbarian' conquest regime. The Mongols were finally driven out of China by the predominantly Han Chinese Ming dynasty in 1368 and, after this serious military reverse, they withdrew to the relative security of their steppe homeland. They strengthened their traditional tribal social and political structures and harassed the military forces of the Ming. Preventing further attempts by the Mongols to reconquer China was a high priority of the Ming dynasty and an important part of its defensive strategy was to strengthen the existing Great Wall network and garrison the border regions with communities that combined the roles of soldiers and farmers. Mongol armies never again posed a serious threat to the Chinese throne.[8]

Even after the Ming came to power as a 'Chinese' dynasty, the influence of the previous rulers was not completely eradicated. Many aspects of the Mongol administration remained in place, including the use of Muslim intermediaries, who were particularly valued at the imperial court for their specialist knowledge of astronomy. The Ming ruling house eventually collapsed after internal factional strife and peasant rebellions: an army of the Manchus, the main historical steppe nomad rivals of the Mongols, 'entered the passes' and marched on Beijing to establish a new dynasty, the Qing, in 1644; to the Chinese this was another 'barbarian' conquest regime. The heirs of Chinggis Khan who had appeared as the all-conquering masters of Asia were now marginalized and confined to the frontiers of China.

Legend of Chinggis Khan

The remembrance of Chinggis Khan remains a central part of Mongol consciousness and is often revived to breathe new life into national sentiment. In the 1930s Owen Lattimore travelled from China into the Ordos region of Inner Mongolia, which lies in the great loop of the Yellow River, in search of the legendary 'sanctuary' of Chinggis Khan at Ejen Horo (*Ezen Xorij*, the Camp or Enclosure of the Lord). In his book, *Mongol Journeys* he relates several versions of legends that describe the death of Chinggis Khan. Although they differ in detail, they all involve him taking a woman against her will, or at least against the wishes of her husband or father, and being castrated and killed when she drew out a knife concealed in her clothing.

Being Chinggis Khan, however, he did not remain dead but disappeared to recuperate so that he could re-emerge when he was required to be the saviour of the Mongol people in times of distress. There are parallels in these stories with the Hidden Imam in the traditions of Twelver Shi'a Islam, or King Arthur in the mediaeval texts known as the Matter of Britain. Beyond these legends there is no hard evidence to corroborate the stories that he died in the manner described but that part of his legend is a powerful metaphor for the condition of the Mongols following the decline of the Chinggisid Empire after the fourteenth century; emasculated by defeat at the hands of the Chinese and reduced to vassal status under the Manchus during the last dynasty of imperial China, the Qing (1644–1911).

There is considerable doubt over whether Ejen Horo was in reality his final resting place, but it became, and has remained, the centre of a cult of Chinggis Khan. Anthropologists reported that religious offerings and pledges of allegiance to the 'world conqueror' were made there by patriotic Mongols shortly after the end of the Second World War as a symbol of Mongol identity. Lattimore participated in, and described in great detail, the complex manoeuvres and intricate rituals that characterized what was as much a political ceremony, a durbar or a jamboree, as a spiritual one. It is impossible to be certain whether these rituals arose from the legend or whether the legend was constructed to explain the rituals.

For the rulers of independent Mongolia, it is politically inconvenient that Ejen Horo, the main centre of Chinggis Khan veneration, does not lie within their national boundaries but in Chinese territory. However another claimant for the resting place of the great warrior, the mountain of Burkhan Khaldun in the Khentii province to the north-east of Ulaanbaatar, does lie in the territory of modern Mongolia. It would be of great benefit for the government in Ulaanbaatar if that claim could be supported by archaeological evidence, but so far none has emerged to substantiate the legends. The tradition that the mountain is a place of spiritual significance long predates the death of Chinggis Khan, who instructed that it was the birthplace of his ancestors and should be revered by his descendants. Shamanic rituals, which for centuries had been performed in front of the sacred mound at its summit, but were banned during the religious persecution of the 1930s, were revived in 2003 and the mountain was declared a World Heritage Site in 2015.[9]

Mongols in the Chinese Empire of the Manchu Qing

Although they are remembered for their wide-ranging conquests, those enterprises were not in the long term a triumph for the Mongols; their military and political forces were overextended, far beyond the limits of their resources: 'The imperial adventure under [Chinggis] Khan and his successors left the Mongols exhausted and disunited politically, and in the seventeenth century they fell, piecemeal, under Manchu domination which continued for over two hundred years'.[10]

The Qing, as the Manchus named their conquest dynasty in China, expanded, at first gradually and then dramatically, to include territory to the west and north of China in which, in addition to Tibetans and Turkic Uyghurs, there were sizeable Mongol communities. In the ethnic hierarchy of China under the Qing dynasty (1644–1911), Mongols were in theory second in importance to their Manchu rulers. As northern nomadic and martial peoples with a religious background of Lama Buddhism and shamanism, their beliefs and culture were much closer to those of the Manchus than to either Muslims or Han Chinese. That does not mean that relations between the two peoples were easy. Some Mongol princes rejected Manchu suzerainty and failed to comply with imperial Manchu protocol and instructions. The political elite of the Qing dynasty has often been referred to by Western historians as a 'diarchy' of Manchu nobles and Han Chinese officials but relations between those élites and nobles of the Mongol banners were also important as the Qing dynasty sought to manage its complex relationship with the Mongols of the steppes. 'Banners' were the traditional Mongol and Manchu tribal units and, as the name suggests, they originated as terms for military formations which mustered and marched behind their own banners.

Mongols and the Manchu banner system

The Manchu military system was organized in banners and this was extended to Mongolia. Separate Mongol banners were controlled by Mongol ruling princes (traditionally *jasag*, but written *zasag* in modern Mongolian – this is also cognate with the *jasag* or *yassa* that refers to the law of the Mongols), to whom the authority of the Manchu court was devolved to enable them to rule their fiefs. These banners retained the traditional stratified social structure of the Mongol tribes and the name banner (*khoshuu* in modern Mongolian) was used for an administrative unit, a subdivision of the prefectural level *aimag* in both Mongolia and Inner Mongolia, until it was replaced by the *sum* (district) in 1931.

The Mongols did not relish Manchu overlordship, but neither was there any effective or unified Mongol resistance. Historically Mongols had been divided into martial tribes that were often at war with each other. The creation of an empire, once Chinggis Khan had unified the tribes, brought about a temporary cessation of this conflict but intense inter-tribal rivalry persisted below the surface. When the Ming dynasty took power in 1368, warfare between the Mongol nobles recommenced and this conflict continued under the rule of the Manchu Qing. The greatest quarrel was between the Khalkh Mongols of the north and the Oirat of the west. When the Khalkh faced defeat at the hands of the Oirat, some Khalkh nobles fled to Inner Mongolia, sought assistance from the Manchu court and, with the aid of Chinese forces, successfully repulsed their western opponents. In the eighteenth century the Manchu Empire effectively eradicated the power of the Oirats. The Khalkh Mongols, while formally accepting the suzerainty of the Manchus, did not accept the status of a conquered people but saw themselves as the core of genuine 'Mongolness'. Something akin to a sense of nationhood and proto-nationalism began to emerge among the Khalkh. The Manchus attempted to discourage any sense of unity among Mongols by preserving territorial divisions, encouraging conflict between tribes and feudal lords, and restricting travel across the borders between Mongol and Chinese lands. This inchoate national sentiment among the Khalkh Mongols was not permitted to develop fully during the Qing period, but it foreshadowed the Mongol nationalism that led to the creation of a genuine modern state in Mongolia in the early twentieth century.

Towards the end of the Qing dynasty the economy of Mongolia began to change. In the early years of Manchu rule there had been little economic activity other than the time-honoured pastoral nomadism, although that appeared to be in a healthy state and less susceptible to the natural disasters that constantly threatened the settled peasant agriculture of rural China to the south.

Mongol aristocrats were aware of the luxury enjoyed by officials at the court of the Manchus and many felt obliged to emulate their overlords. They encouraged Chinese traders to venture into Mongolia to provide them with expensive goods, and employed Chinese craftsmen to build palaces and temples similar to those in the Qing capital. The influence of this cultural interaction persisted for centuries and is apparent in buildings such as the Winter Palace of the Bogd Khan and the Choijin Lama Temple in Ulaanbaatar that are still in existence. Agriculture also developed in some areas of Mongolia, partly to generate revenue for the new expenses of the aristocracy.

After the Opium War of 1839–42 the Chinese economy became increasingly commercialized under pressure from the Treaty Ports, which were controlled by Western commercial interests. This commercialism spread northwards into the steppes and in time began to undermine the self-sufficient economy of the Mongols. From the early nineteenth century, the import of Chinese labour for farming escalated, until significant areas of Inner Mongolia – although fewer in Outer Mongolia – were effectively colonized by Chinese farmers. In the late nineteenth century, the Qing government conscripted Mongols for service in its military units and this additional imposition generated resentment and, on occasion, mutiny. Disaffected soldiers were particularly susceptible to political agitation against ethnic Chinese living in Mongolia, many of them merchants who were seen as wealthy and exploitative interlopers. In 1900, two thousand men in Mongolian military units that had been stationed in Uliasutai to prevent any unrest engendered by the rebels of the Boxer movement in China mutinied over lack of pay and food. Uliasutai, the main town of western Mongolia, was a commercial centre as well as a garrison town; it had a Chinese settlement and the mutineers occupied Chinese market gardens to appropriate food for themselves and their horses. The senior officer in charge of the unit was sympathetic to their plight and not inclined to assist the Chinese. He refused to incriminate the ringleaders and no action was taken against the mutineers.[11]

Pastoral nomadism

The distinctive economy and culture of Mongolia evolved over centuries from the interactions of its people with a challenging geography. Mongolia is usually associated with the Gobi Desert and the herding of stock. Most of the Gobi is more accurately described as semi-desert, rather than true desert as it lacks the sandy expanse associated with, for example, the Sahara, but it was not suitable for the cultivation of rice and vegetables as practised by the Chinese. In the Mongolian language a distinction is made between the *govi* (Gobi) which is the desert in the south of the country and the *khangai*, the afforested steppe in the north. In between these two is the intermediate region of the steppe, the *kheer*, 'steppe' or 'wasteland', a level plain that is also called the *tal*. The grasslands in this intermediate region of the steppe were essential for raising the stock that was the centre of the economic life of the Mongols. Since the Mongolian economy provided the population with little other than the products of horses, cattle, camel sheep and goats (referred to by Mongols collectively as the *tavan mal* 'five animals'), trade with the outside world was essential. Trading routes for camel caravans converged on Kalgan, which is now in China's Hebei province and known as Zhangjiakou. It was Mongolia's main northern gateway through the Great Wall (*khaalgan* means gate in Mongolian), and thence to Beijing and the rest of China.

Trade

The limitations of the nomadic lifestyle made trade essential for the Mongols and even attractive for some. They could supply horses in exchange for tea, pottery and the other refinements of daily life that China could offer. Long-distance trade was carried out with camel caravans that crossed the desert from China. However, these caravans were chiefly managed by Chinese merchants whose economic power was often resented by Mongols, although it was taken advantage of by many aristocrats and officials who were only too willing to borrow from traders who also operated as moneylenders.

Russian merchants were based in Kalgan to carry out their own trade with China. Tea was the principal export to Russia, together with silk and other manufactured goods; in return the Russians sold the Chinese furs, wool and its products, and leather. Russian post offices were established in Kalgan, Beijing and Tianjin to facilitate commerce and communications through Mongolia, and in 1909 a railway line was constructed to connect Kalgan with Beijing. To this day, Kalgan, under its Chinese name of Zhangjiakou, remains an important strategic centre and communications hub. It lies on the trunk route G6 which links Beijing with Ulanqab, Hohhot, the capital of Inner Mongolia, and Baotou, the largest industrial centre in the region.[12]

Climate and the seasons

The climate of Mongolia is of the type known as continental. It is far from the sea and surrounded by mountains and consequently suffers from extremes of weather with changes that can be sudden, unpredictable and often deadly. During the long winters, the temperature can be as low as −40°C, but it can rise to 30°C or even 40°C in the summer. Blizzards and snowfall in the winter are regularly so severe that they are classified as a *tsagaan zud* 'white disaster', a catastrophic natural disaster in which hundreds of thousands of animals are likely to starve as they are unable to reach grass under the snow and herding families find it impossible to get fodder to them. Neither is the complete absence of snow welcomed as that would disturb the ecological balance; it is described as a *khar zud*, a 'black disaster'.

For centuries the pastoral economy was the only economy of Mongolia. It dominated the lives of all Mongols, even the ruling elite. The rhythm of every year was determined by the seasonal needs of the flocks of sheep, cows, horses and yaks as they were moved from winter to summer pasture, accompanied by the nomadic families.

Even though there is now a degree of diversification, the traditional patterns still rule the lives of most of the rural population. In February and March there is normally little edible grass in the pastures. Some winter snow remains, and a late snowfall or heavy cold rainfall can mean death for the animals. Summer lasts from May to September and is enjoyed as a time of green pastures and blue skies when the animals are well fed and the new generation is born. Autumn skies are high and the air is clear and in premodern times this was the traditional season for raids on horseback in search of 'grain, wives and treasure', a practice that is no longer tolerated. Winter begins in November; the animals have to be slaughtered and their meat is dried in preparation for the severe cold weather. The dung of the animals when dried is called *argal* and was the most readily available form of fuel in the grasslands and semi-deserts where there was little or no timber.[13]

The horse in Mongolian culture

Of the five types of livestock the horse was always the most highly valued for its role in war and hunting; for those who were wealthy enough to own one it was the only way to travel any great distance. Horse nomads in Mongolia had more power and prestige than the yak nomads of Tibet, because of their greater mobility and consequently the horse occupied a unique place in Mongolian culture, including among the symbols of shamanism. Camels and cattle, although not prized as highly, were nevertheless essential for carrying loads and pulling oxcarts. The family home, the *ger*, which is of a simple but effective design that has evolved so that it can be erected and taken down regularly, was transported on such carts. Sheep and goats were needed for their meat and wool, but above all for their milk. Milk was an important source of nutrition and mares' milk, when fermented, remains a popular alcoholic refreshment.

It is difficult to overstate the importance of the horse in traditional Mongolia culture. In addition to the practical aspects of Mongols' relationship with their horses, there is a sacred bond that can only be described as quasi-religious. This can be illustrated by the cult of the *khiimori*, the 'wind-horse' prayer flags that are flown outside the *ger* of the nomad families and collectively in larger nomad encampments. The *khiimori*, which have a parallel in Tibet, are essential to ensure the good fortune of the family and represent the need for a traditional Mongol to have a fighting horse that is as fast as the wind and always ready for battle. Some legends link the *khiimori* to the hitching post where Chinggis Khan tethered his horse, and the *ger* flag is a reminder of a smaller flag that is attached to a horse's mane. The wind-horse flag is flown either from the *ger* or from a special platform just outside. It is part of the traditional role of the Mongol man of the house to raise the *khiimori* each morning and to make an offering of juniper, sandalwood and incense in a small box set aside for that purpose. This is done, at the same time as other offerings of food and drink are made, to the sound of a conch being blown. Although these are ancient rituals they are still performed in the countryside and some urban Mongols display a *khiimori* inside their flats or on a window ledge.[14]

Moving the herds

The movement of herds was governed by strict rules. They could only be moved within the territory of their banner group, *khoshuu*; to move outside this area risked armed conflict with nomads from other banners or punishment by the banner authorities. In spring, with the melting of the winter snows, herders sought open high areas for new pastures; in the autumn these might be enlarged to make more grass available to fatten the animals; in winter the favoured site was usually in a depression, or on the southern slopes of hilly terrain, to afford the greatest possible protection against the worst effects of the wind. Migration was a constant process, especially in the spring or autumn: in winter or summer the herders and their flocks remained in one place for longer. These were the traditional patterns of pastoral nomadism and, although technology and collectivization changed them in the twentieth century, they have not disappeared from contemporary Mongolia.

The pastoral economy was supplemented by the hunting of game for food, and mammals for their fur. Some Mongols hunted as individuals, but customarily there were organized communal hunts and the techniques that were refined during this type of hunting were a useful preparation for the mounted warfare for which Mongols were renowned. This preparation was enhanced by the training provided for the manly sports of horse-racing, archery and wrestling. Social, political and religious institutions evolved on the foundations of this economic reality and the Mongols made a virtue out of necessity. In earlier times, even the wealthiest and best educated valued their tough and austere lives in the grasslands more highly than the literate and artistic culture of their settled Chinese neighbours, which they were inclined to regard as effete. Although these attitudes have never completely disappeared, Mongolians did develop their own sophisticated literate and learned culture.

Tibetan Buddhism and the Mongols

Buddhism was central to the life and culture of Mongolia in the past; after a period of enforced atheism in the Soviet period it is recovering much of its former influence. The religious sect prevalent in Mongolia is often referred to as Lama Buddhism, after the lama clergy, although most Mongolians and Tibetans prefer the name Tibetan Buddhism. It became the main religion of Mongolia relatively late in comparison with other parts of Buddhist Asia. Although it has many distinguishing features, it is not a separate and distinct belief system but one branch of the Mahayana Buddhist tradition that prevails across northern Asia, in contrast to the Theravada or Hinayana tradition which is more widespread in South East Asia. The ceremonies, dress and art of Tibetan Buddhism are lively and more colourful than those of more conservative sects of Buddhism and it has idiosyncratic traditions of mystical or tantric thought which draw on the influence of shamanism.

The Gelug or Gelugpa school of Tibetan Buddhism, which is also known as the Yellow or Yellow Hat Sect, is the denomination of Tibetan Buddhism headed by the Dalai Lama. The Gelugpa established itself as the dominant school of Tibetan Buddhism in the late sixteenth century, and became the predominant tradition in Mongolian Buddhism as a result of religious and political alliances between the two peoples. The importance of this relationship can be seen when it is understood that the position of Dalai Lama (literally Ocean or Universal Lama) owes its existence entirely to this alliance. In 1578 the title was bestowed on Sonam Gyatso, a Gelugpa monk of the Drepung monastery in Tibet, by the Mongolian chieftain, Altan Khan. It was also conferred retrospectively on Sonam Gyatso's two predecessors so that, although he was the first to bear the title, he is known as the third Dalai Lama. The fact that the title was conferred by the Mongolian leader, rather than the Wanli emperor of the Chinese Ming dynasty, is of great political significance as it symbolized the alignment of Mongols and Tibetans independently of the authority of the Chinese Empire. The fourteenth and current Dalai Lama, Tenzin Gyatso, is the inheritor of this tradition and his portrait could be seen displayed, prominently and defiantly, in Mongolian Buddhist temples immediately after their ceremonies were reopened to the public in 1990.[15]

Monasteries are normally led by a *khutughtu* (*khutagt* in modern Mongolian), the equivalent of the Tibetan *tulku*. *Khutughtu* is a spiritual title for eminent lamas who are revered as the reincarnations of a saintly figure, or the embodiment of an aspect of the Buddha. It means approximately 'blessed' or 'holy': the term 'living Buddha' which is often used is a translation of the

Chinese word *huofo* and is disliked by many Tibetan Buddhists. The Dalai Lama is at the apex of a hierarchical pyramid of religious authority which can be compared with the relationship between cardinal archbishops and the Pope in the Roman Catholic Church, although the transmission and exercise of authority in Tibetan Buddhism is more diffuse. There is no central authority comparable to that of the Vatican and there are more similarities with the Islamic world.

The doctrine of reincarnation afforded immense power and authority to the senior monks who constituted the executive committee of a monastery and controlled it independently of other institutions. After the death of a *khutughtu* it was necessary to search for a reincarnation in the body of a child – a boy – who would be identified by the application of a precise set of traditional tests, often including the ability to identify objects that had belonged to the previous incarnation. The monasteries had complete autonomy in this process and, although the Dalai Lama was revered as the head of the religion, he did not have the authority to intervene in the process of individual incarnations. After a successful search for the infant reincarnated lama, the senior lamas would arrange for the new *khutughtu* to be educated and groomed in their own likeness.[16]

In addition to spiritual authority the monasteries had at their disposal extraordinary wealth and temporal power. It has been estimated that, across the whole of the Mongolian region, monasteries 'controlled about half of the national wealth', denying a substantial amount of revenue to the state or indeed to any private entrepreneur for development. The land under the control of monasteries – legally they did not own it – entitled them to demand tax revenue from herdsmen; gifts by pious lay people of livestock or other property allowed some individual monks to become very wealthy. From the end of the sixteenth century to the beginning of the twentieth, as many as one-third to one-half of the male population of Mongolia may have been in holy orders at any one time, and these men were therefore not available for productive work. There are many parallels with the condition of the monasteries in Catholic England before their dissolution by King Henry VIII in the sixteenth century:[17]

> Great demands were made upon the people for gifts and sacrifices, and a large institutionalised, unproductive class appeared on the scene. Much of the wealth of Mongolia flowed to the temples and was lost for reinvestment in future development for the society at large. In addition to the unproductive drag of the lamas in Mongolia, there was a great outflow of wealth in pious donations to Tibet, the fountainhead of Lamaist Buddhism. The Mongolian biography of the Zaya Pandita, an

incarnation of the seventeenth century, mentions that on two different occasions over twenty thousand head of horses were gathered in Mongolia and sold to Chinese merchants, and the proceeds were sent to Tibet as a donation.[18]

As a general rule men did not become monks as a result of a strong personal religious vocation in their teens or early adulthood, although this is the case in some cultures, including some sects of Buddhism. Typically, a Mongolian novice lama was introduced to a monastery by his parents as a 7- or 8-year-old child – whether because of the piety or poverty of the family is not always clear – and apprenticed to a senior monk who was assigned as his religious mentor. This happened, among many others, to the future leader of Mongolia, Choibalsan, when he was a small boy. Progress through the lama hierarchy was on the basis of study, discipline and the taking of vows. The vows of an acolyte were marked by the *gesel* level of tonsure and the initiate would proceed to the *gelüng* state after he had taken vows at a higher level. To rise any higher, it was necessary to be recognized as an incarnation; the Mongolian term for any incarnate lama is *gegeen*, which can be translated as 'brilliance' or 'radiance' and there are special titles for even higher ranking incarnate lamas.[19]

The courses at monastic colleges that are designed to guide lamas through all these stages can last for between sixteen and twenty years. As the name of the faith suggests, the language of the courses and the rituals of the monasteries was and remains Tibetan. Knowledge of the scriptures in Tibetan, and the ability to debate them are at the core of a monk's instruction and in some cases are the sum total of his education. This concentration on the Tibetan language, which is completely unrelated to Mongolian in either speech or writing, had a deleterious effect on the study of the Mongolian language. The vast majority of the population in pre-modern times was illiterate in any language – possibly as high as 80 or 90 per cent – and there was no incentive for those who had the ability or the time (as monks did) to study or teach their own language to a high level.

These were among the many complex reasons for the ferocious campaign against the monasteries in the 1930s by the Mongolian People's Revolutionary Party (MPRP) and its government. Comparisons can again be made with Henry VIII's programme of dissolution, although the Mongolian version was considerably more brutal and bloodier and led to the deaths of many thousands of monks. These campaigns are discussed in more detail in Chapter 4.

The influence of Tibetan Buddhism on Mongolian society has been reassessed since the collapse of the Communist government in 1991, and there has been a popular movement to reopen monasteries and restore the prestige of the monks. The role of religion remains controversial and has been criticized by many Mongols and visitors to the country, not only by Marxists, for having been the major impediment to the country's social and economic development and modernization. While some regard the 'spiritual unity' that was produced by the 'universal acceptance of the Buddhist faith in its Lamaist form' as a key factor in the ability of Mongols to maintain a sense of identity during the centuries when they lacked their own state, others are critical of the way in which reactionary lamas blocked social and economic development.[20] 'With the exception of a few devotees of mystical religion, all Tsarist Russian, Western and Chinese travellers described traditional Mongolian Lamaism as 'ignorant, decayed, stagnant, superstitious and economically parasitical.'[21]

The importance of Tibetan Buddhism, or Lamaism as it is often called, to the history of Mongolia is not solely or even primarily as a religion. The religious and political functions of the lamas and the monasteries were inextricably intertwined and it is in the operation of 'ecclesiastical politics' that its full influence was felt:

> I have become convinced [wrote Owen Lattimore in 1962, summarising his experience of Tibetan Buddhism in Mongolia] that the faith and mysticism of the Lama Church are not so important as its ecclesiasticism and that the prime functions of this ecclesiasticism are not religious but political – the control of wealth and power, the operation of a complex apparatus of authority. If you talk much with Mongols, or still better if you keep quiet and listen while Mongols talk among themselves, you will find that there are two kinds of stories and legends about religious events and religious personages (moral tales and folklore). The content of such a story [folklore] is really more political than religious: it shows the way the people feel about the way their society works.[22]

> In Mongolia, where monastic institutions owned territory, collected taxes, and demanded labour services, the 'idle monk', the 'hypocritical priest and the 'grasping abbot' were stock figures of satire as in medieval Europe. It was perfectly consistent to say, 'the living Buddha of that monastery over there is a very holy man and we must reverence him; but we are also entitled to hate the guts of his administrators, who put the screws on us'.[23]

This should not be taken to imply that there are no genuine religious impulses among the population. After stories of the brutality and destruction of the campaign against monasteries in the 1930s and the admiration for the reconstruction and expansion of the monastic system since 1991, it is tempting to assume that Tibetan Buddhism was an unalloyed benefit to Mongolian society and that it has been restored in the interests of the whole population. The tradition of monks, lamas, monasteries, and the *khutughtu* has undoubtedly revived in Mongolia since the Mongolian democratic revolution of 1990–1 but, however strong the devotion of individual Mongols might be to Buddhism, this does not preclude the presence of a degree of ambivalence towards the religious institutions or even a robust anti-clericalism.

Some monasteries, particularly the Gandantegchinlen (Gandan) on the western outskirts of Ulaanbaatar, have become very wealthy. Donations from local worshippers are very important, including parcels of food that are distributed to the monks after services, but it is the support of the state and wealthy benefactors in Mongolia and abroad that provides the funding needed for development. There is a stark contrast between the modernized and opulent new and restored buildings of the Gandan monastery and the poor and often shabby residences of local people that immediately surround it.[24]

Shamanism

Belief in the power of nature, spirits and the lords of heaven was intrinsic to the culture of the Mongol nomads. The religious part of that culture is usually classified as shamanism, a set of spiritual practices that is spread across the whole of Asia but is particularly strong in the north-eastern part of the continent, above all in Siberia, the Mongol lands and Korea. Shamanism preceded Buddhism in Mongolia and was to some extent absorbed into it. The complex system of shamanist beliefs and practices that continued into the age of Buddhism has influenced the way that Buddhism was practised; this influence persists to the present day. In spite of determined persecution, by Buddhists initially, and later also by the Communist government, shamanism continues to exist as an independent religious system in Mongolia.

Shamanism is an unsatisfactory portmanteau term for an assemblage of beliefs and practices that relate human existence to the natural environment and its, sometimes terrifying, power. Shamanism is not confined to Mongolia; it appears in many countries, under different guises and various names. As has been noted, in Asia it has also played an important role in Siberia and Korea, but also in Tibet, where the old pre-Buddhist religion was Bön or Bönpo, a name related to the Tibetan name for Tibet, Bö or Bod. 'There can surely be no doubt [argued Giuseppe Tucci, the eminent Italian Tibetologist] of the existence of certain similarities between the old Tibetan religion and shamanism.[25] The practices of the traditional religions of Daoism in China and Shinto in Japan are plainly related to shamanism, even if they do not use the name. Outside of Asia, Mongolian shamans particularly acknowledge their affinity with the practices of Native American spirit guides, but similar practices either exist or have existed in most parts of the world.

In the mysticism of Mongolian shamanism the prime objects of worship are *tengri*, 'heaven', and *etügen*, 'earth' and it is from these two venerable phenomena that all good and evil emanates. The name shamanism is derived from the practitioner, the shaman: that is not a native Mongol word and it is probably derived from a word meaning 'one who knows' in the language of the Manchus and their Tungusic antecedents. The modern Mongolian word for a shaman is *böö* and its equivalent in the classical language is *böge*; these names strengthen the argument of close links between Mongolian shamanism and pre-Buddhist Tibet. The practice of shamanism is *böölökh*. In the West, it is often called simply 'the way of the shaman'.[26]

The shaman mediates between the realm of humans, the worlds of the gods, demons, evil spirits, and the spirit of the ancestors. A shaman must have a calling for what is seen as a vocation rather than a profession, and many describe having experienced a mystical summons during a period of illness. While unconscious, or even hallucinating, the patient becomes aware that they have been contacted by an envoy from the world of the spirits, often but not always an ancestor. While undergoing treatment a sufferer sometimes perceives a call to the vocation: in that case the patient, having recovered, could then be initiated into the healer's tradition of spells, songs and dances. Although it is not essential for a shaman to have been born into a family with a tradition of the practice, some shamans say that if there is no ancestral spirit line, or if the line has been broken, it will be difficult to work with spirit guides.

A new shaman is equipped with a staff or wand that is carved from birch wood and decorated at the top with a horse's head and at the bottom with a horse's hoof. Strips of cloth attached to the head symbolize the horse's reins and the staff adorned in this way enables the shaman to engage in 'spirit flying'. This suggests obvious parallels with the broomstick of witches in European folklore but emphasizes the reverence for the horse in Mongolian culture. As the initiation of the shaman advances, a drum with a horse's head handle will be added. The essential equipment of a shaman includes a helmet of either felt or iron, often with deer antlers to symbolize speed and the feathers of an eagle or owl for flight, either during the day or at night. Shamans were once clothed in armour but that has evolved into lighter clothing, of symbolic rather than actual protection, which may be brightly coloured and often appears to be tattered. To these garments, the shaman will attach physical objects that are inhabited by the spirits with which the shaman has to work. In modern Mongolian these are called *ongon* – the word means either 'sacred' or a 'guardian or ancestral spirit' – which refers either to the object or its spirit. They can be compared with amulets popular in some schools of Buddhism; in other cultures they would be called fetishes. These objects might be arrow heads, miniature bows, bronze mirrors or bells, but there will also be representations of humans. Shamans have their individual preferences. Dondog a contemporary Mongolian *zairan* – an honorific term used to describe a shaman of high rank – attaches particular importance to the 'painted image of a brown wolf with a circle around it, on a black cloth as background'. He also uses knives, axes, hammers, arrows and tridents and a birch wood staff, to which are tied nine bronze mirrors of different sizes, and an *ongon* in the shape of a human which he finds efficacious in 'extracting black energy and poisons from people'.

Families would summon a shaman when there was an unusually serious crisis to be resolved, whether it was illness, natural or man-made disaster, or some other problem. There are many rituals in shamanism but at the centre of the practice is the trance, aided perhaps by a potent combination of tobacco, medicinal herbs and alcohol, into which the shaman collapses and travels to the spirit world to seek the assistance of whichever gods or spirits are thought to be efficacious. On returning from this spiritual odyssey, he or she is empowered to answer questions or pronounce on problematic subjects. Some shamans are also believed to be able to cure the sick by transferring the sickness into a tree, an animal or some such object. Rivers, streams and other sources of water are also important foci of worship, as is fire. The veneration of ancestors is an integral part of the shamanic tradition and this links Mongolian beliefs to those of China, where 'ancestor worship' predated Confucianism but was integrated into the traditional world view of China, and many of its former tributary states with cultures that are usually categorized as Confucian.

Many of the shamanic rituals described take place within the *ger* of an afflicted person: there are rituals associated with fire and its respectful treatment inside the *ger*, and others that are appropriate at *ovoo* – shrines, sacred mounds, cairns or piles of stones. There are many types of these cairns, including *ovoo* dedicated to the homeland and to one's father; individuals might also have their own personal *ovoo*. The most powerful is the Sky *ovoo* on the sacred mountain Burkhan Khaldun (Mountain of God or Buddha) which is associated with the rise to power of Chinggis Khan and is believed by some to be his birthplace and final resting place. State-sponsored shamans celebrated annual ceremonies at this *ovoo* until theywere outlawed in the

1930s, but there have been attempts to revive the practice in the twenty-first century.

Shamanic rituals were often commissioned by tribal military leaders before a battle so that the shaman could appeal for the protection of the clan's particular martial god. This invocation of shamanic assistance offers at least a partial explanation for some customs that would otherwise appear irrational and bizarre. It also accounts for some of the more repugnant rituals associated with warfare, including the ripping out of the heart of a defeated enemy, a practice that is attested as having taken place as late as the early twentieth century.

Although shamanism is rejected by some devout Buddhists, as is its equivalent in Tibet, it has been a vital component of Mongolian culture for centuries. Contact between Buddhism and shamanism has been so close that in some communities it has effectively created a syncretic religion, especially in the southern part of Mongolia where the rituals and dress of shamans overlap most closely with those of the lamas. One shamanic sect, Yellow Shamanism, was so close to the lama tradition that its rituals were examined and licensed by Buddhist monasteries of the Gelug or Yellow Hat tradition.[27]

Tsam dances

Tsam dances are among the most dramatic and colourful rituals of Mongolian Buddhism. Chinese descriptions of dancing at temple festivals often use the name 'devil dance', a term which Mongolians reject as offensive. They refer to it as the Tsam or Cham festival, using the original Tibetan term; there is not one dance but a range of separate rituals which take place at different times of the year. Neither is it simply a dance but rather a dance drama, which includes the reading of Buddhist scriptures and is considered to be a religious ceremony rather than merely an entertainment. The most popular Tsam ceremony takes place in the sixth lunar month and tells the story of the victory of good over evil, symbolized in the death of an ancient Tibetan 'evil king', Langdharma, who suppressed Buddhism and restored the earlier Bön religion of Tibet. On the following day a statue of the Maitreya, the Buddha of the Future, particularly revered by millenarian sects, is carried during a circumambulation of the monastery.[28]

Individual monasteries had their own variations of the Tsam rituals, but among the best known were those at Dolonor, which is in what is now Duolun in Inner Mongolia and is the site of a monastery built in the seventeenth century for Mongol nobles on the orders of the Qing emperor, Kangxi:

Not long after I arrived in Dolonor [recalled the Living Buddha, Kanjurwa Khutugtu] it was the season for the *cham*, a religious dance festival, mistakenly called by the Chinese *t'iao-kuei* [*tiaogui*], 'devil-dance'. Held in the sixth month of the lunar calendar this was an important occasion, and people gathered from many miles around to participate in the entertainment, the prayers, and a flourishing exchange of goods in the bazaar that sprang up. Together with two incarnations of Dolonor, Shireetü *gegen* and Mendel *gegen*, I attended the *cham* celebrations of each of the two monasteries, Köke and Shira.[29]

Public performances of the Tsam dances were largely discontinued after the establishment of the MPR in 1924, but since 1990 there have been attempts to revive them. Provincial monasteries have also begun to create the special masks used in the dances and it remains to be seen whether the revitalized rituals will develop a genuine religious function or will be primarily to attract tourists.

Mongolia's literary culture

Although Mongols throughout their history, in common with the Manchus and other peoples of the steppes, valued military prowess and the masculine and martial arts – skill in horsemanship, archery and wrestling – overrefined and literary and artistic talents that were considered to be feeble, even effeminate, and of little use in the grasslands, there was and remains a valuable tradition of written and material culture.

The scriptures of Tibetan Buddhism are written in Tibetan, a language that is not even distantly related to Mongolian, and it is these scriptures that are recited to this day in the Buddhist temples and monasteries throughout Mongolia. In the past, many of the most intellectually able young Mongols were directed towards the monasteries and, as has been suggested, there is a strong argument for concluding that the Tibetan religious culture bears a heavy responsibility for the slower development of a secular written culture in the Mongolian language.

For the early and mediaeval history of Mongolia and the Mongols, there is little in the Mongolian language that can be regarded as genuine history, although literary documents that have been preserved are essential for understanding the rise of Chinggis Khan and the thinking of the Mongols. Western historians have often relied on sources in Persian as a more comprehensive and trustworthy account of those lands. Persians were of course among the peoples conquered by Mongols, and Persian scholars were not necessarily well disposed towards their masters. However, Persian was the language of administration across much of central and southern Asia and Persian scholarship persisted after the conquest.[30]

For later periods, despite the prestige of Tibetan, there is a significant body of literature in the Mongolian language. In common with other nomadic peoples, the earliest literary tradition was an oral one of poetry and epics that combined historical fact and legend. The earliest and by far the best-known extant written work of the Mongols is the *Secret History of the Mongols* (*Mongghol-un ni'ucha tobchiyan*), an outline history of the deeds of Chinggis Khan, his ancestors and his son Ögödei Khan, which was produced for the Mongol court sometime after 1240. The original was based on oral testimony and written down in Mongol, but ironically that text has been lost and the earliest extant version is a transcription in Chinese that was made during the Ming dynasty.

The Golden Chronicle (*Altan tobchi*), a compilation of historical records, dates back to the early seventeenth century and the book of *Sagan Sechen*, produced at roughly the same time, is a combination of history and legend. There is a wealth of poetry in Mongolian, much of it epic in form, a reminder of the importance of this type of verse and the oral tradition for a society in which literacy was very limited.

Evidence of a more positive influence of Tibetan Buddhism on writing in Mongolian can be found in another important category of Mongolian literature, the corpus of translations from Tibetan Buddhist sutras and other texts. These works have been the inspiration for a sizeable body of fiction, poetry and drama in Mongolian. The *fons et origo* of this was the translation of the *Kanjur* or *Kangyur*, the canonical collection of Tibetan Buddhist texts that was codified in the fourteenth century as a commentary on the works of the Buddha; this translation defined the style of literary Mongolian for centuries. Chinese works of fiction were also translated into Mongolian, many by way of an earlier translation in Manchu.[31]

The most celebrated Mongolian writer of the nineteenth century was Injanasi, a poet, novelist and historian from the Tümed Right Banner in what is now China's Liaoning province. His father was an official in the banner administration and a prolific collector of books in Mongolian, Chinese, Manchu and Tibetan. Injanasi is renowned for his *Blue History* (*Köke sudar*), an epic fictional prose narrative based on the heroic exploits of Chinggis Khan, but he also wrote fiction that drew heavily on the Chinese tradition of vernacular novels. Two of his books, *One Storey Pavilion* and *Chamber of Red Tears*, were so strikingly similar to Chinese novels that had been written as sequels to the celebrated *Dream of the Red Chamber* (*Hongloumeng*), that he was open to charges of mere translation or plagiarism.[32]

Writing in the MPR throughout the twentieth century was dominated by the Mongolian Writers' Union, which was modelled on the institution of the same name created in the Soviet Union. This encouraged mass literacy and supported the production of great quantities of literature, but it was also responsible for severely constraining the content and the form of that production. The most influential writer of that century, who also served as the chair of the Mongolian Writers' Union, was Tsendiin Damdinsüren, a respected poet, prose writer and newspaper editor. Between 1942 and 1946 he edited *Ünen* (Truth), the Mongolian equivalent of *Pravda*. As a champion of modern Mongolian writing, he was also responsible for the abandonment of the traditional Mongolian script in favour of a modified version of the Russian Cyrillic alphabet, a change that he is said to have deeply regretted in later life.[33]

Two other major literary figures were Byambyn Rinchin and Dashdorjiin Natsagdorj, both of whom became prominent in the development of Soviet-style 'socialist' literature: both incidentally also claimed direct descent from Chinggis Khan.

In his early years, Rinchin was a revolutionary in his home town of Kyakhta. He was an able linguist who served as a Russian-Mongolian translator and interpreter at the first congress of the Mongolian People's Party (MPP) in March 1921. He subsequently studied in Leningrad and was awarded a doctorate in Budapest for his thesis on Mongolian linguistics. He wrote novels and short stories and translated many works of literature from Russian – and from French – and edited publications on shamanism and Mongolian folklore. His statue stands to this day outside the Mongolian National Library in Ulaanbaatar.

The journalist and poet, Natsagdorj, was instrumental in the creation of the Mongolian Writers' Union in the 1920s. He edited the military newspaper *Ardyn Tsereg* (*People's Army*) and was literary editor of *Zaluuchuudyn Ünen* (*Youth Truth*). He was arrested for his unorthodox views in 1932 and was soon released, but he died in 1937 at the age of 31, in circumstances that are still unclear. Natsagdorj was the pre-eminent writer and intellectual of Mongolia in the early twentieth century, an influential member of the Mongolian Academy of Social Sciences and, among many other works, the author of a biography of Sükhbaatar (sometimes written Sukebator). His legacy includes poetry that is still treasured by Mongols, particularly his eulogy on the landscape of Mongolia, *Miniy Nutag* My Homeland) and the libretto of a popular opera, *Uchirtay gurvan tolgoy* (*The Meaning of Three Peaks*), often referred to by the English translation of the Russian version, *Three Sad Hills*. For many years this opera both opened and closed the annual opera season in Ulaanbaatar. A ballet based on the opera was included in the 2017–18 season of the Mongolian State Academic Theatre of Opera and Ballet, the building painted in bright salmon pink that stands on the eastern side of Sükhbaatar Square.[34]

Opera and ballet

Mongolia was introduced to opera and ballet by the Soviet Union; theatres and conservatories were established in Mongolia with Soviet aid and many Mongolian performers studied in Moscow and St Petersburg. Since the 1990s, much of the political legacy of the Soviet era has been rejected and many of the contributions of the USSR to contemporary Mongolia have been contested, but some of the cultural legacy, particularly in ballet, has been positive. Not all the Soviet-inspired culture from this period has been discarded and this reflects the fact that a substantial proportion of the writing and art produced during the 'satellite' years expressed Mongolian national feelings and Mongolian culture as well as pan-Soviet ideals

The wider Soviet cultural legacy

Opera and ballet aside, the influence of the Soviet Union on Mongolian culture was at times extremely damaging. During the 1940s, while Mongolia and its ally the USSR were at war against Nazi Germany – although the USSR did not formally declare war against Japan until August 1945 – Mongolia embarked on a major campaign to abolish and replace cultural relics that were determined to have been imbued with feudal ideology. This drive was effectively a continuation of the political onslaught on the monasteries and the aristocracy that had dominated the 1930s. Religious items that monks had always produced for sale to believers had more or less been wiped out and in 1945 the state inaugurated a series of awards for outstanding herdsmen. Silver animal statuettes were awarded to herdsmen who had managed to produce large herds of 1,000, 5,000 or 10,000 heads of livestock. The statuettes were manufactured by hand in handicraft cooperatives, often by former monks who had been forcibly relieved of their vows and found themselves obliged to find some means of earning a living. As many of the figurines resemble traditional devotional objects, the defrocked monks were well equipped to manufacture them. The awards for herdsmen were accompanied by a silver plaque denoting the level of the award and a wooden pail decorated with silver but, more practically, the families were given material to construct *gers* and livestock enclosures and mowing machinery. A conference of nationally recognized heroic herders was convened in Ulaanbaatar in 1941 to celebrate and promote the award system.

As Mongolia emerged from the Second World War and the Choibalsan era, traditional culture still dominated but efforts to modernize it were already in place. The Cyrillic alphabet had been introduced to replace the traditional Mongolian script and campaigns were launched to ensure that all citizens from the ages of 13 to 45 could read and write in this new orthography. There were claims for a greatly increased literacy rate after these campaigns and it has to be conceded that, although Cyrillic is far from ideal for Mongolian and fails to cope adequately with some of the complexities of the language, it is far easier to read than the traditional Mongolian script which has many ambiguities. In the 1950s, as Mongolia entered the era of Yumjaagiin Tsedenbal, a Cultural Movement sought to expand literacy and introduce modern ideas of hygiene. By 1956, eight years of compulsory education had become the national norm.

Architecture among the Mongols

Until recent times, because all Mongols were dependent on a nomadic pastoral economy, accommodation for the bulk of the population was not in permanent buildings but in *gers*, designed so that they could be readily dismantled and re-erected each time a family's herds were moved from summer to winter pasture and vice versa. Vernacular architecture was limited and fairly uniform, except that some nomads in the north of Mongolia favoured homes that were shaped more like the teepees of indigenous North American Indians rather than the round *ger* favoured in the south and among Kazakh and Kyrgyz nomads. In addition to the ubiquitous small residential *gers*, from at least the thirteenth century onwards, the military elite and nobility on the steppe developed complexes of 'palace *ger*' (*ord-örgö*) that could accommodate thousands of people and were used as military headquarters or as the palaces of rulers. These began as extensions of the mobile architecture of the steppe and, although their design remained tied to the universal and simple techniques of the movable *ger*, they evolved into semi-permanent and eventually permanent structures to which were added various ornamental features for prestige, and fences to provide unity and boundaries. This style of building persisted as late as the early twentieth century and the most powerful Mongolian khans possessed both permanent and mobile residences.

The most important permanent buildings were monasteries and palaces for the ruling religious and secular elite: much of their architecture reflected the influence of shamanism and Tibetan Lama Buddhism as did all other aspects of material culture. The greatest of the early permanent settlements, and the model for much subsequent construction, was the city of Karakorum which now lies in ruins. Karakorum was built on the orders of Chinggis Khan in central Mongolia near to the present-day site of Kharkhorin and the Erdene Zuu monastery. Construction began in 1220 and Karakorum was used by the emperor Ögödei Khan as his capital during his reign from 1228 to 1241. The size of the city can be imagined from the fact that it was surrounded by a wall with four gates that were 3 miles apart. Within the city were at least twelve temples, the buildings of the khan's palace, a military garrison, businesses and housing for the general population. Karakorum was completely destroyed by fire during invasions by Chinese armies and conflict between Mongol nobles: some of the city's original building materials were used in the construction of the Erdene Zuu complex. Evidence of the original size and grandeur of Karakorum depends largely on descriptions by contemporary travellers but much of their observations have been corroborated by archaeological investigations. Joint surveys were carried out by Soviet and Mongolian archaeologists in the early 1930s and in 1948–49 and more recently by a German-Mongolian team but the excavations are still a work in progress.[35]

The architecture of temples and monasteries owed much to the basic construction methods of the *ger*. In time, as stone and brick supplemented and, in some cases, replaced timber, more elaborate forms of construction became possible. Temples such as the complex at Erdene Zuu were strongly influenced by Tibetan architectural styles. A wall built for defensive purposes around that monastery, the earliest such wall in Khalkh Mongolia, had four gates, like Karakorum, and on the walls were erected 108 stupas. These rounded tomb-like structures are traditionally the resting places for the relics of deceased lamas and are also the focus of meditation. The interior of the monastery provides examples of different traditions of architecture: native Mongolian, Tibetan and even the classical Chinese style.

The origins of the modern capital of Ulaanbaatar lie in the administrative and religious centre of Ikh Khüree (the Great Enclosed Monastery) which changed its location twenty-one times over the years before it finally settled on its present site on the north bank of the Tuul River. The original buildings were all in the style of *gers* which surrounded a central area that contained the palace, the main temples and residences for lamas. There was also a wooden temple like a pavilion, in front of which was left a wide square that could be used for religious observances. Mongolian residences occupied the south of the city and in the eastern and western suburbs were the houses and the businesses of Chinese traders. Even when the site of Ikh Khüree, or Urga as it was also known in the Russian form of its name, had been roughly established, many of the main buildings were not permanent: in 1756 they were moved some distance to the west and a new monastery the Gandantegchinling was constructed on a nearby hill. This monastery, generally called simply Gandan, is now the main centre for Tibetan Buddhist worship and education not only in Ulaanbaatar but in the whole of Mongolia.

From the early twentieth century, primarily under the influence of the Soviet model of modernization, a new style of building appeared, initially in the premises of foreign businesses and the residences of their managers: some of these were converted for use by Mongol institutions. Western architects, German and Hungarian respectively, produced designs for the State Printing House and a theatre. As Soviet aid and influence grew, so did the number of buildings in a European – or more specifically Russian – fashion, especially in the 1940s.

Mongolian students increasingly travelled to the USSR for their professional and technical education in architecture and construction techniques, among other subjects. Soviet models of town planning and infrastructure development became the norm and, by the end of the 1950s, the central Sükhbaatar Square in the capital Ulaanbaatar was surrounded by monumental constructions, including the joint mausoleum of the early Communist leaders, Sükhbaatar and Choibalsan, the party and government complex behind it and the Ulaanbaatar Hotel, all of which were built in the Soviet style. Construction on the Soviet model continued throughout the 1970s and 1980s, but Mongols began to resent the fact that little attempt had been made to design buildings that made any concession to traditional Mongolian styles of architecture.

Mongols in the capital Ulaanbaatar and other cities became accustomed to living in blocks of flats but the *ger* remained the normal home for most of the rural population. Even in the cities, including the capital as has been observed, the *ger* is still a common sight. In the second decade of the twenty-first century, there are still isolated *gers* in urban centres and extensive compounds on the outskirts where rows of *gers* set behind wooden stockades act as a bridge between traditional and modern concepts of housing and lifestyles.[36]

Zanabazar (1635–1723) and the high religious art of the Mongols

Mongolia is rarely associated with works of art of the finest quality although many examples can be found in the National Museum and other museums.

In the monasteries, lamas of the lower ranks worked to produce devotional objects for the faithful; these items, which were often of indifferent quality, included amulets, *thangka* religious images, sculptures, figures from shamanic dance ceremonies and family altars that were designed to be used inside the *ger* homes of often poor nomad families. The production of these artefacts was seriously affected by the destruction of the monasteries in the 1930s.

One individual, however, stands out in the production of art and artefacts of the finest quality. The sculptures cast in bronze and copper that were created by Zanabazar and his school in the seventeenth century can only be described in those terms. Zanabazar was an artist of extraordinary genius but he was also a man of great political and religious influence. He played a decisive role in the power play between Mongolia, Tibet and the Manchu conquerors of China in the late sixteenth and early seventeenth centuries and the no less important internal struggle for supremacy between the Khalkh Mongols of the east and the Oirats of west Mongolia.[37]

Zanabazar was born in 1635 and probably died in Beijing in 1723 or 1724. His father, the Khalkh Mongol Prince Tüshet Khan Gombodorj, was himself the son of Avtai [Abadai] Khan who is credited with having introduced the Gelugpa Yellow Sect of Tibetan Buddhism to the Khalkh Mongols. Zanabazar was identified as the reincarnation of Javzan Darmnat (Jebtsundamba) with the support of the Manchu Qing government and the Tibetan hierarchy. All of these powerful figures sought to use Buddhism as a political tool for stabilizing and controlling Mongolia and diminishing the authority of what the modern Mongolian historian Baabar (B. Batbayar) has called the 'primitive rites of shamanism' in order to 'open up for Mongolia prospects for sharing in the cultural wealth of India and Tibet. In this way the coming of Buddhism marked a breakthrough for the Mongolian society of that period'.[38] The Mongolian aristocratic elite supported the identification of Zanabazar as an incarnated *khutughtu*, in the belief that with his recognition Mongolia would enjoy the stability of a centralized spiritual and temporal government at a time of dangerous division.

Leaders of the disparate warring Mongolian tribes had attempted to resist the power of the expanding Qing Empire which took control of China in 1644. The Mongols were far from united and the bitter competition between the Oirats of the west and the Khalkh of the east has already been mentioned. Zanabazar effectively became the leader of the Khalkh Mongols in 1655 after the death of previous khans but fled southwards to Inner Mongolia to solicit support from other tribal leaders in his struggles against the Qing. In 1688, by which time the Qing had already consolidated its power throughout China Proper, Zanabazar, with the support of other Khalkh nobles, finally agreed to accept the overlordship of the Qing. A ceremony to mark the integration of Khalkh Mongolia into Qing China was held at Dolonor on 2 May 1691. Zanabazar and his most influential supporters in the Khalkh nobility were received by the Kangxi emperor amid the strictest security. The Khalkh nobles were rewarded with gifts of silver, brocaded silk and other sumptuous garments but in return had to accept their new status as 'bondsmen of the Manchu emperor'.

'In the person of Zanabazar two different Mongolian concepts of heredity converge'.[39] As the son of Gombodorj and the grandson of Avtai Khan, he could claim direct descent from Chinggis Khan and this accorded him precedence among the Mongolian aristocracy. Because of this genealogy he became an influential political figure but his religious status, conferred by the recognition of his incarnation, was at least as important for the exercise of his authority and is more enthusiastically celebrated today. He is known to modern Mongolians by the title of Öndör Gegeen which best translates as 'exalted enlightened one', an honorific applied to an incarnate lama. As the sixteenth incarnation of Jebtsundamba, one of the original disciples of the Buddha, Zanabazar was known as the Jebtsundamba Khutukhtu – the title inherited by the Bogd Khan in the early twentieth century – and was recognized as the supreme spiritual leader of the Khalkh Mongols.

Zanabazar was also responsible for the creation of the Soyombo characters for writing the Mongolian language, a system which was based on the Devanagari characters in which Sanskrit, the sacred language of Hinduism but also of Buddhism, is written. It was used primarily for the translation of Buddhist texts from Sanskrit and Tibetan (and it bears some resemblance to the Tibetan script), but its complexity prevented it from being adopted for everyday writing and the 'Uyghur' script replaced it. The Soyombo script fell into desuetude but what remains of Zanabazar's creation is the Soyombo symbol; it was originally used to mark the beginning and end of a text but is now the ubiquitous symbol of Mongolia and forms part of the design of the national flag.[40]

Choijin Lama Temple

The most valuable works produced by Zanabazar and his pupils are kept in the Amugalan Temple (the Temple of Peace) which is part of the Choijin Lama Temple complex in the capital Ulaanbaatar. It is now a museum and is situated just to the south of Sükhbaatar Square, in the shadow of the ultra-modern Blue Sky Tower. It is not an ancient foundation but was originally a group of temples constructed between 1904 and 1908 under the sponsorship of the eighth incarnation of the Jebtsundamba Khutukhtu (the

Bogd Khan) – and thus at least in theory the spiritual heir to Zanabazar – for his brother, Luvsankhaidav, who served as the State Oracle of Mongolia. Initially the temple complex was exclusively a place of worship and was noted for traditional oracle trances carried out under Luvsankhaidav's supervision. The temple was closed in 1937 during the brutal campaign against religion, but the buildings survived and were reopened as a museum the following year, the intention being that it would serve as a reminder of the iniquities of the feudal past. There were plans to demolish it – and there is photographic evidence of partial destruction in the late 1930s when many monasteries and other buildings belonging to the feudal order were torn down – but, because it had such an important educational and political function for the regime, it was preserved. For a major national institution, it appears dilapidated from the outside and the grounds are not well kept, but the exhibits are immaculately preserved and securely displayed.

Representations of Zanabazar himself can be seen in statues, paintings and ornamental bosses that are held in several museums in Mongolia. They are often described as 'self-portraits' but since there are records of his disciples enquiring how they should represent him and his hand gestures, which have precise religious symbolism, it is safe to presume that most are from his school. The gilt bronze statue of Zanabazar displayed in the Choijin Lama Museum depicts him in the robes of a monk and holding a *vajra* or ritual tool in his right hand and a bell in his left. Other statues include: the youthful and perfect form of the Buddha Ratnasambhava in gilt bronze, wearing a five-point diadem embossed with the mythical Garuda bird and in a meditative posture; the gilt brass Maitreya, the Buddha of the future standing on lotus and moon discs; and the Amitabha Buddha, the principal Buddha in the Pure Land sect in gilt bronze. The most intriguing and unexpected masterpiece is of joined gilt brass figures of Heruka, the White Cakramsavara of the Tantric tradition. 'Holding the vases of jewels in his two hands he embraces his consort, a dakini', a 'sky dancer' or priestess in that tradition. The use of the word 'embrace' conceals a greater degree of intimacy than is usually meant in English. The most impressive sculpture that is not purely figurative is the Bodhi Stupa which commemorates the attainment of enlightenment by Sakyamuni, the Buddha, beneath the Bodhi tree in Bodhgaya in what is now India's Bihar state, after he overcame the temptations of the world. It is 32 centimetres high in gilt brass and the Buddha is depicted 'sitting in meditation posture on a lion throne'.

The most recent catalogue of the Zanabazar pieces displayed in the temple was produced in 2015 to commemorate the 380th anniversary of the birth of the master sculptor, but in addition to the artefacts attributed to him and his disciples, the Choijin Lama Museum is also the repository for some of the most important Buddhist works of art and artefacts in Mongolia, although others can be seen in the Zanabazar Museum of Fine Art and the National Museum of Mongolia, both of which are also in Ulaanbaatar. The works of Zanabazar on display at the Choijin Lama Temple and the other museums are a reminder of the existence of a highly sophisticated artistic culture in Mongolia, from at least the seventeenth century, and the depth of influence of the Buddhist tradition that Mongolia had received from India by way of Tibet. The history of the building in the twentieth century is a chronicle of the continuity of Buddhist (and indeed shamanistic) practices, their suppression during the period of the MPR and, if not yet the revival, then the preservation and display of the finest products of that religious tradition.[41]

*

Mongolia, as it entered a period of revolutionary change in the twentieth century, was a land of apparently simple pastoral herding folk, but with complex social, cultural and religious traditions, underpinned by profound respect for the Buddhist faith inherited from Tibet. The country struggled to establish itself as a modern state, accepting that it was only realistically able to do so in an alliance with the Soviet Union. It had to grapple with Stalinist policies but also with its own cultural legacy which inhibited modernization and development but could not be jettisoned as it also contained the essence of what it meant to be Mongol.

2

Revolutionary Mongolia in the early twentieth century

The modern state of Mongolia was created during an epoch of dramatic and violent change that engulfed the whole of eastern Asia during the first two decades of the twentieth century. The war between Japan and Russia in 1904–5 was followed by the collapse of the Chinese Empire in 1911 and the revolutions in Russia first in 1905 and then the dual revolutions of February and October 1917, all of which affected Mongolia. The old order in Asia was coming to an end, and such was the extent of the political and social transformation in Mongolia after 1911 that it cannot be described as anything other than a revolution. By 1924 a new state – the Mongolian People's Republic (MPR) – which was closely allied with the Soviet Union, and a single ruling party – the Mongolian People's Revolutionary Party (MPRP) – had emerged from this revolution. The state and the party remained in place until Mongolia's democratic revolution of 1990–1.

Geopolitics cannot be ignored; it always influences, and often determines, the destiny of nations and a weaker country such as Mongolia, lying between two powerful states, is particularly susceptible to the ebb and flow of geopolitical movements. The Mongolian people have always lived in the border regions between China and Russia, and their destiny has depended on the fluctuating relative strengths of those two great powers and the vagaries of their foreign policies. The position of modestly sized Mongolia has been variously described as being a buffer, a link or a cushion. For most of the twentieth century it was so closely allied to Russia and subsequently the Soviet Union that it has usually been described as a 'satellite' of the USSR. This relationship had drawbacks, some of which were severe but, as far as the majority of Mongols were concerned, it had the great benefit of keeping China at arm's length.[1]

Mongolian antipathy towards China led it inevitably to seek aid from, and alliances with, governments in Russia. This did not, however, mean that the revolutionary changes that began in 1911 were simply the result of Russian intervention and manipulation. As Thomas Ewing argues:

This revolution was the logical culmination of a growing nationalistic consciousness of the Mongols and of the [Qing] mismanagement of Mongolia in the final decade of its existence – aggravated to no little degree by the misrule of Mongolian princes and a deteriorating economy.[2]

Mongolia actively courted Russia as a counterweight to the greater threat of China, and this continued long after the 1911 revolution.

Princely residence to Red Hero

In the early twentieth century, Mongolia – the whole of the land occupied by Mongols beyond the Great Wall – was a powerful magnet for diplomats, merchants and adventurers who had been in China and had tired of the splendours and claustrophobia of imperial Beijing, its stultifying bureaucratic rituals and the political intrigues and infighting of the Qing court and its republican successor. Adventurous spirits headed north in search of the desert, the steppe and the broad blue skies of Mongolia's wide open spaces. Many of them left behind descriptions of what they found. These are of varying value for analysing the changes that were affecting Mongolia, the quality depending on the vision and perspicacity of the travellers and their ability to communicate with Mongols. Most have some merit for the contemporary images they offer of the land and its people.

The main objective for these travellers was the Mongolian capital. It has had many names throughout its history, but by the twentieth century was generally referred to by foreigners as Urga. Urga is the Russian form of *Örgöö*, the residence or tent of a prince. The prince was Mongolia's last aristocratic ruler, the strange and anomalous Bogd Khan. To Mongols the city was usually Ikh Khüree, the Great Monastery, which more accurately reflects the Bogd Khan's original spiritual authority. When Mongolia became independent of Chinese control in 1911, the name of the city was changed to Niislel Khüree, Capital Monastery, and that name remained in use until China temporarily reoccupied Mongolia in 1919. After the revolution of 1921–4 which led to a close alliance between Mongolia and Soviet Russia, the revolutionaries decided to change the name of their capital again, this time to Ulaanbaatar, Red Hero, and it has been known by that name ever since.[3]

Bogd Khan: The Living Buddha of Urga

The temporal ruler of Mongolia, the Bogd Khan, is often referred to as the Living Buddha of Urga as he was also the eighth incarnation of the

Jebtsundamba Khutukhtu and consequently the successor to the cultured artist and statesman Zanabazar: he could hardly have been more different. As has been observed, 'Living Buddha' is not a Mongolian usage but a translation from the Chinese which is disliked by Mongolians. It has however been used frequently in English-language accounts of the Bogd Khan.

The Swedish missionary, Frans August Larson, studied the Mongolian language in Beijing and then spent twenty years in Mongolia where he made the acquaintance of many lamas, including the Living Buddha. The Bogd Khan was born in Tibet and taken to Urga as a baby by lamas, to whom it had been revealed that he was to be 'God on earth to the Mongolian people'. Although he was educated in Mongolia, the Tibetan lamas acquired influence and authority in Urga through his presence. Larson expected an austere and spiritual figure but found him to be 'fun-loving' and partial to practical jokes. His status as a 'living god' theoretically precluded marriage, but this convention was circumvented by designating his intended bride a goddess. Larson acknowledges that the Bogd Khan lived a life of luxury and privilege at a time when most Mongols were desperately poor but also paints a positive portrait of his friend as a charitable man and a great ruler, an image that was not shared by other Westerners or Mongols who knew him well.[4]

When the Bogd Khan was enthroned as Khan in 1911 after the Manchu Qing Empire collapsed and Outer Mongolia declared itself independent, he was already a high-ranking lama, a recognized incarnation at the highest possible level, a *khutukhtu* (*khutagt* in modern Mongolian) which means 'holy' or 'saintly', not an entirely accurate description of the man himself. The Bogd Khan was the head of the Tibetan Buddhist order in Mongolia for a total of forty-nine years and for thirteen of these he was simultaneously head of state. He was an eccentric choice to be at the head of the revolutionary government that took over in 1921, but Owen Lattimore explained the political thinking behind his elevation:

With Manchu authority gone, none of the great regional nobles could be promoted to act as Head of State, because that would have made his peers jealous. Therefore, this new office was assigned to the most eminent religious leader in the country, the Jebtsundamba [Kh]utukhtu or 'Living Buddha of Urga'. As he was a Tibetan by birth, he was not even related to any of the noble families. He took the title of Kaghan [Khan] and the reign style of 'Elevated by All' – an historical fiction, suggesting that he had been recognised by the acclamation of the chiefs and warriors, in the ancient tribal tradition. As a lama he was supposed to be celibate, but in his new secular capacity his concubine was also officially given a title, making her a sort of queen. This anomaly did not bother anyone any more than the comparable goings-on bothered people in Europe in the days of the Medici Popes.[5]

The treatment of the Living Buddha of Urga by the revolutionaries reflects the caution with which they approached the task of establishing a new regime. Instead of removing the Bogd Khan as head of state in 1921, they retained him in deference to the continuing influence of the more conservative nationalists whom they wished to win over. However, his executive authority was taken away and reassigned to a cabinet of ministers, which in turn was by and large under the authority of the revolutionaries. 'In this way deference to a symbol of continuity was combined with a decisive shift in the distribution of real power. The balance of compromise thus established lasted until the death of the Living Buddha in 1924.'[6]

The Bogd Khan was a transitional figure whose authority collapsed during the period of invasion and internal conflict between 1919 and 1921, when there were attacks on Urga by both Chinese troops and White Russian army units under Baron Ungern-Sternberg, the notorious 'Mad Baron', whose violence in attacking Bolsheviks and any other opponents verged on insanity. During the Mongolian revolution of 1921, which was carried out with assistance from the Bolsheviks, the Bogd Khan was detained by Sükhbaatar, the revolutionary hero sometimes referred to as the 'Lenin' of Mongolia, who had served in the Khan's forces before rebelling. Sükhbaatar died in mysterious circumstances in 1923 but his legacy lingered on. The organization of which he was one of the founding members, the MPRP, was to remain the single ruling party in Mongolia till 1990 and the renaming of Urga as Ulaanbaatar (Red Hero) was in his honour. The Bogd Khan was permitted to remain as ruler until his death in 1924, but the limited authority that he exercised after the foreign invasions was restricted even further. His Winter Palace, which is situated to the north of the Tuul River in Ulaanbaatar, is now a museum, although the corresponding Summer Palace south of the river was destroyed in the early years of the Choibalsan period. The Bogd Khan had been a symbol of continuity but paradoxically during his rule a certain amount of political and social change had taken place, notably, 'the creation of a Western-style government, staffed with a permanent professional bureaucracy instead of the rotating service which was the normal pattern for Mongolian officials.'[7] It was not, however, an effective administrative body. As long as the Bogd Khan lived, the revolutionaries were not enthusiastic about confronting the power and wealth of the monastic system which was his earliest and greatest source of support.

Some traditional biographies of the Bogd Khan gave a full and respectful account of his religious and secular authority and his importance as a transitional figure and that is repeated by some contemporary scholars, including Batsaikhan Ookhnoi, who seek to replace the Communist-era government with a revived monarchy.[8]

A less flattering version by Owen Lattimore, based on his association with people who knew the leader, reveals a darker side to the Living Buddha of Urga:

> From the age of about 17 he began to surround himself with dissipated youngsters and to drink, carouse, smoke, gamble, and frequent the company of women. Even at this age, he was cruel. One of his escapades was to burn the hair and beard off an old retainer with kerosene. Podzneev [a Russian traveller, writer and eminent Mongolist], who saw him in 1892, describes his expression of childish wilfulness, but also notes that nothing he could do could lessen the people's infatuated religious faith in him.
>
> In his later years the Jebtsundamba Khutukhtu was a besotted drunkard. For many years he was blind, probably as a result of syphilis. He made no attempt to hide his depraved sexual life. When he became the ruler of Autonomous Mongolia, his most important consort was treated with imperial honours.[9]

For Lattimore this state of affairs demonstrated the persistence of 'mediaeval conditions' and a 'mediaeval psychology' in the Mongolia of the twentieth century. The Bogd Khan's lifestyle was no different from the way that emperors of China – and many other states – had behaved for centuries. Another contemporary 'living Buddha', the Dilowa Khutkhtu – 'a man as chaste and even saintly in his life as the Jebtsundamba Khutukhtu was depraved', in Lattimore's estimation – explains in his own autobiography that, in spite of the Bogd Khan's private idiosyncrasies, he had a reputation for being able to perform his religious duties satisfactorily; because he was the eighth incarnation he was regarded as a spiritually powerful figure. As the Qing dynasty's rule over China waned, he gave his religious imprimatur to the creation of a unified Mongol state and this was why he was allowed to remain as the head of a political and religious coalition that ruled an independent Mongolia until his death in 1924.

The most recent and detailed account of the career of the Bogd Khan in English is the consciously revisionist history by Batsaikhan Ookhnoi of the Mongolian Academy of Sciences. It fails to address, in fact it completely ignores, misgivings about the lama's private life but seeks to highlight 'the accusations and false judgements widespread in socialist propaganda and perpetuated in modern democratic Mongolia'. The book, which makes full use of Mongolian and Russian archives, concentrates on the Bogd Khan's role as ruler and his successes in diplomacy and gives him much greater credit for the successful creation of a modern Mongolian state than most previous accounts.[10]

Winter Palace of the Bogd Khan

The Winter Palace, which unlike the Summer Palace and a State Yellow Palace survived fires in 1924, is in the southern suburbs of Ulaanbaatar between the Dund and Tuul rivers. Today it stands in its own grounds just across the road from a very modern shopping centre, which houses a variety of commercial enterprises including a Korean coffee shop. The palace was constructed between 1893 and 1903 and was converted into a museum in 1926 after the death of the Bogd Khan and the confiscation of his property by state officials of the MPR. Choibalsan, who later became the dictatorial ruler of Mongolia as prime minister, was given the responsibility of selling off the property at a public auction, but it was later decided that some of it should be preserved for posterity in the new era and used as a negative example of how the feudal elite had lived.

The building complex remains intact as a museum: the buildings have clearly seen better days and the grass between them has not been well looked after, but the artefacts are carefully preserved. The museum is regularly visited by parties of local schoolchildren as well as foreign tourists. The actual palace – the residence of the Bogd Khan – is not very palatial. It is a two-storey building based on a design produced by a Russian architect and resembles the country house of a European nobleman. The Manchu emperor of China, Guangxu (or more likely his aunt, the interfering and intimidating Empress Dowager) criticized it for being in the style of a foreign religious tradition, so additional Buddhist ornamentation was added to the roof and lotus patterns were painted on the walls to make it appear less alien. The Bogd Khan and his queen, Dondogdulam, used the palace as their winter quarters for twenty years and the contents of the museum reflect their lives and their, sometimes bizarre, tastes.

The Waiting Room which was used by those who were seeking an audience with the Bogd Khan has on its wall a silk banner inscribed with a *magtaal*, a eulogy or, in the words of the museum's curator, 'traditional song of praise, describing the Bogd Khan's virtue in bringing prosperity and auspice [sic] to the Buddhist faith and the people'. There is also a painting commissioned by the Bogd Khan in 1912 from an artist, Jugder, of the city that was then still known as Niislel Khuree (Capital Monastery) as imagined seen from the air. In natural pigments it depicts the Winter Palace, the Summer Palace, the

State Yellow Palace, the White Palace, Gandan monastery, Maimai Town (the Chinese trading area) and the Manzushri Monastery. This gives a powerful impression of the domain of the Bogd Khan in the first year of Mongolia's independence from China.[11]

The Reception Room is dominated by the seat of the Bogd Khan, raised to a great height so that he would tower over even the most senior lamas and officials. He received these subordinates in private, and they were seated to his left on red and yellow seats if they were lamas and to his right on blue seats if they were secular nobles. The height was achieved by layers of cushions, twenty-five in all, to represent the titles and honours that he had accrued. The throne was decorated with a nine-dragon motif, presented to the Bogd Khan by the Guangxu emperor of the Manchu Qing dynasty.

Other rooms contain portraits of the Bogd Khan and his queen consort, his concubine until he married her in 1911 after Mongolia achieved its independence; clothing worn by both when they were performing official and religious duties; and ceremonial religious artefacts. Thrones from the State Yellow Palace, which was destroyed by fire in 1924, were transferred to the Winter Palace together with other artefacts and documents including the Bogd Khan's royal decree and the Mongolian declaration of independence from the Manchu regime in China: many of these can be viewed in the museum.

The Bogd Khan had an interest in animals and was given an elephant by a nobleman who had bought it in Russia. He also had a collection of stuffed animals, mostly those that were not native to Mongolia; this was specially created for him in Hamburg in 1901. These creatures occupy a room in the palace museum today as does the leopard skin *ger*, a potent symbol of 'Mongolness' for this high lama of Tibetan origin.

The Western-style palace building is set to the eastern side of the main complex which, in complete contrast, is a group of seven Buddhist summer prayer temples, built in a traditional East Asian style and arranged on a north-south axis. There are two smaller buildings which contained respectively the religious library and accommodation for visiting government and Buddhist officials during the reign of the Bogd Khan; three ceremonial gates mark the southern approach. The traditional Buddhist temple setting serves to emphasize the primacy of the Bogd Khan's religious status but also his temporal functions, many of which were performed under religious auspices.[12]

The Thirteenth Dalai Lama in Mongolia

Tibetan Buddhism has played a vital role in Mongolian society for centuries, but that does not mean that relations between the Mongolian and Tibetan religious hierarchies have always been amicable. This became apparent in 1903 when the thirteenth Dalai Lama (the immediate predecessor of the current holder of that title) took refuge in Ikh Khüree (Urga) after fleeing from the Younghusband expedition, a military incursion into Tibet launched from India by British forces under the command of Lieutenant-Colonel Sir Francis Younghusband. The express purpose of this expedition was to examine ways of countering potential Russian expansion that might threaten the stability of the Indian Raj. This followed concerns raised by the visit to the Tibetan capital, Lhasa, of a Buryat Mongol, Dorjiev, who had been enlisted to further the interests of Tsarist Russia in Tibet and who also acted as an informal adviser to the Dalai Lama. Younghusband was also given the task of establishing diplomatic relations with the deliberately isolated and cloistered Lhasa government. Sir Charles Bell, sometime British Political Officer for the Indian Civil Service in Sikkim, subsequently special envoy to Tibet in 1920, and the doyen of British Tibetology in the early twentieth century, conceded that the fear of Russia was somewhat exaggerated and that 'a Russian army could not have crossed Tibet and invaded India'. Nevertheless, rumours surrounding diplomatic negotiations between China and Russia alarmed the government of India and provoked Lord Curzon into dispatching a 'mission with an armed escort'. The mission's advance was resisted by Tibetan forces but was then reinforced so that it effectively became a military expedition (as evidenced by the issue of a war medal 'with clasps for the principal actions' to troops who had taken part).[13] The initial encounter between British and Tibetan forces resulted in at least 300 deaths and many injuries. In the eyes of the government in Lhasa, this was nothing short of an invasion and the Dalai Lama and his entourage sought sanctuary in Mongolia. The British were able to reach Lhasa without much difficulty and the outcome was an agreement, the Anglo-Tibetan (Lhasa) Convention, which was signed on the Tibetan side by a high lama, Tri Rimpoche, acting as Regent for the Dalai Lama, who by his absence was able to distance himself from the negotiations. Although it was a Tibetan who signed the agreement in the absence of the Dalai Lama, Tibetan politics was effectively dominated by representatives of the Manchu Qing government, the *ambans*, who had unsuccessfully advised negotiations with the British. Melvyn Goldstein, a leading historian of Tibet observed that,

> At that time the Dalai Lama was languishing in exile, spending time first in Outer Mongolia and then in the ethnic Tibetan areas of what is now Qinghai province. His overture to the Russian czar had proved futile and his position in exile was somewhat precarious as he had been 'deposed' by the Chinese government in 1904 because of his flight.[14]

On 26 July 1904 the Dalai Lama left the Potala Palace in Lhasa at two o'clock in the morning, under the cover of darkness to ensure secrecy. Travelling by camel, and after brief stays at the monasteries of Amarbuyant and Lama in Sain Noyon *aimag* (now in Arkhangai in central Mongolia), he finally arrived in Urga on 14 November, accompanied by his escort of fifty Tibetan lamas and servants. He was received by an enthusiastic crowd, but not by the Bogd Khan, the Jebtsundamba Khutukhtu, and went immediately to the Gandan monastery where he was being accommodated.

There are differing accounts of the relations between the Dalai Lama and the Jebtsundamba Khutukhtu, who was not yet the temporal ruler but was the highest spiritual authority in Mongolia and, like the Dalai Lama, was of Tibetan origin. There were serious tensions from the outset. There was even speculation that to avoid conflict the Jebtsundamba Khutukhtu might find it necessary to move far away from Urga to the Erdene Zuu Monastery near Kharkhorin in the Orkhon river valley. The Dalai Lama was unquestionably the senior spiritual figure, and he was able to exercise his authority in the traditional religious disputations that accompanied examinations in Mongolia for degrees in Tibetan Buddhism. As a result of these disputations in 1905, some Mongolian lamas became direct disciples of the Dalai Lama, a move that was perceived by the Jebtsundamba Khutukhtu as undermining his own religious authority in Mongolia.

Two further factors must be added to the personal froideur between the two grand lamas. First, there was competition for political influence by those diplomats in Urga who represented either the Manchu Qing court in Beijing or the Russian Tsar. Some meetings that did take place between the two high lamas were held in secret, at night, in a *ger* on the Tasgan Hill outside Urga, mainly to avoid their conversations being overheard by Manchu spies. Both senior lamas were deeply suspicious of the intentions of the Chinese government which was still controlled by the Manchu Qing court. Secondly, some Khalkh aristocrats who had previously followed the Jebstundamba Khutukhtu as the leader of a movement to achieve an independent Mongolia (under Russian protection) also began to cultivate the Dalai Lama as a possible alternative focus of political authority.

The uncomfortable exile of the Dalai Lama in Urga ended in the summer of 1905, when he moved to the monastery of Wang Khuree in the town now called Bulgan, which is in the north of Mongolia, some 300 miles from Urga. From this vantage point he established direct contacts with Russian officials and in August 1906, as Russia and Britain began negotiating on the future of Tibet, he returned to his homeland and took up residence temporarily at the important monastery of Kumbum in the Tibetan region of Amdo. Amdo, which in 1935 was the birthplace of the man who would later be recognized as the fourteenth Dalai Lama, was later integrated by the government of the People's Republic of China (PRC) into Qinghai province.

In 1908, the Dalai Lama visited Beijing in an unsuccessful and mortifying attempt to arrive at an agreement with the Chinese government. He returned to Lhasa the following year, but by then a Chinese military force had already been despatched to ensure Qing control over Tibet. That army, under Zhao Erfeng, a Qing government official and a Han Chinese bannerman, entered Lhasa in February 1910 and the Dalai Lama was obliged to flee again, this time to Darjeeling in British India. It was ironic that India became his refuge after his humiliating flight before the advance of the Younghusband expedition which had been launched from India. China was beginning to exercise real authority over Tibet, but this rapidly came to an end with the collapse of the Qing regime after the Revolution of 1911 in China. The tribulations of the thirteenth Dalai Lama illustrate how closely the affairs of Mongolia were linked to those of Tibet, but also to the great power politics of China, Russia and Britain which became far more important. In 1913 Tibet and Mongolia signed a treaty of mutual recognition to assert their independence but this was ignored by the great powers.[15]

Revolutionary herdsmen, the partisans of 1921

After the demise of the Chinese Empire in 1911 Mongolia achieved formal self-rule with the Bogd Khan as head of state. However, it was the action of revolutionaries ten years later that ensured the country's genuine and long-term independence from China and the beginning of its close association with revolutionary Russia. In 1921 Mongolian partisans, with the support of the Russian Red Army, drove the remnants of Ungern-Sternberg's anti-Bolshevik White Guards out of Mongolia and created the Mongolian Provisional Government. They permitted the Bogd Khan to remain in office but with greatly reduced powers. Although the ultimate result of the Mongolian revolution was the creation of a state that was closely allied to the Soviet Union, there is no doubt that the chief impetus for the revolt was Mongolian nationalism in opposition to China.[16]

This priority and the legacy of the partisans dominated Mongolian thinking for decades. In 1961 Mongolia celebrated the fortieth anniversary of the revolution that had extricated Mongolia from Chinese control. In the same year the MPR was finally admitted to membership of the United Nations, which had been created in 1945 at the end of the Second World War. It had taken fifteen years to persuade the United Nations that Mongolia was sufficiently independent of the Soviet Union to qualify as a bona fide nation state and was not the equivalent of one of the constituent republics of the USSR. Among the publications issued by the Mongolian government to celebrate the anniversary were a staid official history, *Forty Years of the Mongolian People's Revolutionary Party and the People's Revolution* (*Mongol ardyn khuv'sgalt nam ba ardyn khuv'sgalyn döchin jil*), and the more interesting *Narratives of the Mongolian People's Volunteer Army – Partisans* (*Mongol ardyn juramt tsergiin durtagaluud*), both of which were published under the names of editorial collectives.

Owen Lattimore saw this latter book, a collection of reminiscences by 200 of the Sükhbaatar partisans when he visited Ulaanbaatar in 1961 and was impressed by the fact that there had been no attempt to iron out discrepancies in the published recollections: 'it was history in the raw'. The background of the partisans was varied: many had served in a military unit; some had been Buddhist priests or monks; a number had been farmers and there was a small group of educated men who had worked in the lower ranks of the civil or military government. By far the largest category consisted of men who had worked as 'hired herdsmen, hunters, caravan men, cart-drivers in the old official transportation service and stage-riders in the courier service'. Their style of life had made these men tough and mobile and they were accustomed to protecting themselves and their charges in a harsh environment.[17]

Magsarjav (1877–1927): Indomitable hero or barbaric warrior?

The earliest revolutionary leader was not the celebrated Sükhbaatar, whose contribution will be examined in more detail later, but Sandagdorjiyn Magsarjav who was described by Lattimore as 'a strange, romantic and sometimes savage figure'. Magsarjav had a particular following in western Mongolia where his early military operations were based. He was born into an impoverished family of the minor aristocracy in the province of Bulgan in the north of the country. His background was not in herding but in farming, which was not unusual in that part of Mongolia. He turned to soldiering to fight the Chinese and served in a variety of ragbag units including, surprisingly, those under the command of the 'Mad Baron', Ungern-Sternberg, who is usually viewed as the sworn enemy of all Mongols. The deranged Baltic German-Russian aristocrat was at the time fighting a Chinese warlord and was able to persuade some Mongols to join him to fight a common enemy. Eventually Magsarjav joined a band of partisans associated with Sükhbaatar and Choibalsan, although he was older than either of them and was senior enough to have been considered a partisan leader in his own right. He died in 1927 when the MPR was still in its infancy, and it is the other two who are celebrated as the victorious leaders of the revolution.

The relegation of Magsarjav to a lower status in the revolutionary pantheon could also have resulted from his character and particularly his behaviour in the field which was uncomfortably close to the savagery of old-style Mongol warfare. A regime that wanted to present itself as modern, and the harbinger of a new type of civilization, might not want to praise his methods too fulsomely. Owen Lattimore characterized Magsarjav as a 'ruthless warrior who like Ja Lama [a contemporary of Magsarjav and a brutal warlord] revived the ancient shamanistic "magical" practice of tearing the hearts out of enemies killed in battle'.[18] Magsarjav, he declared,

> put prisoners to death, sacrificing their blood and their hearts to the battle standards of his troops ... It is my belief that men like Magsarjav [for he was not the only one and Ja Lama was even more barbaric, killing prisoners specifically for this ritual] stirred up these memories [of warrior folk heroes who enhanced their performance with magic including blood sacrifice] in order to create a new morale of battle to the death, converting passive heroism ... into merciless retaliation against the callous cruelty... of those against whom he was leading his men.[19]

Nevertheless, a biography of Magsarjav that was written by, or at least appeared under the name of, Mongolia's then leader, Choibalsan, was published in 1942 in the middle of the Second World War by the MPRP Central Committee's Department of Propaganda. It dwells on the positive and patriotic features of this national hero but otherwise provides a full amount of his life and does not flinch from describing the blood sacrifices, confirming Lattimore's account.[20]

Born in 1877 into an aristocratic but impoverished family in what is now Bulgan *aimag* in north central Mongolia, Magsarjav worked for a more powerful lord who was willing to allow him to get an education. At the age of 25 he inherited the title of 'duke' but this came with neither real authority nor money, so he continued to work tending livestock but also growing wheat and barley in this region in which there was settled agriculture as well as pastoral nomadism. As a literate young man, he had also carried out administrative work for the local banner office, and in 1911 he was able to abandon farming and work for the Mongolian civil service under its Manchu overlords. He was attached to the Khalkh Regular Service, in the western city of Khovd, with responsibility for official and military supplies and collecting debts for Chinese merchants. The year 1911 was the final year of the decaying Manchu Qing dynasty which ruled Mongolia as well as China. Magsarjav was well placed to play a major part in a Mongolian uprising against imperial rule that had been simmering for years and finally came to the boil in November of that year, when the Mongols established their independent provisional government under the Bogd Khan.

In the summer of 1912 Magsarjav was instructed by the Mongolian revolutionaries to remove all Manchu and Chinese officials from the western region around Khovd and to 'transfer all official business in the Khovd region to the office of the Khalkh Regular Service'. The officials from China, unable to accept the loss of their authority, refused and threatened to arrest Magsarjav who galloped to Niislel Khüree (Urga and later Ulaanbaatar) to report to the new Mongolian central government. Magsarjav and another hero of the revolution, Manlaibaatar Damdinsüren, were appointed Commanders of the Expeditionary Forces of the Western Frontier and returned to Khovd with orders that troops be mobilized under their command. When they had amassed sufficient forces, they attacked the city, killing many of the garrison, and taking many Chinese troops prisoner:

> Commander Magsarjav chopped the heads off the two Chinese captured earlier, together with those of the three who had just been captured, five in all. In order to raise the morale of the Mongol soldiers, Magsarjav paraded all his soldiers. Then he had the bodies of the Chinese soldiers opened and their hearts taken out to be sacrificed to the standard of the Commander-in-Chief of the Mongolian Army. Then Magsarjav and other officers tasted the blood of the five Chinese soldiers. He also ordered the Mongol soldiers to taste it, in order to show their heroic determination.[21]

After a failed attempt to breach the city walls with explosives, the Mongol cavalry launched a murderous onslaught and Khovd surrendered on 9 July 1912. The Manchu viceroy, his deputy and the local Chinese military commander were all captured, and the shops of Chinese merchants were looted, although Magsarjav, who had been on friendly terms with some traders, had given orders that there was to be no plunder.

Magsarjav also sacrificed the hearts of Kazakh bandits when his troops were operating in the Uriankhai region during the chaotic revolutionary period. He also led troops into Inner Mongolia to attack Chinese garrisons but in 1915, after the signing of a trilateral Russian-Chinese-Mongolian treaty that ceded Inner Mongolia to China, he retreated to Niislel Khüree and was appointed commander-in-chief of the Mongolian armed forces.

In the summer of 1919, the Mongolian forces encountered a group of White Russians, who had escaped from the new state being created after the Bolsheviks' seizure of power. Magsarjav was ordered to resist their incursion and did so successfully with the assistance of Red Army units that had been deployed in pursuit of the Whites. In spite of his military prowess and his successes in reforming the organization, discipline and supply of the army, Magsarjav was not a favourite of the Bogd Khan and his position was undermined by other feudal lords. His estrangement from the new government and its aristocratic supporters drew him into the revolutionary movement and it was his association with Sükhbaatar that established his reputation as one of the precursors of the movement. It was also as a result of this association with Sükhbaatar that he was arrested when the Chinese, who had been increasingly intervening in Mongolia for two years, mounted a further incursion in 1920. This resulted in a formal transfer of sovereignty from the Mongolian government to the Chinese in February 1920, an act that triggered the formation of new and determined nationalist revolutionary associations in Mongolia.

Magsarjav was released after the armies of the White Russian adventurer, the 'Mad Baron' Ungern-Sternberg, captured Niislel Khüree (Urga) in February 1921 and the Baron appointed him commander-in-chief of his Mongolian auxiliaries. As Ungern-Sternberg had suspected, Magsarjav was in sympathy with the revolutionaries and switched sides: the units under his command began to fight the Baron and drove his troops out of northwestern Mongolia. Magsarjav threw in his lot with Sükhbaatar and Choibalsan who were in the process of creating what would become the MPRP. He eventually became a member of the party's Central Committee and minister of war in the government that it dominated. He died on 3 September 1927 and was buried in his home district of Bulgan in a mausoleum built in the shape of a *ger*. In his 1942 biographical essay on Magsarjav, Choibalsan, Mongolia's premier from 1939 to 1952, redefined this brilliant but barbaric warrior as a revolutionary precursor of the MPRP. This brought him into the Mongolian revolutionary pantheon but also demonstrated how traditional attitudes, sustained by shamanistic beliefs, persisted during Mongolia's emerging nationalism and were not completely abandoned even during the spread of a new way of thinking based on the doctrines of the Soviet Union during the Stalin period. Modern accounts of the Mongolian revolution, such as B. Batbayar Baabar's *History of Mongolia: From World Power to Soviet Satellite* ignore or downplay the more barbaric elements in the methods of leaders like Magsarjav.[22]

3

Establishing the Mongolian People's Republic: Sükhbaatar and Choibalsan (1921–4)

Out of the maelstrom emerged two figures whose names have been indelibly linked with the creation of the new Mongolian state. Sükhbaatar (1893–1923), honoured as the principal hero of Mongolia's battle for independence from China, did not even live to see the creation of the Mongolian People's Republic (MPR) in 1924, but the presence of his statue in the very centre of Ulaanbaatar testifies to the resilience of his legacy and the myths that surround him. Choibalsan (1895–1952) outlived his comrade Sükhbaatar and eventually became head of the government and the absolute ruler of Mongolia until his death, subject only to the approval of Stalin. Reassessments of the history of this period since the Mongolian democratic revolution of 1990–1 have raised questions about the role played by these two men in the 1920s, and of others whose contribution has arguably been suppressed, but there remains no doubt about their importance.

Sükhbaatar is still acknowledged in Mongolia as the 'supreme hero' of the revolution of 1921 that paved the way for the establishment in 1924 of the MPR, formally independent but closely allied to the Soviet Union. Because there are parallels in their chronologies and both died young within a year of each other, Sükhbaatar has often been spoken of as Mongolia's Lenin, which is convenient as his successor, Choibalsan, again with the convenient concurrence of dates, can be thought of as Mongolia's Stalin. These are simplistic and not entirely helpful comparisons and do not accurately reflect the roles or the authority of either man. Sükhbaatar's statue occupies the centre of the main square of Ulaanbaatar which is named after him. It was briefly renamed Chinggis Khan Square in 2013 but the change was unpopular and in 2016 it officially reverted to its original name, which most people in the capital had in any case continued to use.

Sükhbaatar growing up

Sükhbaatar was born on 2 February 1893 in Maimaicheng, a Chinese name which literally means 'trading town'. It was close to Urga (Ikh Khüree) and, as its name suggests, was a Chinese commercial settlement and is now within the south-eastern suburbs of present-day Ulaanbaatar. Sükhbaatar's family were originally poor pastoral nomads but his parents had moved to the capital in search of work and, it seems, to avoid his in-laws who disapproved of their daughter's marriage to a man with such poor prospects. The ancestral grazing grounds of his parents' home banner in Tsetsen Khan *aimag*, were in the east of what was then Outer Mongolia and close to Manchuria, and the family owed the feudal rulers of that *aimag* unpaid corvée labour and other duties. Sükhbaatar's father, Damdin, was a personal serf of Taij Ilden who was an aristocrat and a *tuslagch*, a high-ranking assistant to a *zasag*, the ruling prince of a banner, in the highly stratified feudal administration of traditional Mongolia.

The district in which Sükhbaatar was born is now known as Amgalanbaatar and is home to the Sükhbaatar Birthplace Garden, a monument to his memory. His name at birth was probably simply Sükh (Axe), which is said to have been given to him after his father lost an axe in the river. Mongolian given names are sometimes chosen for superstitious reasons and can appear strange to outsiders. Sükhbaatar means 'Axe Hero' and he is often referred to as D. Sükhbaatar, short for Damdiny Sükhbaatar, the patronymic formed from his father's name, Damdin. In Mongolia most people are known simply by their given name and the patronymic or initial is rarely used, except on formal occasions or when it is necessary to distinguish different individuals with the same given name.

Damdin worked as a night-watchman for Chinese shopkeepers in Maimaicheng and looked after their animals, but in 1898 when Sükhbaatar was only 4 years old the family moved to be closer to the centre of Urga. They found a space to set up their *ger* near the Russian Consulate which was in the east of the capital, overlooking the River Tuul which flows westward through the southern outskirts of the city. The administrators of Tsetsen Khan *aimag* tried to insist that Damdin return to his ancestral place to carry out his feudal obligations but, with the help of his friend Davaa, he managed to obtain a post as a 'servant and fire-tender' in the office of the *aimag* representative in Urga. As this was work for the *aimag* administration it was considered equivalent to feudal service, so he did not have to leave the city. The family remained poor, managing with just a felt door to their *ger* when most other people were able to buy wooden ones. Inside, they could manage to acquire only one hide to cover the floor and there was little furniture.

As a young child Sükhbaatar had no formal schooling, but he acquired some basic knowledge of the Russian language while playing with the children of Russian families who lived around the consulate. The teenage Sükhbaatar persuaded his parents that he should have at least a basic education and in 1907, at the age of 14, he began to learn to read and write Mongolian with the assistance of a tutor, Jamiyan, who was a *zaisan*, a minor official in the office of the Bogd Khan, the Living Buddha of Urga. Jamiyan also instructed the young Sükhbaatar and other boys in arithmetic at an informal *ger* school that he ran. He later played an important role in negotiations between the Bogd Khan and the revolutionaries and, after the revolution, was appointed to the Institute of Scripture and Manuscripts in what later became the Mongolian Academy of Social Sciences. It is remarkable that Sükhbaatar gained any education at all as his parents could not afford to pay tuition fees. He benefited from a tradition that tutors would occasionally teach an able boy from a poor family without charge. This was not pure altruism: if that boy eventually became an official, the tutor would have acquired a valuable connection.

The tutoring lasted until Sükhbaatar was 16, when his parents found paid employment for him as the family desperately needed an extra income. Sükhbaatar worked as a guide and rider for the Horse Relay postal courier system, riding the postal route between Urga and Burgaltai and acting as guide and companion to travellers who were not familiar with the route. Although this work attracted a low wage it was not a normal job, but a feudal obligation to which all families were subjected in rotation, and which was hated and avoided where possible. Sükhbaatar complained of being overworked and frequently ill-treated by his aristocratic superiors and after a few months moved to another Horse Relay station in Urga itself. To supplement his wages from the relay and help support his family he earned additional money by delivering meat from the market and selling firewood and hay to families that raised livestock.[1]

Sükhbaatar the soldier and Mongolian secession in 1911

The disintegration of the Manchu Empire in the autumn of 1911 and the creation of a national Mongolian army was a critical moment for Mongolia, and for Sükhbaatar. Anti-Manchu sentiment had been growing among the general population which had been dominated by a range of powerful and wealthy individuals – Manchu officials, lamas, feudal lords and Chinese traders. By October 1911, when the uprising in China against the Manchus broke out, much of the authority of the Manchus in Mongolia had already evaporated and many lamas and nobles, whatever their previous allegiances, were effectively lining up with nationalist revolutionaries. An independent Mongol state was proclaimed in Urga (Ikh Khüree) at noon on 30 December 1911 by the Western calendar, and the final representative of the Manchu overlords, the *amban* Sandowa, fled to Beijing with his officials. The Living Buddha of Urga, the Jebtsundamba Khutukhtu, who had until then exercised only spiritual authority as the Bogd Gegen (Holy or August Radiance), was now installed as head of state with the title of Bogd Khan and acquired the temporal powers of a monarch. Some Mongol historians refer to him as the Emperor, one possible translation of Khan.[2]

The new regime in Urga took the name of Provisional General Office for Khalkh Affairs but it was often simply called the Mongolian Autonomous Government. Its autonomy was far from unqualified: in two international treaties, the Sino-Russian Accord of 1913 and the Treaty of Kyakhta of 1915, which it signed with Russia and China, Mongolia conceded that it would accept the status of autonomy under Chinese suzerainty rather than insist on genuine independence.

The Mongolian government had created a new army by mobilizing troops from the four Khalkh *aimags* and Sükhbaatar was conscripted into this new formation which was trained by Russian officers. Initially he served in the menial positions of cook and batman to an officer in units stationed in the countryside, but he was later transferred to the capital garrison in Urga. As a literate Mongol, who also knew Russian and had some mathematical knowledge, he was a natural choice for the Military Training School that was established in 1912 at Khujiburlan, to the east of Urga, with the assistance of Russian advisors. Sükhbaatar displayed a talent for military tactics, excelled at horsemanship and was a first-rate shot with the rifle. He graduated in the 'fifth rank with a white glass button and a peacock feather in his hat'; this signified that he was the fifth of the five leading cadets who were each appointed to command a platoon. It was at this time that he met and married Yangjmaa: they set up home in a *ger* near the college, and Yangjmaa supplemented their income by milking cows owned by Russian officers who were in charge of training the troops with whom her husband served.

Sükhbaatar saw service on the Mongolian border where his unit repelled attacks by both regular Chinese soldiers and bandits. In 1917 he was deployed to the eastern frontier under the command of the infamous Magsarjav, promoted to the rank of captain and put in command of a machine gun company. In addition to his nationalist and anti-Chinese sentiments, he had become deeply conscious of the poor conditions under which rank-and-file soldiers served. Wages were low, discipline was brutal and the food was poor. Sükhbaatar was not afraid to stand up to bullying officers, however senior, and was influential in a brief but successful protest by the troops of his unit when they were supplied with meat that was even more rotten than usual. His involvement was discreet – an officer could not be seen to be inciting a mutiny – but his sympathy for the rank-and-file troops did not go unnoticed. In 1918 he was transferred by the Ministry of Defence to the Mongolian Autonomous Government, to assist in the publication of legal codes and Buddhist texts. This unusual career move was partly because he was literate and partly because his former teacher, Jamiyan, later the first president of the Mongolian Committee of Scientists, directed the official publishing office and pulled strings on his behalf. An additional factor, however, was that officials at the ministry had not forgotten his involvement with the food protest and thought it prudent to separate him from the troops who had shown dissent. He served for a total of nine years in the army until his regiment was demobilized in 1919. Popular perceptions of Sükhbaatar's status as a gallant and heroic warrior were enhanced by stories such as the occasion of the great *naadam* – the Mongolian equivalent of the Highland Games – of 1922 when he 'rode down the field at full gallop, leaning from the saddle to pick up silver dollars from the ground – a show to delight the cavalryman in every Mongol heart'.[3]

By 1919 he had become a radical anti-Chinese nationalist and was increasingly concerned about social justice, but he was in no sense a Marxist or indeed an adherent of any political philosophy. This was in contrast with his colleague and successor, Choilbalsan, who had been influenced by Russian Communists at an early stage in his career. Sükhbaatar remained in contact with many of his military comrades, some of whom subsequently joined him in one of the groups of nationalist partisans that emerged to resist pressure from China.

China reoccupies Mongolia in 1919

After the forces of General Xu Shucheng reoccupied Mongolia in 1919, resistance to China became the overwhelming priority of the Mongolian revolutionary movement. This paved the way for an eventual alliance with Russia that would last for decades.

When Russian influence in the east declined in the turmoil of the revolutions of February and October 1917 and the ensuing civil war, China took the opportunity to reassert its claims to Mongolian territory. The government of the Republic of China (1911–49), anxious to regain all the territories of the defunct empire, was determined to crush Mongolia's autonomous government. By the middle of 1918 the Urga regime had been weakened by a combination of Chinese political pressure and internal factional conflict.

Even the limited autonomy enjoyed by the Urga regime was annulled when military officers acting in the name of the Republic of China decided to incorporate Mongolia into its administrative structure. In November 1919, military units of the Northwest Frontier Defence Army, commanded by General Xu Shuzheng a subordinate of the Chinese warlord Duan Qirui, captured Urga and obliged members of the Mongolian regime to relinquish power. Members of the Upper and Lower Houses of the Mongolian parliament met to decide on their response to Xu and, although Sükhbaatar was not a member or either house, he became involved in an intervention in favour of resisting the Chinese.

On 19 February 1920 there was a formal ceremony for the liquidation of the autonomous government and the Bogd Khan was obliged to prostrate himself in front of an image of the Chinese president. This high-handed behaviour left the Mongol leadership utterly humiliated and fuelled a new wave of anti-Chinese sentiment. As the army of the Mongolian government was disbanded, Sükhbaatar found himself out of a job so he and his family moved back to Urga to stay with a relative. Back in the capital, Sükhbaatar had become involved with East Urga (*Züün Hüree*) one of two clandestine groups that were contemplating resistance against the Chinese occupation. Members of East Urga were mainly low-ranking government officials. The other group was Consular Terrace (*Konsulyn Denj*), sometimes called Consular Hill, which consisted primarily of commoners, one of whom was Choibalsan; this group was led by the lama, Bodoo, who had taught Mongol at the Russian Consulate. Choibalsan had studied in Irkutsk, so the Consular Terrace group was well placed to make the first approaches to the Russians. The two groups began to cooperate in the spring of 1920 and put up posters denouncing the Mongolian ruling élite for betraying the people and somewhat naively entreating General Xu to return their rights to them. East Khüree concentrated on influencing the Bogd Khan but also cultivated Russian contacts.

The independent monarchy was formally restored in 1921 under what Charles Bawden pithily characterized as the 'brutal, though historically irrelevant, régime of the white Russian leader, Baron Ungern-Sternberg', universally known as the 'Mad Baron'. Another provisional government was established in Kyakhta, the town in the Mongol Buryat region of Russia close to the Mongolian border which was a major crossing point for trade between Russia and China. The new government restored the constitutional monarchy, this time with the assistance of units of the Red Army from revolutionary Russia, and this regime lasted until the death of the Jebtsundamba Khutukhtu, the Bogd Khan, in 1924.[4]

Russian revolutionaries and the Mongolian People's Party

It was at this time that Sükhbaatar became involved with Russian revolutionaries who were supporters of the Bolsheviks. Contacts with Russia were not entirely new. In the summer of 1911, a delegation of Mongol princes and high lamas, conscious that their feudal loyalty had been owed not to China in general but to the now deposed Qing emperor, journeyed to St Petersburg to seek support for Mongolian independence. Russia itself, between the two revolutionary years of 1905 and 1917, was a nation in flux and, although there was some support for the idea of an independent Outer Mongolia, the government in St Petersburg was not willing to confront China over its claims, particularly to Inner Mongolia. The Russo-Chinese Joint Declaration of 1913 'recognised Chinese suzerainty over an autonomous Outer Mongolia' and the arrangement was formalized in the Tripartite Agreement between Russia, China and Mongolia in 1915.[5]

Russian attitudes changed after the October Revolution of 1917, although overtures from Mongolian radicals were still received cautiously. The Soviet government was more concerned with defeating the anti-Bolshevik military intervention on its western borders. In the summer of 1919, however, a message from the new Soviet government invited Mongolia to send delegates to meet the Red Army and repudiated the Tsarist Joint Declaration of 1913. The Bogd Khan administration, no doubt preoccupied with pressure from China, failed to respond to this approach.

Sükhbaatar and his fellow activists agreed to send representatives to what became the Eastern Bureau of the Communist International, the Comintern. According to the official chronology, on 25 June 1920 the members of the two clandestine groups, East Urga and Consular Terrace, united under the name of the Mongolian People's Party (MPP). In April 1920, representatives of both groups met the Russian representative, I. V. Sorokovikov, who was about to leave Irkutsk for Moscow to report on the situation in Urga. When Sorokovikov returned to Irkutsk 20 June he was officially the representative of the Comintern and urged the Mongolians to send delegates to the Comintern's Far Eastern Secretariat. By the end of June there was a functioning MPP but, notwithstanding its connections with the Russians, it was not a creation of the Comintern. It was not even Marxist or socialist: its members all subscribed to a form of anti-Chinese nationalism, but some remained committed to working with the existing Buddhist hierarchy. As Fujiko Isono pointed out, 'not only was the whole life of the Mongols steeped in Lamaism, but the Lamaist religion and the Bogd had become symbols of anti-Chinese nationalism and autonomy. The MPP had formed around a set of 'Ten Oaths', which committed the members to the abolition of exploitation, restoration of 'our lost political power and [defence of our] religion'. The ambiguity of the oaths permitted individuals to interpret the document in whatever way was convenient to them.[6]

It is important to remember that Russia, then as now, was a multi-ethnic society. Although most of the leading Bolsheviks were, if not all ethnically Russian, then primarily Russian speakers of European origin, members of other ethnic groups supported their opposition to the Tsarist regime. The group most relevant to the Mongolian revolution was the Buryats, recognized as ethnic Mongols and speakers of what has been classified as either a separate Mongol language or a dialect of Mongol. Progressive Buryats, that is those sympathetic to the Bolsheviks, were an important conduit between the Russians and the Mongols of Mongolia.

Recent research, drawing on Mongolian documents that have become available since 1991, has cast doubt on some of the details of the foundation of the MPP. particularly the prominence accorded to Sükhbaatar, the official hero of the Mongolian revolution. Hiroshi Futaki has argued that the memoirs of Dansrangiin Dogsom, one of the founding members of the party and later head of state should be relied on for determining the date that the two separate groups amalgamated to constitute the party. Futaki uses different names, calling East Urga the 'Civil Servants' Group' and Consular Terrace the 'People's Group'. These are attempts to describe the composition of the two groups and not the names by which they were known at the time and invite confusion. More significantly, he argues that they amalgamated earlier than 25 June 1920, the date given in official accounts. It was, he suggests, 'a day in the middle month of spring 1920' and in the residence of Dogsom rather than Danzan as is usually recorded. At this point, he argues, the Mongolian revolutionaries contacted the Russian military adviser Sorokovikov and 'a relationship with Soviet Russia became realistic'. While this does not invalidate previous arguments about the move towards Russia, it does downplay the role of Sükhbaatar in the initial months of the MPP.[7]

Two delegates, Choibalsan and Danzan, were chosen by drawing lots to travel northwards to meet representatives of the Bolshevik government in the Far Eastern Republic but, after a clandestine meeting on the steppe, it was decided to increase the number of delegates, and Sükhbaatar and four others were chosen to accompany them. The journey to seek the backing of Russia was supported by some Mongolians but opposed by others. It was dangerous, as the delegates had to contend with Chinese troops and secret agents. They also had to finance the journey out of their own meagre resources and Sükhbaatar is said to have sold his own *ger* and left his wife and son to live in a shed.

The delegates left Urga towards the end of June 1920 and reached Kyakhta on 18 August. Kyakhta is on the border between Russia and Mongolia. In

1920 it was divided into a Russian settlement in the north which was called Troitskosavsk (Deed Shivee in Mongolian) and a Mongolian one in the south, now called Altanbulag. Troitskosavsk was in Buryatia, just across the border from Outer Mongolia, although the border seems to have been more notional than real at that time; it later reverted to its original name of Kyakhta. Some visitors and writers continued to use the name Kyakhta for both sides of the border and reserved Troitskosavsk for the original fortified Russian encampment to the north of the commercial area.[8]

With considerable difficulty Choibalsan and Danzan located the elusive Russian consul who sent them by steamer on the Selenge river to Verkhneudinsk (now the Buryat Republic's capital of Ulan Ude). On arrival in Verkhneudinsk, they were treated with great suspicion but eventually met the premier of the Russian-controlled Far Eastern Republic, Boris Shumyatsky, whose caution verged on paranoia. The Russians insisted that any request for assistance should be under the seal of the Bogd Khan and after some delay this was provided. On 10 August five more MPP members, including Sükhbaatar, arrived in Verkhneudinsk and the Mongols were instructed to travel by train to Irkutsk for a meeting with staff of the Comintern. They were well received when they arrived on 15 August, but it became clear that the Russians in Irkutsk were more interested in a request from a potential allied political party than a formal document from the Bogd Khan. This required difficult negotiations among the delegates, mainly about the significance of the Bogd's seal, but a document was agreed upon in which the delegates requested financial assistance and arms and ammunition. A subsequent document maintained their aim of retaining the Bogd as a constitutional monarch but included the recognition of the need for a social revolution and a struggle against the secular Mongol aristocracy. Attacks on the Lamaist establishment were either not envisaged or diplomatically deferred in the light of the deep respect for Buddhism in the Mongolian population.

Sükhbaatar and Choibalsan remained in Irkutsk for advanced training with the Russian Red Army and political education from Comintern officials, while their colleagues visited other areas under Bolshevik control. The group were particularly impressed by Lenin's clearly expressed views that ethnic minority groups should be allowed considerable autonomy within their own territories.[9]

Enter the Mad Baron

The new and embattled Soviet regime was reluctant to involve itself deeply in Mongolian politics as the political situation in the Russian heartland and on its European flank was still unresolved. The Mongolians wanted arms to assist them in resisting the Chinese, but the Bolsheviks wanted cordial relations with China and encouraged Mongolian progressives to find common cause with nationalist Chinese. There was no incentive for the Bolshevik leadership to invade or control Mongolia and Fujiko Isono's argument that, 'the theory [prevalent for most of the 20th century] of a Soviet-inspired Mongolian revolution gives too much credence to the efficiency and organisational ability of the Soviet government and the Comintern', is persuasive.[10] It was only the capture of Urga by White Russian forces under Baron Ungern-Sternberg and the restoration of the Bogd Khan supported by Mongol princes, that persuaded them to change their minds. Ungern-Sternberg had planned to use Mongolia as the launch pad for a grandiose plan that involved a counter-revolution against the Bolsheviks and a restoration of the monarchies of Russia, China and Mongolia. His forces eventually captured Urga in early February 1921 and the Bogd Khan was spirited away to a mountain monastery under close guard by Ungern-Sternberg's troops. Meanwhile, the Mongolian revolutionaries, who were in touch with the Bogd's administration, were making their way back to Urga and had reached Kyakhta.

The Bolsheviks were by then even less willing to support the Mongolian revolution for fear of Chinese reprisals and were more concerned about maintaining the security of a nominally independent Far Eastern Republic as a buffer state. The initiative was now with the Mongolian revolutionaries and their embryonic military forces.[11]

Building the party and partisans

Sükhbaatar 'personally visited several frontier watch-posts to the west of Kyakhta to recruit volunteers for the People's Army', of which he had been appointed commander-in-chief on 9 February 1921.[12] Some were drafted from the banner units on the frontier, but most were volunteers; many had received military training and possessed their own weapons. The majority were from poor herding families, a background very different from the peasant armies of China, and their ability to ride horses and hunt was a great advantage for the military. These 'partisans', who initially only numbered about 400, were soon in action against the Chinese army and Choibalsan was given command of partisan units in the west of Mongolia.

The formal inaugural conference of the MPP did not take place until 1 March 1921, when it was held in the Russian sector of Kyakhta. A representative of the Comintern attended, as did a group of educated Buryats sympathetic to the Bolsheviks. Delegates agreed on a Party Platform that was more radical than the original Ten Oaths and clearly showed the influence of the Buryats who were well-versed in the use of Marxist terminology in Mongolian. Differences between delegates who were more revolutionary or more nationalist were temporarily smoothed over in the interests of a unified party and they agreed to form a Provisional People's Government and, as a priority, to liberate Kyakhta from the Chinese.

The plan to free Kyakhta from Chinese control came to fruition on 15 March 1921 and the defeat of the Chinese the following day is commemorated as the date of the birth of the Mongolian People's Revolutionary Army. Soviet troops were held in reserve and the fighting was carried out by Mongolian partisans, although many had Soviet weapons. The revolutionaries, and their Mongolian People's Provisional Government, now had control over a substantial section of northern Mongolia but, in the words of an official biography of Sükhbaatar, the remainder of the country 'was still under the control of Baron Ungern, the treacherous Government in Khüree and groups of Chinese bandits'.[13] Ungern-Sternberg had moved his forces north, and, under the command of a Mongol prince, they attacked Kyakhta in May 1921. The initial resistance came from Mongolian partisans and, with support from the Bolshevik troops in Siberia, the Mongolian forces were able to repel Ungern-Sternberg's White Russians. The partisans, whose numbers had now risen to 700, marched on Urga at the end of June 1921 and were able to enter the city without resistance as the Bogd Khan and his administration had decided to receive the revolutionaries peacefully. They entered Urga (Niislel Khüree), and in a spirit of cooperation, flew the yellow flag of the Mongolian Autonomous Republic over the palace of the Living Buddha, the Bogd Khan. A constitutional monarchy was proclaimed, which retained the Bogd Khan as head of state, but his authority had been much reduced by his inability to resist the Chinese and he was thenceforth confined to dealing with religious affairs. Ungern-Sternberg retreated into Russia where he was tried and executed by the Bolsheviks, probably in Novosibirsk in September 1921, although an alternative account put his execution in Irkutsk. Western Mongolia had remained in the hands of White Russian forces and the Oirat and other groups of that region were suspicious of the intentions of the dominant Khalkh Mongols in the east. This conflict was resolved when the military leader, Magsarjav, staged a coup d'état in Uliastai and threw in his lot with the other revolutionaries. Hostilities finally ceased in January 1922 with the capitulation of White Russian forces.[14]

Acknowledging the vital importance of Russian support for their new government, the Mongolians had sent a delegation to Moscow via Ulan Ude and Irkutsk. On 5 November 1921 a Treaty of Friendship was signed between the Mongolian government and what would the following year become the USSR; Lenin received the revolutionary herdsmen at the Kremlin.

Meanwhile in Mongolia there was opposition to Sükhbaatar's control over the party and the government, both from within the MPP and from the conservative ruling elite around the Bogd Khan. Early in 1922 Sükhbaatar purged a group of his opponents as suspicions grew about Chinese and Japanese attempts to destabilize Mongolia; there were constant rumours of a coup against him. Among those executed was his rival Bodoo who had led the Consular Terrace group in the creation of the MPP. On 20 February 1923 Sükhbaatar died following a severe cold and fever: he was 30 years old. Earlier versions of his official biography blamed his death on poisoning by his enemies, but these claims were dropped later.

The National Museum of Mongolia in Ulaanbaatar preserves Sükhbaatar's traditional *deel* or gown and his *xantaaz*, the short sleeveless jacket usually worn over it. This jacket is decorated with a pattern of the *ulzii* or eternal knot, an important symbol of continuity and interdependence in Tibetan Buddhist culture. These garments are displayed alongside a box made of wood, leather, silver, coral and the ornamental gem, turquoise; in this box he carried his official seal as commander-in-chief of the armed forces.[15]

Even before the victory over the White Forces, the People's Government had begun to issue decrees: these included the transfer of land and natural resources to the state and the abolition of the institution of *khamjilga* that bound commoners in service to the nobles; the hereditary status of these nobles was also threatened but it was not abolished at this stage. These decrees announced policies that were relatively mild and did not portend the collectivization of livestock that was to follow in the years from 1929 to 1931. When the Bogd Khan died in May 1924, the constitutional monarchy died with him and Mongolia was proclaimed a people's republic. These developments were not accepted without opposition, some revolutionaries disagreed about the speed of change: the executions, following what was claimed to be the unmasking of a plot against the MPP by Bodoo and other party members, have already been mentioned. There was also obstruction from the aristocracy and the high lamas but by 1925 the new government felt confident enough for Soviet Red Army units to be withdrawn.[16]

Choibalsan's childhood

It is necessary to retrace our steps to assess the role in the Mongolian revolution played by the other major figure in the country's twentieth-century history, Choibalsan. In official histories of the MPR, the name of Choibalsan is inextricably linked with that of Sükhbaatar from the earliest days of the revolution. In common with his close colleague and many of the other revolutionaries, Choibalsan came from an impoverished family background. He was born on 8 February 1895 in the countryside around the eastern Mongolian city that now bears his name but was then called Bayan Tumen. When he was 13 years old, he was placed in a monastery by his mother: this may have been for reasons of piety, as she wanted him and his elder brother to study the Tibetan language and Buddhist scriptures, but it was also a practical proposition as the family would not have to pay for his keep. He found the strict monastic regime intolerable, especially the impossibility of having any independent thought; when he was 17 he escaped with a friend. Although without any footwear they walked all the way to Niislel Khüree (Urga), a journey of 1,000 kilometres. With no contacts in the capital they slept either in the marketplace or in the shelter of the remains of the city walls. This monastic background and his determination to escape from it is one of many interesting parallels between his career and that of his subsequent Soviet mentor, Joseph Stalin.

The pair earned what money they could by delivering meat from the market or acting as night-watchmen. Somehow Choibalsan was able to gain entry to a school run by a Buryat Mongol, Jamsrano (later the founder of the Mongolian Academy of Sciences), to train translators and interpreters in the Russian language. He was successful enough to be able to transfer to a more advanced course at a secondary school in the Siberian city of Irkutsk; consequently, much of his education at this most impressionable age was influenced by Russians. When the October Revolution broke out in Russia in 1917, he was able to observe the impact that the uprisings in St Petersburg and Moscow had on the Russian Far East. In Irkutsk he witnessed demonstrations, became aware of meetings attended by radical workers, and began to appreciate the significance of the political activities of the Bolsheviks. Choibalsan and the other Mongolian students were, however, recalled to Mongolia by the Autonomous Government in Urga which was concerned at the potential influence of Bolshevik ideas on its own security. In 1918, Choibalsan briefly attended the Communications School in the Mongolian capital which trained staff for the newly established telegraph service. He was literate in both Mongolian and Russian, he had a certain level of education, but he was not considered to be an intellectual.

Choibalsan and Sükhbaatar: A revolutionary apprenticeship

It was at this point that China decided to eliminate the Mongolian Autonomous Government and Choibalsan became part of the Consular Terrace clandestine revolutionary group that was organized in Urga to defy the Chinese. The cooperation between Consular Terrace and Eastern Urga, the group to which Sükhbaatar belonged, was the basis for the foundation in 1920 of the MPP, which was renamed the Mongolian People's Revolutionary Party (MPRP) in 1924. Both men recognized that a military organization was essential to ensure political success, and that Soviet Russia was the only possible external source of support for Mongolia's resistance to Chinese aggression. Both travelled to Russia; both enrolled in the Military Training College of the Red Army in Irkutsk; and both were members of the MPP when it held its inaugural congress on 1 March 1921 and resolved to combine national liberation with a degree of social revolution. Sükhbaatar and Choibalsan then led separate units of partisan and regular troops in successful actions against the White Russian and Chinese armies. In July 1921 the revolutionaries were able to establish an independent regime based in Urga. They retained the old Bogd Khan as head of state, in recognition of the respect he enjoyed among pious Mongols, and this restricted their longer term aims of displacing the existing structures of power and the traditional culture that the Living Buddha of Urga represented.

Succession to Sükhbaatar

It has long been assumed that after the death of Sükhbaatar on 20 February 1923, Choibalsan became the principal leader of the party and the government until his death in 1952. This belief was encouraged by the official media during the life of the MPR because it strengthened the analogy with Lenin and Stalin in the Soviet Union. In fact, the transition to what became Choibalsan's autocratic rule was slow and disorderly: it required the removal of potential rivals and opponents through purges in which Choibalsan was in all probability involved, although he did not always play the leading role. In the words of Choibalsan's political heir, Tsedenbal, 'Under the leadership of Choibalsan the Party liquidated its enemies and then pushed the revolution to the second stage'. This was a way of describing a comprehensive purge of all party and government organizations including the Central Committee, to which Choibalsan reported on 20 January 1925, identifying the internal and external enemies who he believed threatened their authority. The result of this wholesale removal of troublesome or disloyal individuals was a division within the party into two factions, the Capital and Rural: Choibalsan sided with the Rural faction against what he and his supporters designated as the 'right wing' Capital group.[17]

Sükhbaatar had been much more of a military leader than a politician. After his death and the establishment of the new regime, the focus of the revolutionaries shifted from military considerations to the consolidation of the MPRP and the need to construct an effective government to rule the MPR. It was difficult to achieve a clear succession to Sükhbaatar. As the 1930s were succeeded by the 1940s, Choibalsan came to dominate Mongolia but his rise to power was gradual. For much of this period he was not sufficiently powerful to exercise supreme authority and several lesser known individuals served as heads of the government and the party.

4

Mongolian People's Revolutionary Party in power: The Choibalsan years (1924–52)

In the fifteen years before Choibalsan finally achieved power in 1936, Mongolia experienced wild policy swings, the destruction of Lama Buddhist monastic power, a decline in the economy and a violent conflict that was only ended by the intervention of Moscow and the Comintern. The canonization of Sükhbaatar and Choibalsan as the Lenin and Stalin of Mongolia, symbolized by their joint mausoleum in the style of Lenin's tomb at the north end of Ulaanbaatar's Sükhbaatar Square that was not finally demolished until 2005, has obscured the confusion and turmoil of the 1920s, ignored or underplayed the role of other revolutionaries and blamed Choibalsan exclusively for all the errors and crimes of those years when responsibility should really have been spread more widely.

At the time of Sükhbaatar's death on 20 February 1923 the Mongolian People's Revolutionary Party (MPRP) chairman was Ajvaagijn Danzan who had held the post from 2 January 1923, was ousted on 31 August 1924 and then enjoyed a brief career as a diplomat. Danzan was replaced by Tseren-Ochiryn Dambadorj, a young and educated Marxist who rose through the Mongolian Revolutionary Youth League and remained in post until 1928. During this period there were no great policy changes, but local government was restructured, and a modern system of taxation introduced.[1] The private economy continued to flourish and relations between the government and the Lama Buddhist establishment could be described as mutually accommodating. Dambadorj, despite his Marxist background, sought to broaden Mongolia's international links and aimed to reduce the regime's dependence on the Soviet Union; in the end this resulted in his downfall. In the prevailing relatively tolerant and broad-minded atmosphere, it was possible for someone like Tsyben Jamsrano (1880–1942), a democratic socialist and expert on shamanism who worked at the precursor to the Mongolian Academy of Sciences, to advocate openly that the revolutionaries should allow a reformed Lama Buddhism to exist since, in cooperation with the state, it would serve to protect humanity. This period of tolerance did not last.

At this point, Choibalsan cannot be described accurately as a dictator, but neither did he lack power: he was a member of the Central Committee of the MPRP from 1924 to 1940 and had a place on its ruling presidium. In addition, he was able to exercise his authority as commander-in-chief of the Mongolian army for much of the time from 1924. He began to acquire real political power when he served as minister of internal affairs from 1936 to 1940 and this was consolidated when he was prime minister from 28 March 1939 until his death on 26 January 1952. In terms of real power and authority, however, for most of this period the political direction of Mongolia was controlled not by anyone in the Mongolian leadership but indirectly by Stalin and his agents from Moscow and Irkutsk.

Choibalsan's reputation is more tarnished than Sükhbaatar's, because of the purges and mass killings of Buddhist monks and others who were considered a threat to the regime in the 1930s. These took place after Sükhbaatar's death. In a resolution passed by the MPRP Central Committee in January 1962, ten years after Choibalsan's death and during the de-Stalinization movement inspired by the Soviet leadership under Khrushchev, Choibalsan was formally accused of complicity in all these purges and executions. While he cannot be absolved from blame, as he was a senior party and government official for much of this time, his role was complicated and somewhat ambiguous. He was away from Mongolia for much of the worst period of repression and did not take up his formal appointment as minister of internal affairs until the worst of the purges were already over. He could certainly be criticized for allowing a cult of personality to develop around him, although even the adulation of Choibalsan was mild in comparison with the wider veneration for Stalin in Mongolia. Although far from guiltless personally, it can be argued that in death he became a useful scapegoat for the collective errors and crimes of the 1930s, so that others could be exonerated, and their transgressions conveniently forgotten.[2]

Buryats

The political leadership of the MPR during the twentieth century was Mongolian in its origin but it also included some Buryat Mongols whose homeland was in Russian territory. Many were judged by Mongolians to be closer to the Soviet Communist Party than to their Khalkh cousins from the Mongolian People's Republic (MPR). Ironically the Buryats were also a target of Stalin's venom, primarily because of the large numbers of Buryats who had fled Russian territory after the October Revolution. From the outset the emerging Mongolian élite was manipulated from Moscow, using the influence of Buryat intermediaries, until it was aligned as closely as possible with the structure of the political elites of the European and Asian republics of the Soviet Union. Mongolian attitudes to the Buryats, and even to those who were born from mixed Buryat and Khalkh marriages, are complicated. They were thought not to be genuine Mongols because of their closeness to Moscow, but did not initially suffer the same discrimination as Mongolians who were thought to have Chinese antecedents. This did not last and during the great purges of the 1930s, Buryats who had occupied prominent positions in the leadership were accused of being counter-revolutionaries and Japanese spies; many were arrested and executed.[3]

Soviet intervention

Choibalsan is described by the historian Baabar, who is no enthusiast for the MPRP and its legacy, as 'one of the most stable, polite and calculating of the Mongolian revolutionaries'.[4] As far as he could, he kept out of the limelight during the MPRP's internal conflict in the 1920s although there are suggestions that he was directly implicated in the purge of Danzan. He attended a military school in the USSR in 1923 and returned to Mongolia to hold senior posts in the newly emerging Mongolian army, becoming at some point its commander-in-chief.

The intervention of the Soviet Union, and in particular the part played by Kliment Voroshilov, proved decisive for Choibalsan's career. Voroshilov was appointed People's Commissar for Military Affairs in the USSR in 1925 and was acutely aware of the strategic importance of Mongolia, situated as it was on the eastern border of the USSR. In September 1928, a Special Commission from the Comintern arrived in Ulaanbaatar unexpectedly. Baabar prefers to describe this delegation as 'in reality, a gang of Stalin's men who came to Mongolia to carry out a coup d'état'.[5] The aim of the team was to remove from the Mongolian leadership people who were not loyal to Moscow and who could be attacked as 'right-wing opportunists', and to insist that the Mongolians should follow the policies of forced collectivization and attacks on monastic institutions that were underway in the Soviet Union. The MPRP party leader, Dambadorj, was sent to Moscow for training and never returned. He became ill and died there in 1934. Choibalsan was identified by the Comintern team as a possible successor and on 28 November 1928 the Mongolian Affairs Commission of the Soviet Communist Party recommended that he be released from his role as commander-in-chief and elected MPRP general secretary. He was released from the army but was not elected to the leadership of the party. Instead he was appointed to head a low-level committee to manage the confiscation of the property of feudal landowners. This demeaning demotion was followed by a series of low-level appointments which reveal his political weakness and the domestic opposition that he faced.[6]

Stalin's choice

This changed in 1934 when Choibalsan was summoned to Moscow to give evidence in the trail of Jambyn Lkhümbe, who had briefly been Secretary of the MPRP Central Committee. Lkhümbe was executed in 1934, accused of having been a counter-revolutionary. Choibalsan came to the attention of Stalin and began to rise in power under Stalin's patronage. At this time Peljidiin Genden was Secretary of the Mongolian Central Committee and prime minister but he fell into disfavour with Stalin as he was adamantly opposed to the stationing of Soviet Red Army units in Mongolia; Stalin considered this essential for the security of the Soviet Union. At a meeting between Stalin, Genden and Choibalsan in Moscow in the autumn of 1934, Choibalsan was appointed Genden's deputy. Genden had a bitter quarrel with Stalin, was removed as prime minister in 1936 and executed on 26 November 1937.

This left Choibalsan, who had now acquired the highest military title of Marshal, as Stalin's choice to run Mongolia. On 26 February 1936 he was appointed minister for internal affairs. From this point onwards Choibalsan had the title and the responsibility for the policies that were being carried out in Mongolia but, even then, his authority could only be exercised with the approval of his Soviet mentors. The new Ministry of Internal Affairs that he headed was completely dominated by Soviet advisers, trainers, translators and interpreters. Many of these were drawn from the Soviet NKVD, the People's Commissariat for Internal Affairs, which in the 1930s ran the Soviet Union's prison camps and was responsible for thousands of extra-judicial killings in the USSR during the mass purges of 1936 to 1938.

The only remaining obstacle to Choibalsan's rise to the top of the Mongolian leadership was Gelegdorjiin Demid, who had replaced him as commander-in-chief of the army. The solution was to invite Demid to Moscow; mysteriously he died of food poisoning on the railway journey from Ulaanbaatar. Several other members of his party were also poisoned and one other died. Demid's funeral was held on 2 September 1937. Choibalsan became commander-in-chief again and concurrently minister of defence.[7]

Mongolian great purge

Stalin needed an acquiescent leader in Mongolia and this need became more urgent after the Japanese invasion of China on 7 July 1937. For Stalin it was imperative that the Red Army be stationed in Mongolia to protect the eastern flank of the Soviet Union and the Mongolians were pressured into accepting this. The arrival of the troops was followed by a large-scale purge in Mongolia which initially targeted the intelligentsia; members of the Central Committee; members of the Lesser Khural (the lower house of parliament that was in existence between 1924 and 1951 and then again briefly from 1990 to 1992); and ministers and army officers. The targets were based on a list of 115 names of 'counter-revolutionaries' drawn up by the Soviet Deputy Minister of Internal Affairs, Mikhail Frinovsky. Of these individuals, sixty-five were arrested immediately but the purge continued for months and expanded into the wider Mongolian society. Buddhist lamas suffered most: as many as 16,000 were detained and many, if not most, were shot and killed. At least 800 Buddhist monasteries and temples were destroyed during this period. The assets of the institutions were also seized; this included sacred artefacts that were precious in the religious sense and in many cases of considerable monetary value. Religious books were also confiscated and burned.

In the middle of the purge, Choibalsan left Ulaanbaatar for Moscow on 30 August 1938, ostensibly for medical treatment. He met Stalin who instructed him to take over as prime minister, replacing Anandyn Amar who had served as head of state from 1932 to 1936. Choibalsan returned to Mongolia at the end of January 1939 and signed the indictments for a trial of Amar who was accused of spying for Japan. The case was handed over to the NKVD; Amar was tried in Moscow and executed in 1941.

The targets of the purges in Mongolia changed in line with the increasingly irrational swings of political culture in the Soviet Union. Suddenly the purge was redirected against those who were judged guilty of 'overzealousness'; many Mongols, who had assumed that they were loyally following the policies of their own government and that of the USSR, found themselves arrested and taken to Moscow for investigation.

The purges and the terror ended in the spring of 1939, partly because they had generated so much anti-Soviet feeling in Mongolia. Choibalsan apologized for what had been done in his absence in Moscow: as many as 20,000 people had been executed in the previous two years. He returned to Moscow in the latter part of 1939, this time accompanied by Yumjaagiin Tsedenbal who had been identified by the Comintern as a likely future leader of Mongolia, to request economic aid, including support for railway construction. They eventually met Stalin on 3 January 1940 and it was becoming apparent that Choibalsan and Tsedenbal were the only two Mongols that Stalin felt he could trust. Choibalsan had wanted to reduce his political responsibilities, possibly as a result of the purges in which he had acquiesced even if he had not directed them. Stalin would not hear of this and when the two returned to Moscow, Choibalsan was prime minister and commander-in-chief of the armed forces and Tsedenbal was general secretary of the MPRP. In Communist political structures the post of party general secretary was conventionally the more senior position but that was not the case in Mongolia.

In 1940 Stalin awarded Choibalsan the Order of Lenin, an unambiguous endorsement of the satisfactory way that the Mongolian leader had carried out Soviet policies. The historian Baabar has argued that the 'hysteria of espionage and counter-revolution that overwhelmed Mongolian society reflected Choibalsan's own paranoia', but also conceded that Choibalsan was used by Stalin as a 'symbolic cover' for the purge in Mongolia that had been instigated and carried out according to instructions from, and by, agents of Moscow. Choibalsan, he claimed, was essentially a tool of the NKVD, the Soviet secret police.[8] The cult of the personality of Choibalsan began in earnest at this time, partly based on his early association with Sükhbaatar, and partly as he was presented as the saviour of Mongolia from Japanese invasion, having supported Stalin's insistence on stationing the Red Army in Mongolia, although he had little choice in the matter.

Choibalsan's legacy

The joint mausoleum of Sükhbaatar and Choibalsan in Ulaanbaatar's Sükhbaatar Square is no more as it was demolished in 2005 to make way for a statue of Chinggis Khan. However, despite the denunciation of Choibalsan in the 1960s his presence has not been completely erased from the capital: a statue of him still stands in front of the Mongolian National University in Ulaanbaatar.[9]

The MPR that had been established in 1924 lasted until 1990. The regime fell in the wake of the collapse of the Soviet Union and its Eastern European dependants, but the immediate cause was its own internal democratic revolution. The MPR was a one-party state, controlled by the MPRP. Although it was formally independent, in comparison with its close neighbours such as Kazakhstan and Kyrgyzstan which were constituent republics of the USSR, this independence was limited. Such was the scepticism with which it was treated in the early years of the MPR that, although the independence of

Mongolia had been accepted by the victorious allies at the end of the Second World War, Ulaanbaatar's application for membership of the United Nations was not accepted until 1961.

Two political figures dominated the life of the MPR, Choibalsan until his death in 1952 and then his chosen successor Tsedenbal. It is customary to refer to these rulers as dictators although, as has been demonstrated, it took Choibalsan over a decade to consolidate his own power and both he and Tsedenbal could only rule with the consent of others in the MPRP hierarchy and, more importantly, the leadership of the Soviet Union.

This period of Mongolia's history is difficult to assess. Struggling to summarize the often tumultuous events of seventy years, the editors of the National Museum of Mongolia's thoughtful guide argue that: 'The intricate co-existence of positive as well as negative developments characterises this period'.[10] It is widely acknowledged that official histories published during the existence of the MPR are distinctly unreliable guides to the realities of power and the impact of the government's policies on the population of Mongolia. In particular they undoubtedly airbrushed out much of the brutality of the purges and the campaigns against the clergy that took place in the 1930s. As Mongolia seeks to find its place in the modern world after the end of what is still referred to as the 'socialist period', it also struggles to come to terms with this past. During the present-day intellectual and ideological struggles there have been many attempts to redress the balance of previous unreliable narratives. In some cases they have rejected the entire official history of the MPR and, in doing so, run the risk of creating a different category of distortion. It is not possible to understand the history of the period from 1924 until 1990 without careful consideration of the history of the only political party, the MPRP.

Mongolian People's Revolutionary Party

The Mongolian People's Revolutionary Party (MPRP), as the Mongolian People's Party (MPP) was renamed at its Third Congress in 1924, emerged from the partisans and the work of Sükhbaatar and Choibalsan and became the most powerful organization in Mongolia. It was the ruling party, and indeed the only political party, until 1990. It was never called a 'Communist' party, but that was not uncommon in the countries allied to the Soviet Union; Mongolians considered it to be the equivalent of any of the other Marxist-Leninist parties. When a delegation from Ulaanbaatar led by Sükhbaatar visited Moscow in 1921 they proposed changing their name to include the word Communist; Lenin dissuaded them on the grounds that, in a predominantly nomadic society, a proletarian party would not be appropriate to Mongolia's needs.

In the revolutionary movement Sükhbaatar was an inspirational Mongol nationalist who could mobilize popular support, while Choibalsan was more of an organizer whose strength was in developing links between the revolt in Mongolia and international revolutionaries, primarily in Russia but also with others who had been influenced by the Russian Revolution. The revolutionaries who became the bedrock of the MPRP were drawn from the increasing number of impoverished individuals who had lost confidence in the ability of the old order of powerful aristocrats and tribal organizations in the banner system to provide for them and their families. For Choibalsan particularly, an alliance with the newly emerging regime in Russia was the only way forward: not only would it protect the Mongols from any possible new threats from China, it would also ensure that they were on the winning side of a great global struggle.

Sükhbaatar and Choibalsan had belonged to different clandestine organizations, but these forces were combined during the winter months of 1919 and 1920, following the intervention of Innokenty Sorokovikov, the representative of the Comintern's Far Eastern Secretariat in Irkutsk. The merger was marked by the carving of an official seal containing the Soyombo symbol in a piece of sandalwood. The wood was taken from the leg of a table owned by S. Danzan, who became the first chairman of the MPP but was executed in 1924 because he was too closely connected with Chinese businesses. The first party newspaper, *Uria* (The Call), appeared on 18 July 1921 and a woodcut designed for its masthead depicted a soldier in traditional Mongolian dress blowing on a conch shell. The conch is called a *tsagaan büree*, 'white trumpet' in Mongolian and was sounded in traditional Buddhist rituals; it can still be heard in the Gandan and other monasteries. It became a symbol for the party that was calling the Mongolian people to arms, a clear example of the use of traditional symbols in what was intended to be a modern revolution. An ancient rifle owned by the partisan L. Gombojav, displayed in the National Museum alongside these mementos, vividly illustrates the primitive weaponry available to the revolutionaries.[11]

Sükhbaatar and Choibalsan established a close relationship that was both political and personal: the combination of Sükhbaatar's Mongol nationalist partisans and Choibalsan's organization that included both Mongols and Russians proved to be a powerful force. There can be no doubt that the involvement of Russia and Russians at this early stage was critical for the direction of the Mongolian revolution and the forerunner of the close link that would last until 1990. A cautious assessment of that period by contemporary Mongolian scholars concludes that, 'The new developments in policies and government structures were not equally liked by all policymakers. The Soviet Comintern saw to it that Russian interests in Mongolia were being protected'.[12] On the orders of Moscow's agents, the MPRP Chairman Danzan, the first Prime Minister Bodoo, and others who opposed the extent of direct Soviet involvement were executed. In spite of this submission to the wishes of Moscow, at this stage it was still possible for the political leadership of Mongolia to retain a degree of independence and to put into practice policies that reflected the needs of Mongolians rather than just the Comintern, although Comintern representatives were a constant presence in Ulaanbaatar, particularly during important meetings of the MPP.

The revolution was a continuous process: it began in 1911 with the initial break from imperial China; genuine independence from China became a reality in July 1921; and Mongolia's relationship with Moscow was confirmed in 1924 when it became a people's republic. Even then the process was bedevilled by internal conflict between factions, conventionally labelled 'left' and 'right', that was not even partially resolved until 1929.

Once in power the MPRP was faced with two potential opposition power blocs, one religious and one secular. The religious hierarchy based in the monasteries was not universally popular but there was genuine antipathy towards the secular authority of the aristocracy. This was primarily because of heavy taxation and the labour, military and courier services that the nobles could demand from the lower orders – the *khamjlaga* (retainers or serfs) and *albat* (servant) classes. These demands had often been enforced with great brutality so there was understandably widespread support for restricting or abolishing the privileges of the aristocrats. This assault on the traditional order of the 'feudal' nobles was the cornerstone of the policies of the new government between 1921 and the death of two of the major political figures of the period, Sükhbaatar in 1923 and the Bogd Khan – the Living Buddha of Urga – in 1924. The policies of this period were not an unqualified success: in spite of attempts to create popular forms of government, aristocrats were still able to exercise considerable influence over the new political organizations. As the revolution deepened, and the property of the wealthiest nobles was confiscated from 1929 onwards, this naturally affected their social position, authority and political influence. However, the aristocracy was not eliminated and many of the noble families found alternative ways of earning a living, often by moving into commerce and displacing Chinese traders whose position had been undermined by the growth of Mongol nationalism. This was the starting point for the evolution of a modern mercantile Mongolian middle class.[13]

An unplanned but dramatic outcome of the reforms was a great increase in internal migration, primarily from eastern Mongolia towards the west.

Herdsmen, who had previously been bound by the restrictions imposed by their feudal lords, were now free to lead their livestock to a wider range of seasonal pastures. Some left Mongolia altogether and crossed the borders into Chinese or Soviet territory.[14]

The initial assault on monastic authority

After the death of the Bogd Khan in 1924, and the decision by the revolutionaries at the Third Great Khural (National Assembly) in 1926 that there would be no official recognition of a Ninth Incarnation – or indeed any further incarnations of 'living Buddhas' – the government was reorganized to exclude all representatives of religious authority. The way was open for a determined assault on the religious hierarchy. The clergy were among the most literate of the population, although their interests were primarily in Tibetan religious texts. However they also had the ability to operate with Mongolian documents and the experience of running the complex bureaucracies that administered the great wealth of the monasteries, and through which their authority was exercised.

While the primary target of the revolutionaries had been the dominance of what they referred to as the feudal aristocracy, they had not neglected the traditional power structures of the monasteries, the 'yellow feudal' system as it was known after the conventional colours associated with the Gelugpa sect of Tibetan Buddhism. Over the centuries, monasteries had acquired land and property, although technically they did not own land, and the right to levy taxes, either in money or in kind. Some lamas became wealthy, particularly the 'living Buddhas' who presided over the larger monasteries.

The monastic bureaucracy was complex and rigidly hierarchical. At its apex were learned monks, religious intellectuals who had earned their position by years studying sacred Tibetan texts. They presided over a much larger group of officials who administered the monastic estates and the artists and artisans – 'painters, metal workers casting bronze images, carpenters and builders'.[15] The monasteries also required the support of, and supported, large numbers of staff who were engaged in menial or less skilled work. Critics of the monastic system focused on the concentration of wealth and the number of staff required who might otherwise be involved in work of more tangible benefit to ordinary Mongolians.[16]

The political assault on the Tibetan Buddhist clergy and the attempts to 'liquidate' them as a powerful group is now universally accepted as having been a catastrophic error that was both politically and morally unjustifiable.

The 'struggle against religion' had its roots in the 1920s but it reached its height in the 1930s during the period in which Choibalsan was beginning to consolidate his authority in the government. As Owen Lattimore pointed out,

> In the last four or five years of the process, the disintegration of the once powerful church was unbelievably rapid. Of the 767 monasteries and temples, some were burned and some torn down, to use their materials for other buildings; some were adapted for use as offices and schools. This part of the 'liquidation' was shockingly destructive; not even enough buildings were left to make it possible to study properly the differences between Tibetan, Chinese and Mongol architectural principles and workmanship.[17]

Similar assaults on the religious establishment have taken place in neighbouring China, particularly during the Cultural Revolution which Mao Zedong launched in 1966 and which lasted for about a decade. Lattimore's account will also seem oddly familiar to anyone with even a limited knowledge of the mediaeval and early modern history of Great Britain. The dissolution of the monasteries on the orders of King Henry VIII between 1536 and 1541 transformed the religious, social and economic structure of England and Wales, and, to a lesser extent, Ireland. The secular political authority of the Catholic Church was virtually eradicated and replaced by that of the Protestant Church of England, of which King Henry was declared the head. The dissolution broke up some of the largest landholdings in the country and greatly increased the finances of the court.

In the words of one of the most venerable historians of Tudor England:

> The really surprising thing is not that there was some dislocation – even at times a good deal of it – but that the dissolution passed off so easily... [it] destroyed the last possible refuge of papalism, enriched the crown, and anchored the new order firmly in the self-interest of the land-owning classes who purchased the estates.[18]

The 'lama question'

The 'dislocation' in Mongolia 400 years later was more dramatic and much bloodier. For Christopher Kaplonski, however, the 'really surprising thing' is not that there was a concentrated assault on the Buddhist institutions but how long it took the revolutionaries to begin the process:

For almost two decades, from the revolution of 1921 until about 1940, the socialist government struggled to claim legitimacy for itself and to answer the question of the lamas. These two issues are inextricably linked. The last Mongolian emperor, who had ruled from 1911 until the revolution of 1921, had been a Buddhist 'living god', one of the highest ranking incarnations in Tibetan Buddhism. His death in 1924 would not mark the end of roughly three hundred years of Buddhism in Mongolia, but it would signal, perhaps, the start of the end.'[19]

As has previously been noted, the most ferocious phase of the assault took place in the late 1930s with 'the killing of approximately eighteen thousand lamas in the space of eighteen months, from late 1937 to mid-1939'.[20] The 'repressions of the late 1930s were ... an endpoint of a long process of engagement, confrontation and conflict between the socialists and the Buddhist establishment'. In the same period a further 18,000 people also met their deaths; most of these were Buryat Mongols. The most contentious issue in interpreting the reasons for these killings is determining the culpability of, on the one hand, the Mongolian leadership, and on the other, Stalin and his functionaries in Moscow. Was it 'merely the imposition of Stalin's will', and, in that case, were the Mongolians 'merely geopolitical puppets'?[21]

Revolutionaries in conflict: 'Right Deviation' and 'Rural Opposition'

By the end of the 1920s the government of Mongolia was essentially in the hands of revolutionaries. The more radical elements, however, insisted that it was still dominated by a conservative elite that was drawn in some cases from the very feudal aristocracy that the revolutionaries had attempted to destroy. This elite group had its power base in the bureaucracy of the party and the state and was based primarily in the capital, Ulaanbaatar, which had acquired this new name (Red Hero) in 1924. The group was subsequently classified, in the Stalinist terminology of the period, as a 'right deviationist' trend. Also known as the Capital City faction, it was led by Dambadorj (1899–1934) who was Russian-educated but was also in favour of improving ties with China. He was therefore at odds with much popular opinion in Mongolia.

A series of political battles broke out between the Capital City faction and the 'Rural Opposition', which was led by Choibalsan and, as its name suggests, drew its support mainly from the countryside. At the decisive

Seventh Congress of the MPRP in 1928, the 'Rural Opposition' defeated the Capital City 'right deviationists' in a vote on a Central Committee report that, if it had gone the other way, would have drawn Mongolia closer to the China of the Guomindang nationalists. This would have been in line with policies of Stalin's Comintern in the immediate aftermath of the expulsion of Trotsky and his alleged supporters. In the event the rejection of ties with China aligned Mongolia even more firmly with the USSR.

The victory of the 'Rural Opposition' led to a wide-ranging purge of officials in both the party and the government who were deemed to have been supporters of the Capital City faction. New regulations were drawn up for membership of the MPRP and these gave priority to recruitment from the poorer classes of hired or poor herdsmen, workers and soldiers, categories that described the natural power base of the 'Rural Opposition'. In 1929 the government ordered the confiscation of the property of 669 prominent and powerful aristocratic families which had until then been able to retain their wealth and some of their political influence.[22]

Moscow takes control: Seventh Party Congress 1928

The Seventh Congress of the MPRP that took place from 23 October to 10 December 1928 was a defining moment for Mongolia, not only for its defeat of the 'right deviationists' but also for the relationship between the party and Moscow. The victory of the 'Rural Opposition' had not simply been the outcome of the domestic factional struggle, but was brought about by the dramatic intervention of the Comintern. The quasi-republican government that had overthrown the theocratic monarchy of the Bogd Khan in 1924 had restricted the political power of the secular aristocracy but had not seriously limited its control over the economy. Mongolia had been supported by Moscow but the Comintern and the Soviet Union had not exerted significant direct influence over the government in Ulaanbaatar.

By 1926 the escalating dispute in the Soviet Union between Stalin and an increasingly unified opposition was reaching a climax. Leon Trotsky, who had been largely responsible for the victory of the Red Army in the Russian civil war and was the most prominent left oppositionist in the Communist Party of the Soviet Union (Bolshevik), was expelled from Stalin's Central Committee and forced into exile, first in Kazakhstan and then in Turkey. Stalin emerged as the unchallenged leader of the USSR. Both the lethal internal dispute and the subsequent Stalin dictatorship had serious ramifications well beyond the borders of the Soviet Union as Communist parties and their allies were obliged to take sides in the dispute and, if they were to remain close to the Soviet Union, to adjust their national policies to those approved by Moscow.

In September 1928, a Comintern Special Commission 'landed in Ulaanbaatar unexpectedly' determined to reverse the policies that were now classified as 'right-wing opportunism' and replace the leadership with individuals who were demonstrably loyal to Moscow. Dambadorj, the chairman of the Central Committee of the MPRP, was sent to the USSR for training and never returned. He died in Moscow in 1934, possibly, but not unquestionably, from natural causes. From 1928 to 1940 there was no Central Committee chairman and three secretaries were appointed to work as a collective leadership, leaving the party with reduced authority. This absence of a leadership greatly facilitated domination by Moscow. The commission had demonstrated its authority but had engineered what was effectively a coup d'état by forming an alliance with radical elements in the rural organizations of the MPRP, the group that became known as the 'Rural Opposition'. They were persuaded that the country was ripe for the creation of a socialist economy, in line with the concept of 'bypassing capitalism' that had been formally adopted by the MPRP in 1925.[23]

Following this takeover, the Comintern issued instructions that completely reversed the gradualist policies that had been in force since 1924. A Comintern document, 'Letter 2452', ordered the MPRP to emulate the radical collectivization programme that was being enforced in the USSR and to attack monastic institutions and the power base of the feudal aristocracy. Collectivization was on the whole disastrous for the herding economy, which was Mongolia's primary source of wealth. Mongolia's economy was to be linked inextricably with that of the Soviet Union and gradually the USSR became its only major foreign contact. From 1929 Mongolia was 'obliged to the USSR for all foreign trade, for military supplies and training, for higher education facilities, medical help and so on'. Internally there was a comprehensive purge of the MPRP, to remove the lamas, aristocrats and business people who had become members. The instructions of the Comintern were formally endorsed by its Central Committee in the summer of 1929.[24]

The official narrative of the Seventh Congress claimed that 'foreigners' – meaning primarily anyone with possible Chinese ancestry or connections but also Buryats – had been excluded from the leadership and that power had passed from the secular and religious aristocracy to Mongolian commoners. Nationalism and xenophobia reigned, and trade and economic relations with countries other than the USSR were discontinued. Notable examples which had a severe impact on Mongolian development included a brick company and a power station, both of which had been due to be built with German funding but were abandoned.[25]

Class struggle, chaos and civil war

The events that followed the Soviet intervention of 1928 have been described by Baabar as 'communist hysteria', by Bawden as a 'socialist fiasco' and were later repudiated by the MPRP as a 'leftist deviation'.[26] A 1930 poster celebrating the Eighth Congress of the MPP announced that the party was 'poised to solve all questions and problems regarding the revolution' and that 'enemy classes' would be overthrown and destroyed.[27] The first acts of the new administration were attacks on the feudal aristocracy, who were an easier target than the clergy; there were fewer of them, they were less well organized and they enjoyed little popular support. The initial expropriations of 1929 were followed by a second wave from 1930 to 1931, when a further 837 families suffered the confiscation of their property. Most of these belonged to the secular aristocracy but 205 were the families of senior lamas. The actions against the property-owning classes were more violent than in 1929 and over 700 heads of households were imprisoned or executed, having been accused of opposing the government and the MPRP. Since the 'liquidation of the nobles as a class' had been accomplished without any serious resistance, the MPRP felt confident enough to mount a devastating attack on the authority of the Lama Buddhist establishment and then to move directly towards socialism by imposing a policy of collectivization. A class struggle was declared between the commoners (*ard*) and the nobles. Choibalsan, who otherwise maintained a low profile throughout this period, made a brief appearance as chairman of a committee to decide on the confiscation and redistribution of aristocrats' property.[28]

The drive to undermine the authority of the monasteries was initially limited to confiscating the herds owned by the lamas, farming them out to poorer families and paying wages to the commoners who looked after then. These moves were followed by more violent assaults, which culminated in, 'a wild spree of desecration of lamaseries, putting out the eyes of Buddha statues, distributing sacred vessels and vestments to the ordinary herdsmen as private property, [and] taxing lamas, rich and poor'.[29] These attacks were carried out by the poor, uneducated and illiterate who were often terrified that if they did not obey orders they were likely to be in serious trouble in a later campaign.

The government began to tax the property and income of lamas irrespective of whether they were wealthy or poor. As Owen Lattimore pointed out after his extensive investigations in 1961, they

> did not discriminate between the property and power of the church – if they had done so, they could have utilised the anti-clericalism which

is always latent in highly clerical countries – and the religion itself which most of the people still regarded as their own religion, not just the property of the lamas. The result was to rally people to support the church and look to the lamas for leadership.[30]

It was not only the nobles and lamas who were targeted in these campaigns. Taxes were also imposed on small businesses, private caravan traders and artisans in crude measures that did not distinguish between those who were earning a modest income and wealthy and powerful businessmen.[31]

Anti-government demonstrations

These actions by the MPRP government triggered an equally violent resistance and some of those who opposed the government fled from the areas under closest MPRP control. The discontent turned into an armed revolt and then escalated into a full-scale civil war that resulted in a great loss of life. The resistance to these crude and repressive policies crystallized into armed uprisings in 1931 and 1932, notably in the Arkhangai region in the centre of the country. These revolts were followed by further repression and the resistance was eventually suppressed by the Mongolian People's Revolutionary Army under the control of the MPRP.

A modern copy of a 1932 poster displayed in the National Museum illustrates vividly how the party envisaged the campaign. It depicts a soldier on a tank attacking lamas and the wealthy nobility following the uprising of that year.

The combined effect of these hasty and ill-thought-out policies was to trigger a violent reaction that was described in the official publication, *Forty Years of the Mongolian People's Party and the Peoples Revolution*, as 'a severe struggle, continuing for several months; it was the sharpest manifestation of the class struggle in our country, which reached the scale of civil war'[32]. Many thousands of lives were lost, and the conflict was most violent in the west of Mongolia which had retained its traditional reputation for independence and was the goal of many of those who had fled repression in the eastern part of the country.

Mongolians and others have fiercely debated who was responsible for the disasters of this period. Some have argued that it was simply a result of following too closely the instructions of the Comintern without due consideration for the specific social and economic conditions of Mongolia. Others have blamed overenthusiastic and overconfident supporters of the 'left deviation' policies. They were accused of using Comintern directives to show the Soviet Union how committed they were to achieving socialism in a short period of time, without necessarily having cleared their actions with Moscow. Choibalsan's position was characteristically equivocal. He had been an influential figure in the 'Rural Opposition' that struggled against the 'right deviation' but was also one of the first to voice opposition to the 'left deviation'.

There was barbarism on both sides in this internal conflict, including the continued use of the shamanist rituals of ripping the heart out of live prisoners. The People's Revolutionary Army was deployed to put down the insurrection but was unable to do so without assistance. Order was finally restored after the intervention of the Soviet Red Army which deployed motorized regiments and air power in support of infantry and police units. The outcome was a crisis of confidence for the MPRP. Not only was the Mongolian state unable to suppress an uprising on its own account but some of its supporters, and even members, had participated in the revolt. Many ordinary Mongols who did not necessarily approve of the exactions of the lamas were horrified by the crude and arbitrary attacks on the monasteries. Thousands of MPRP members were purged, especially in the west of the country where the rebellion was most tenacious.[33]

The new turn

In what, with a nod to the earlier New Economic Policy of the USSR, became known as the 'new turn' (*shine ergelt*) of 1932–4, the mindless assaults of the 'leftist' deviations were condemned at a combined meeting of the MPRP and its youth wing. The more radical Mongolian Revolutionary Youth Union (*Mongol huv'sgalt zaluuchuudyn evlel*) had played a leading role in the violence, including the arrests and executions. There are resonances of the later attacks of youthful Red Guards on traditional Chinese culture in the 1960s in the name of Mao Zedong. In Mongolia there was no attempt to restore the privileges or status of the monasteries; righting some of the wrongs of this period was eventually enforced in another intervention from the USSR and the Comintern in June 1932. Moscow had become increasingly concerned at the strategic weakness of Mongolia as a critical component of its eastern front against Japanese expansion and was providing training for the Mongolian army.

The 'new turn' of 1932 was a political volte-face that was devised to camouflage the reversal of the previous disastrous policies. It followed an intervention by both the Comintern and the Central Committee of the Communist Party of the Soviet Union, which was able to muster sufficient ideological firepower to persuade the leadership of the MPRP that they should mend their ways. A document from these two bodies, criticizing the 'left deviation' but supporting Choibalsan, was sent from Moscow to Ulaanbaatar on 29 May 1932 but its receipt was not formally acknowledged by the MPRP Central Committee until the second half of June. The delay suggests considerable internal conflict in the MPRP and complicated manoeuvring between Moscow and Ulaanbaatar. All the indications are that Choibalsan requested help from the Comintern to resolve what was essentially a factional struggle within the Mongolian party, albeit one that had implications for the international Communist movement as a whole and for the defence of the Soviet Union. Choibalsan was at that time acting as both minister of foreign affairs and Mongolia's ambassador to the Soviet Union. With the backing of Moscow, the Mongols called a joint special session of their own Central Committee and Central Investigative Committee: the 'left deviation' was overturned and the 'new turn' was declared. Official accounts make a distinction between the periods of the 'left deviation' and the 'new turn' but this was cosmetic. Although radical and violent anti-clericalism was no longer state policy that did not mean that it had ceased. Continuing the persecution of lamas and the expropriation of monastic property and lands was undoubtedly in the interests of some individuals or groups in the government and party.[34]

This 'new turn' also finally established Choibalsan's dominant position in the MPRP. Although he has since been regarded as second only to Sükhbaatar as an acknowledged founding father of the Mongolian revolution, until this special session he was merely one senior figure among many. After the factional battles of the summer of 1932 his authority continued to grow; by 1939 his control of both the Mongolian government and the MPRP was undisputed and his accession to power drew Mongolia even closer to Stalin's Soviet Union in practice and in style.[35]

Domestic stability was restored and a decision was made to replace political compulsion by 'persuasion, propaganda and education', but in the longer term the 'new turn' did not bring an end to violence, persecution or death – particularly in the world of the lamas. Many monasteries and temples were badly damaged and some were demolished entirely so that by 1961 there was only one fully operational monastery in the whole of Mongolia – the Gandantegchinling in the north-western corner of Ulaanbaatar, now vastly expanded and one of a greater number of rebuilt monasteries. Before the 'liquidation' of the monasteries began there were perhaps 100,000 lamas in total throughout Mongolia. By the end of the process, less than 10 per cent of these remained in the monasteries. Of the rest many had been obliged to move into cooperatives or become herders, but countless monks were also killed in the process.[36]

By the 1960s, after the deaths of Stalin and Choibalsan and the reverberations of Khrushchev's 'secret speech' in which the errors and crimes of the Stalin period were revealed and denounced, it became possible to reinterpret the conduct of the government between 1929 and 1932 as a period of Stalinist excess. The whole period was designated as a 'left deviation' and the 'Rural Opposition' with which Choibalsan was associated was no longer an opposition but was in power and controlled both government and party.

The policy of collectivization in this period was handled in a similar crude and overhasty fashion. Families were simply instructed to join cooperatives without being given any understanding of what a cooperative was, what they would have to contribute to it, or how they might benefit. In practice the cooperatives were forced into existence by simply amalgamating the herds of different families and those confiscated from aristocrats, lamas and the wealthy. When this was combined with punitive taxation on privately held livestock it created a crisis in the pastoral economy in which as many as 10 million cattle were either slaughtered, or died due to inappropriate care. The number of livestock in 1930 was estimated at 23.6 million while in 1932 it had fallen to 15.1 million and the herds did not recover until 1940. Taken as a whole it is difficult to find anything positive to say about Mongolian or Soviet policies during this period.[37]

Threat from Japan

The fate of Mongolia in the 1930s, in common with its close neighbour China and much of the rest of Asia, cannot be understood without considering the rapid expansion of militarist Japan in the first quarter of the twentieth century. In 1931 Japanese forces had invaded Manchuria, the north-eastern region of China which was also home to significant populations of Mongols. This region was declared to be Manzhouguo (Manchukuo), a state independent of China (although not of Japan). Other provinces, which are now included in the Chinese region of Inner Mongolia, were targeted by the Japanese with policies designed to separate that region from China. Mongolia itself felt under threat and the only realistic defence against this was its alliance with the Soviet Union. In 1937 Japan invaded and occupied most of eastern China: the threat of an attack on Mongolia from Manzhouguo and Inner Mongolia was felt even more keenly.

The impact of the Japanese threat on internal policy was far from clear-cut. Japanese agents operated in Mongolia, many covertly, and constantly intrigued in support of pan-Mongolian independence which, it was thought, would benefit Japan's control over north-east Asia. In neighbouring

Inner Mongolia there were radical political movements demanding self-determination and separation from China, some of which were sponsored directly by the Japanese. Other organizations were more independent, notably the group led by Prince Demchukdongrob (De Wang or Prince De) which the Japanese attempted to control. The involvement of Japan also created a climate of paranoia in Mongolia itself, encouraged, some would argue, by the Comintern. Political opponents of Choibalsan were accused of assisting the Japanese in their attempt to conquer Mongolia and many were arrested and executed in a purge that began with mass arrests on the night of 10 September 1937. Victims of this and other political persecutions are commemorated on this date every year in Mongolia today and a permanent monument to their memory stands outside the National Museum in Ulaanbaatar.

In this paranoid atmosphere the Mongolian security agencies, which had already built up their authority in the campaigns against the aristocracy and the monasteries, became even more powerful. The purge extended far beyond internal political opponents of Choibalsan, and included intellectuals, writers, scientists, and yet more lamas. Between 1933 and 1953 the number affected by ongoing purges may have been as high as 36,000.

Battle of Khalkhyn Gol

The tensions with Japan eventually led to military conflict at the battle of Khalkhyn Gol, the Khalkh River, near the village of Nomynkhan or Nomonhan which is now on the border between Mongolia and China's Inner Mongolian Autonomous Region. The Soviet Union needed to ensure that Mongolia remained independent and out of Japanese control to protect Lake Baikal and the Trans-Siberian Railway. Throughout the 1930s it had been clear that the MPR was a vital link in Stalin's comprehensive defence system for the Russian Far East.

After a statement by Stalin in 1936 that the USSR would support Mongolia if its territorial integrity were threatened, Moscow and Ulaanbaatar signed a treaty of mutual aid and Soviet troops were dispatched to Mongolia. This was far from universally popular and could only take place after those Mongolian politicians who opposed the increase in Soviet influence had been physically or politically eliminated.

In all, 2,000 Mongolian men were conscripted into a modern army, which was trained by Anatoliy Ilyich Gekker, who had previously served as a military advisor to the MPR. It was placed under the overall command of Vasily Konstantinovich Blyukher, the Commander of the Soviet Union's

Far Eastern Special Army. His family had assumed that surname in commemoration of the Prussian General Blücher who fought Napoleon at the battles of Leipzig and Waterloo. Because the two most senior Mongolian officers were Gelegdorjiin Demid and Jamjamgiin Lhagvasüren, both of whom were graduates of Soviet military academies, the Mongolian military was able to function like a Soviet army.

The semi-autonomous Japanese Guandong (Kwantung) Army in Manzhouguo was charged with strengthening the defences of the puppet state by establishing new military bases on the borders. On 11 May 1939, in an attempt to create a new frontier favourable to them, 10,000 Japanese troops occupied Mongolian territory on the left bank of the Khalkh River, the Khalkhyn Gol, on the border between Mongolia and Manzhouguo. In a counter-offensive, Mongolian and Soviet forces forced the Japanese to retreat to the original border by 29 May. The conflict escalated, more Soviet units were mobilized under Georgy (later Marshal) Zhukov who deployed motorized armoured units and artillery, supported by the Mongolian Eighth Cavalry Division and an artillery unit. The Mongolian contribution was relatively insignificant but so were their losses.

Japanese forces were routed at Bayantsaagan in early July and forced to retreat but they brought in reinforcements from Manzhouguo. Zhukov responded with additional tank and artillery regiments and air support. His order of battle was superior to that marshalled by the Japanese forces which were wiped out in a major Soviet offensive on 20 August.

On 12 September Japanese units attacked again but, after diplomatic manoeuvres in Moscow, a ceasefire was agreed on 15 September. Japan had lost at least 17,000 troops, either killed or wounded, and its forces were not able to advance further in this part of northeast Asia. Khalkhyn Gol was a decisive victory for the Soviet forces and the Mongol units that they had trained and supported. Mongolia assisted the Soviet war effort not only with troops but by providing horses, ammunition and military articles made from wool and leather.

A treaty signed in 1941 between the Japanese foreign minister, Tōgō Shigenori, and Vyacheslav Molotov, the minister of foreign affairs of the USSR stabilized the frontiers of Mongolia until the end of the Second World War. While the result of the military and diplomatic manoeuvring was to give the USSR even more influence over Mongolia's domestic and foreign policy, the only possible alternative at that time for Mongolia was accepting occupation by Japan. For Mongolia's long-term political alliance, as Charles Bawden put it, 'The definitive choice having been taken in 1921, all logic was on the side of Mongolia's continuing loyalty to Russia'.[38]

The emergence of the Choibalsan dictatorship

From the detailed accounts of Choibalsan's activities in Mongolia and his relations with Moscow, it is possible to arrive at a judicious assessment of what has been called his dictatorship. This will require some reiteration of the narrative of his rise to power and more detailed consideration of his role in the purges. The official narratives that present Mongolia's successive leaders as having emerged from a normal bureaucratic process are clearly unsound. As has been shown, after the death of Sükhbaatar in 1923 Choibalsan did not immediately succeed his colleague, the revolutionary hero; it took him well over a decade to arrive at the pinnacle of power and his rise was only achieved after a brutal and prolonged period of faction fighting, political purges, and assassinations camouflaged as legal executions. All of this was subject to the agreement of the Comintern from Moscow, with the constant threat of direct Soviet intervention.

Choibalsan had attended a military school in the USSR and had become a senior officer in the Mongolian army, but he kept out of the political limelight until 1934. He had been involved in the purge of Danzan in 1924 and by 1928 he was so close to the Soviet leadership that the Mongolian Affairs Commission of the Communist Party of the Soviet Union recommended that he should step down as commander-in-chief of the Mongolian armed forces and be appointed general secretary of the MPRP. Only the first of these happened and he was instead given a minor role of heading the commission that decided on the confiscation of feudal property.

Choibalsan's name appears during these tumultuous years as a supporter of the swing to 'the left' and he spoke at the Seventh Congress of the need for close friendship with the USSR, but he was still not a significant political actor. A range of party and government positions are ascribed to him during this period, but even if they were genuine appointments at the time rather than retrospective designations to improve his political curriculum vitae, they do not help to establish to what extent he was able to exercise real authority. It is most likely that he was waiting in the wings and it should be remembered that Baabar, whose historical approach is resolutely anti-Communist, described Choibalsan as 'one of the most stable, polite and calculating of the Mongolian revolutionaries'.

In 1932 the individual who had emerged as the most powerful figure was Genden. He enjoyed the support of Stalin, was appointed premier and was entrusted by Moscow to pilot the 'new turn' which claimed to emphasize the development of the existing local economy rather than emulating Soviet development. It was supposed to usher in a period of relaxation in policies on religion and the confiscation of land or stock and trade, but it was not universally supported in Mongolia; some in the leadership wished to continue the attacks on the religious establishment. Genden was unwilling to countenance any further assault on Buddhism or the monasteries and their lamas but he eventually fell out with Stalin, primarily over his opposition to the stationing of Soviet Red Army troops in Mongolia.

In 1934 Choibalsan was summoned to Moscow as either a witness or, some have suggested, a suspect in the case of Lkhümbe, briefly the head of the MPRP, who was eventually executed for counter-revolutionary activities and collusion with the Japanese. The Mongolian government was not able to act independently. Trials and executions of traitors and counter-revolutionaries were either carried out in Stalin's Moscow or in accordance with instructions from the Soviet authorities. The purges in Mongolia were part of the wider process of purges and show trials carried out in the USSR during the 1930s. Choibalsan did not initiate the purges in Mongolia and did not carry them out directly, but he was an accomplice, albeit in a subordinate role and often in absentia. It is nevertheless clear that he benefited from the outcome. The Lkhümbe affair marked the beginning of Stalin's patronage of Choibalsan who evidently persuaded the Soviet leadership that he was not a counter-revolutionary. Some sources allege that he proved his loyalty by interrogating other Mongols who were accused of collaborating with Lhumbe.

Choibalsan returned from Moscow with the title of Marshal: this was presumably conferred on him by the authority of Stalin rather than any Mongol. On 26 February 1936, on Stalin's insistence, he was appointed minister of internal affairs, leading a full ministry that had been built on the basis of the former Internal Affairs Committee, but was effectively under the control of the Soviet NKVD, which provided training staff and translators and dominated the Mongolian ministry. The Soviet NKVD had been transformed in 1934 into the main internal security force for the whole Soviet Union: it was the successor to the Cheka – the secret police of the Bolsheviks between 1917 and 1922 and was responsible for the Soviet purges of the 1930s and for running the prison camps of the Gulag and other organs of repression. The Mongolian purges were a natural extension of their work.

From this point, Choibalsan was Stalin's henchman in Mongolia but his appointment as minister of internal affairs made him effectively deputy to Genden. This was much against Genden's wishes so he was purged in 1937, accused of having been excessively lenient towards anti-Soviet attitudes among the lamas; of spying for the Japanese; and personal improprieties which principally involved alcohol and other men's wives.

At this point the minister of war and commander-in-chief of the armed forces was Demid, who was deeply suspicious of Soviet intentions towards Mongolia. He was invited to Moscow and on 22 August, while travelling on the Trans-Siberian Express, died of 'food poisoning' at Tayga station which is to the north-east of Novosibirsk in Siberia. Demid was later accused of having betrayed Mongolia to the Japanese. By 2 September, the day of Demid's funeral, Choibalsan had taken over both of his positions and the following day issued Order 366, which condemned the influence of Japanese spies and provocateurs on Mongolian traitors.

Stalin had decided on 13 August that Soviet troops should be stationed permanently in Mongolia. This was a high priority for Moscow as the USSR looked to defending its eastern flank against possible Japanese invasion as part of a comprehensive system of defence the in Far East. A Soviet delegation had arrived, unannounced as was their wont, in Ulaanbaatar on 23 August, the day after Demid's demise, and the following day an invitation to station Soviet units was issued in the name of the State Lesser Khural, the lower house of parliament, and the Council of Ministers. By this time, units of the 17th Army of the Red Army, the field army that defended the Soviet Far East during the Second World War, had already moved into Mongolia at the border crossing points of Altanbulag and Ereentsav. The 17th Army deployed two mechanized motor brigades, an infantry division, a cavalry brigade and support units, totalling almost 30,000 troops. Stalin had got his way.[39]

Mongolian purges

On 10 September 1937, the anniversary of which is now set aside to remember the victims of Stalinist repression, the great purge of the party and the government was launched. During this campaign most of the members of Mongolia's intelligentsia were expelled from government and party offices. On 28 March 1939, after the completion of this purge, Choibalsan was declared premier. In most countries that follow the Soviet model of party and government, it is the general secretary of the party who wields the most power but this was the period when the party leadership was weak and divided and Choibalsan's dictatorship was built on his leadership of the government rather than the party.

Although Choibalsan was the ruler of Mongolia from 1939 until his death in 1952, even then he could only exercise his authority with the express permission of Stalin and the Politburo of the Communist Party of the Soviet Union (CPSU) in Moscow. Choibalsan was a close contemporary of Stalin (who died in 1953) and is often compared with the Soviet leader, especially in terms of the personality cult that developed around him, although eulogies to Choibalsan in Mongolia were dwarfed by those to Stalin. He possessed however nothing like the political muscle of Stalin.

Choibalsan has been held personally responsible for the repression and purges of the 1930s, including the destruction of monasteries and the deaths of thousands of monks. While he was undoubtedly part of the political structure during the appalling 1930s, he was not by any means the most senior Mongolian official when the worst of the atrocities were committed. His responsibility for the turmoil and atrocities, which began in the early 1930s well before he became premier, must be shared with other political figures in Mongolia, but even more with Stalin and agents of Stalin's Comintern for their chaotic and confusing interventions and for their failure to act to stem the tide of violence.[40]

The original list of 115 individuals to be eliminated from the power structure in these purges was drawn up not by a Mongol but by Mikhail Frinovski, who was the deputy head of the NKVD and second-in-command to the infamous Nikolai Yezhov who controlled the NKVD from 1936 to 38. Frinovski referred to Choibalsan as being 'alone in the struggle' to rid Mongolia of these 'counterrevolutionaries'. On 11 September 1937 instructions on the targets of the purge were issued in Choibalsan's name and he reported back to Yezhov, on the success of this first trawl. The first 65 of those detained were intellectuals, members of the Central Committee and the Lesser Khural, ministers and senior army officers. The campaign then moved against the Buddhist establishment: in 1937 and 1938, 16,631 lamas were persecuted and most of them were executed in mass shootings. When burial grounds near Mörön were excavated in 1992, the remains of over 1,000 lamas were uncovered. Special attention was also paid to Buryat Mongols and Kazakhs who had fled to Mongolia from the USSR to escape Stalin's offensive and who were regarded by the Mongols as well as the NKVD as actual or potential traitors.[41]

Choibalsan did not initiate the purges or even control the way in which they were carried out. He was not even the head of the Mongolian government; the prime minister from 1936 to 1939 was Amar. Choibalsan was summoned to Moscow at the height of the purges and left Ulaanbaatar on 30 August 1938. His visit was ostensibly for medical treatment as his health was considered to have suffered from overwork and indeed, he spent a month in Sochi, the popular resort for the Soviet elite on the Black Sea in an area that had been fought over by Russian and Caucasian forces during the nineteenth century. He met Stalin twice during this stay in the USSR and was told that he was to replace Amar as prime minister of Mongolia.

Choibalsan returned to Ulaanbaatar in January 1939 and on 6 March at an enlarged meeting of the Lesser Khural he introduced an indictment that accused Amar of counter-revolutionary activities. Although Choibalsan had signed the indictment, the denunciation was as usual managed by the head of Moscow's mission to Mongolia and the Soviet staff of the NKVD. Amar was sent to Siberia and then to Moscow where he was put on trial in July 1941, accused of spying for the Japanese. There were many rumours about his fate but it later transpired that he was sentenced to death by the Military Collegium of the USSR Supreme Court and executed on 27 July. When his trial was reviewed after Khrushchev's secret speech of 1956, it was judged that there had never been any genuine evidence against him and he was posthumously rehabilitated. Details of this miscarriage of justice and the fate of another thirty-one Mongolian leaders dispatched in this way were made public by the Russian government after the collapse of the Soviet Union in 1991.

Choibalsan had not ordered these purges and executions but he cooperated with the Soviet authorities in carrying them out. He was a weak man and a willing tool and benefited from them politically and personally. He was not, however, a free agent but a 'symbolic cover' for the actions of Moscow and the NKVD. The Mongolian elite had succumbed to an atmosphere of paranoia, which Choibalsan shared. Fears of counter-revolution and espionage by Japan were rife; although most were unsubstantiated, they provided a useful pretext for accusations and purges.

After the dismissal of Amar, on Stalin's orders, Choibalsan held both posts of prime minister and minister for internal affairs. This gave him formal political authority and effective control over the security services, in addition to his continuing responsibility for the military and for foreign relations. At this point another delegation arrived from Moscow with new instructions: it was time to end the reign of terror. Moscow had concluded that there had been 'overzealousness', but there is no doubt that the degree of anti-Soviet feeling that had been generated by the purges was a major factor in this dramatic volte-face. As Choibalsan had spent a great deal of time in Russia at the height of the purges, he could be absolved of personal, direct responsibility for the persecution and death of many innocent people; on 20 April he apologized for what had been done in his absence. He dismissed his deputy, dissolved the Extraordinary Commission which had managed the purges and mounted a new purge of those who could be convicted of 'overzealousness'; many were sent to Moscow for trial.

All told, the terror had led to the death of between 36,000 and 45,000 individuals within the space of eighteen months. This was accompanied by the destruction of almost all the 800 monasteries and temples in Mongolia; the confiscation of monastic assets including precious religious artefacts; and the burning of religious books.[42] The number of victims of the purges varies and it is unlikely that there will ever be a figure accepted by all. Morris Rossabi uses a much lower figure:

> Estimates of lives lost during this repression vary considerably, but the most reliable figure hovers around 25,000. The number of executed Buddhist monks within that figure is also in dispute, but specialists concur that of the 100,000 or so monks in the early twentieth century, fewer than a thousand continued to serve in the monasteries by mid-century. Most were defrocked, but some were killed, and the vast majority of the monasteries were either destroyed or severely damaged.[43]

Choibalsan returned to Moscow in late 1939 to report on the political situation and request aid for economic development in Mongolia, including a link to the Soviet railway system. On this mission he was accompanied by his acolyte Tsedenbal and they left Ulaanbaatar on 18 November, but did not manage to see Stalin until January 1940. Choibalsan pleaded to be allowed to relinquish some of his responsibilities but Stalin would not agree. Choibalsan had been the only Mongol that he was willing to trust but now Tsedenbal was added to this very short list. When they returned home Choibalsan established a new ruling team with himself as prime minister and commander-in-chief of the army and Tsedenbal as general secretary of the MPRP. A 'personality cult' of Choibalsan, modelled on the Stalin cult in the USSR, began to develop around the suggestion that Choibalsan had saved the nation from the Japanese, but the cult of Stalin was even more prevalent in Mongolia. In 1940 Stalin awarded Choibalsan the Order of Lenin.[44]

Did Choibalsan have any choice in his alliance with Stalin? The MPRP, within which he operated, had begun as an independent nationalist organization but it relied so heavily on the support of the Comintern and the Soviet Communist Party that it functioned almost as a creature of Moscow; almost all of its leaders had been trained in the Soviet Union. Charles Bawden argued that,

> True national independence for Mongolia in the thirties was never a practical proposition. In theoretical terms the choice lay between alignment with the USSR, with whom she had thrown in her lot in 1921 and again in 1929, and penetration by Japan, whose sphere of imperial ambition was beginning by now to embrace Mongolia.[45]

The only other option was an accommodation with China but that was unthinkable: the raison d'être of the original Mongolian revolution in 1921 had been to escape the clutches of China and, in the 1930s, China still claimed Mongolia for its own, was even more nationalistic, and was in any case fighting what at the time appeared to be a losing battle with Japan.

After Choibalsan's death in 1952 he was succeeded by Tsedenbal who headed the government from 1952 to 1974 and was general secretary of the MPRP from 1958 to 1984. When there was a decision in 1961 by the MPRP Central Committee to 'liquidate the harmful consequences' of the Choibalsan cult of personality, the analogy with Stalin's rule could not have been closer. Although Choibalsan owed his position to Stalin, the Soviet Union and the Comintern – in addition to political support from within Mongolia – Choibalsan and Stalin were not identical in background, outlook or policies.

Owen Lattimore argued that 'it would be a misreading of history to describe Choibalsan as nothing but Stalin's shadow over Mongolia'.[46] In a conversation with a former political prisoner, he told him,

> Well I met Choibalsan in 1944, and he didn't seem to me at all the intriguing or plotting type. In fact, I thought there was a lot of the good old-fashioned Mongol about him – you know, bluff, straightforward. Couldn't he stop all that stuff? Or couldn't he at least intervene in the cases of people he knew? [His interlocuter replied] 'Choibalsan was all right, He was a good man. But he was under heavy pressure, and his authority was limited'.

Choibalsan liked nothing better than attending traditional Mongol games or stopping at the *ger* of some random herdsman to drink copious quantities of fermented mare's milk and talk at great length. Nevertheless, he was content to use the shadow of Stalin to rise to power and to use it, or allow it to be used, ruthlessly.[47]

Images of Choibalsan

The images of Choibalsan that are on display in the National Museum of Mongolia in Ulaanbaatar are strikingly different from the way in which his predecessor is portrayed. Sükhbaatar is represented by his traditional uniform of *deel* tunic and jacket as commander-in-chief; he is very much the image of an old-fashioned herdsman-warrior. Choibalsan appears as a modern leader – but modern in the Soviet style – in photographs on horseback with his infant son Nergui in 1940; with the commander of Soviet troops in Mongolia; alongside the Soviet commander, Field Marshal Zhukov in 1939; and with Defence Minister Tsedenbal, his eventual successor in 1944. Choibalsan's marshal's uniform and sword are impressive but not gaudy, although his impressive tasselled epaulettes serve to emphasize his exalted rank. A special decoration, the Order of the Golden Star of the Marshal of the MPR, that was awarded to Choibalsan in 1944 to commemorate his military achievements, is also displayed prominently in the National Museum.[48]

5

Post-War Mongolia: The Tsedenbal (1952–84) and Batmönkh (1984–90) years

A 1944 photograph of Choibalsan and Tsedenbal shows Choibalsan in full uniform and with the epaulette rank badges of a Mongolian army marshal. Seated on his right is his successor Tsedenbal, in a uniform that bears the insignia of a lieutenant-general, and at the age of only 28 looking extremely youthful for someone of such a high rank. He appears to be gazing at Choibalsan with reverence and affection, and as if he were seeking guidance from his commanding officer.[1]

By the time Tsedenbal succeeded his mentor in 1952 and became premier (chairman of the Council of Ministers) he had achieved a more mature look and was photographed in a Western-style suit, and wearing only two decorations, with the other members of the Mongolian People's Revolutionary Party (MPRP) Central Committee. This change of image was not entirely coincidental; the rise of Tsedenbal heralded a break with the militaristic and Stalinist past and inaugurated a period of planned economic development, albeit development that corresponded closely with the post-Stalin policies of the Soviet Union.[2]

Referendum of 1945

By 1945 Mongolia was tied firmly to the Soviet Union, but its status was far from being accepted by the international community. China in particular felt that it had a historical claim to the territory and wished to recover the whole of Mongolia (Inner and Outer) that had been a part of the Chinese Empire under the Qing dynasty. China at that time was still formally ruled by the Chiang Kai-shek regime. During the war with Japan it governed little more than its temporary capital in Chongqing, but it was still recognized as the legitimate government of the whole of China by the international community. It was treated as one of the great powers by virtue of its alliance with the United States and the other partners in the war against both Japan and Hitler's Germany. The Soviet Union, which was also part of this alliance, did not wish to see Mongolia revert to Chinese control for ideological, strategic and geopolitical reasons, and this coincided with the general will of the Mongolian population which had no intention of being ruled again by China. China was powerless to insist on its claims but, to save face, Chiang Kai-shek agreed to accept the independence of Mongolia if Mongols expressed that wish in a referendum or plebiscite. There was an understanding that, in return, China would retain control over north-eastern China – Manchuria – a region with a history of border disputes with Imperial Russia and its successor, the Soviet Union.

The Lesser Khural, effectively a presidium elected by the Great Khural, duly passed a resolution when it sat in February 1945 calling for a referendum on Mongolian independence. The proclamation was printed in traditional Mongolian script; although Cyrillic was now the official script in favour, the assumption was clearly that only the traditional version would be understood by most literate voters at that time. A poster publicizing the referendum was also in the older script and featured a herdsman, in a traditional felt hat and *deel* robe with his right arm raised, superimposed on an outline map of Mongolia. In the top left of the poster is a new state emblem that briefly replaced the popular mystical *soyombo* device in the 1940s, in the interests of 'radically renewing society'. This emblem, approved by Stalin, featured a 'mounted horseman carrying a lasso pole riding toward the sun … surrounded by the remaining four traditional livestock animals'. All this was in a circular frame decorated with a traditional Mongol pattern.[3]

The poster informed Mongols that in the referendum they were invited to vote for or against the statement: 'I am a citizen of the Mongolian People's Republic and it is my sincerest wish to be constantly ready to guard the independence of our country with body and mind. I salute the independence of my country.' The referendum took place on 20 October 1945. Referendum day was designated a national holiday and followed a massive propaganda campaign by the state. Voting was carried out under the scrutiny of outside observers, including some from China. The ballot was organized through a total of 3,304 local voting committees and the result was that not a single vote was cast against independence: 487,409 voters, many of whom were illiterate and had to indicate their preference with their finger prints, 'unanimously declared their wish for independence'.[4]

For the historian Baabar, the referendum was a 'political farce'; the result had never been in any doubt so the ballot could easily have been conducted under fair and democratic procedures. Although the mechanics of the election could be called into question, the outcome was not contested and the

Republic of China, formally if reluctantly, acknowledged the independence of the Mongolian People's Republic (MPR). The campaign had built on and encouraged the anti-Chinese nationalism or patriotism that had suffused the Mongolian revolution since 1911. The MPR was now independent of China – and indeed Chiang Kai-shek's government was too weak to do anything other than to accept the reality – but not of the USSR on which it remained dependent for its economy and defence. Stalin agreed not to incorporate Mongolia into the Soviet Union but one region, Uriankhai, which had been renamed Tannu Tuva in 1921 and did not regard itself as part of traditional Mongolia – its language is more Turkic than Mongolian – had already become part of the Soviet Union in 1944. As Tuva, it remains a republic of the Russian Federation.[5]

Tsedenbal comes to power

Yumjaagiin Tsedenbal (1916–91) succeeded Choibalsan as prime minister in 1952 and served until 1974. There was no alternative candidate and no overt opposition to his succession. He served as president from 1974 to 1984 and concurrently as general secretary of the MPRP from 1958 to 1984 when he was eventually removed from power and forced to retire to Moscow. He ran Mongolia for thirty-two years and the reign of the MPRP lasted only for another six years after his enforced retirement.

Born in the Davst district of Uvs on 17 September 1916, Tsedenbal was the first leader of the country to have lived entirely in the post-revolutionary period. Tsedenbal's family were Dörvöds, members of a small ethnic minority that are part of the Oirat (Oyrd) group of western Mongols. His early life was strongly influenced by connections with the Soviet Union: Davst is in north-western Mongolia, on the border with what is now Tuva in the Russian Federation. Tsedenbal attended the Institute of Finance and Economics in the Siberian city of Irkutsk and graduated in 1938. He spent some time travelling in the Caucasus before returning to Mongolia to start work as a teacher at Ulaanbaatar Financial College. Within a very short time he had been appointed deputy director of the college and then to the post of deputy finance minister in the Mongolian government.[6]

Tsedenbal's rapid rise to power at such a young age reflects the small pool of available leaders in Mongolia who were considered both able and politically reliable in the eyes of Moscow. It also stemmed from his long and close association with his predecessor, Choibalsan, who, together with the Soviet leadership, had treated him as the crown prince. A member of the Mongolian Revolutionary Youth League in 1931, Tsedenbal had joined the adult MPRP in 1939 and only a year later was selected to its Central Committee and Presidium. He took over as general secretary of the MPRP on 8 April 1940 and among other things was responsible for the decision to abandon the traditional Mongolian writing system in favour of the Cyrillic script. From 1941 to 1945, the years in which the Second World War had the greatest impact on Mongolia, he held military posts, rising to the rank of lieutenant general and was deputy commander-in-chief of the Mongolian People's Army and head of its Political Directorate.

Tsedenbal had come to the attention of Comintern officials in 1938 while he was still a student, although when he was first invited to Moscow with Choibalsan that summer, he could not be found and was unable to go. A year later he did accompany Choibalsan, at the invitation of Stalin, leaving Ulaanbaatar on 18 November, but not meeting the great man until 3 January 1940. At the age of 24, Tsedenbal was regarded by the Kremlin as second only to Choibalsan in a ruling duumvirate and, on their return to Mongolia, he was formally designated the general secretary of the MPRP Central Committee at the party's tenth congress (20 March–5 April 1940). This followed the purge of the leading figures in the party, including the previous secretaries of the Central Committee, Khas-Ochiryn Luvsandorj, who was executed in Moscow as a counter-revolutionary, Banzarjavyn Baasanjav who died in prison and Dashiin Damba who survived.[7]

When Tsedenbal inherited the leadership of Mongolia on Choibalsan's death in 1952 he also inherited a measure of opprobrium for the excesses of pre-war Mongolia and the dictatorial style of Choibalsan's rule. This did not however prevent him from permitting the emergence of his own personality cult, albeit on a more modest scale. He arranged to have himself awarded many honours in both Mongolia and the USSR, including the title of Marshal in emulation of his mentor, Choibalsan.[8]

Although the MPRP continued to control Mongolia as a one-party state, the political culture of the Tsedenbal years was less brutal, gradually reflecting the de-Stalinization of the Soviet Union under Khrushchev. Tsedenbal did not hesitate to eliminate political opponents but in general they were not executed but dismissed from office, incarcerated or exiled.

Tsedenbal's wife, Anastasia Ivanovna Filatova (1920–21 October 2001) was not only Russian but close to the family of Leonid Brezhnev, the general secretary of the Soviet Communist Party from 1964 until his death in 1982. She exerted considerable influence on her husband, who was in any case accustomed to follow closely the political trends of the USSR.

Tsedenbal had come to power without opposition and ruled Mongolia for over thirty years but it should not be assumed that he never faced political challenges. Mongolia's closeness to the Soviet Union meant that its own leadership and intelligentsia were aware of the growing dissent that had been legitimized when Khrushchev's 1956 'secret speech' revealed the evils of the Stalin period, and the partial de-Stalinization that followed it. The leadership in Ulaanbaatar faced similar criticisms from intellectuals and some senior members of the MPRP but these were ruthlessly resisted by the government and the internal critics were denounced as 'erroneous intellectuals', rightists and counter-revolutionaries, who were 'corrupting the social agenda'.[9] They were removed from any positions of influence and effectively silenced in a move that mirrored the treatment of intellectuals during the Anti-Rightist Movement in China at about the same time, although there is no evidence of a direct political connection.

Socialist construction in the Tsedenbal era

During Tsedenbal's rule Soviet-style quotas were introduced for the production of wool, meat and milk and these quotas became the main forces driving the herding economy. From this developed a national industry based on the processing of raw materials obtained from livestock. New factories were built and companies were established on the model of Soviet industrial combines, all with Soviet aid. At Khatgal, on the southern shores of Lake Khovsgol, a new wool-washing plant was built but there were also similar developments in the capital, Ulaanbaatar. There is no doubt that this industrialization was closely tied to the needs of the Soviet economy, but Mongolia also benefited: among the new installations that appeared were a major power station, radio broadcasting plant, veterinary services, hospitals, kindergartens, a postal service, theatres and cinemas.[10]

Towards the end of the 1950s, again following the Soviet model, certain areas of Mongolia were designated as 'virgin lands' to be ploughed for growing cereal and vegetables. This was part of an attempt to steer the country away from its absolute dependence on animal husbandry. Between 1957 and 1959 there was a drive to collectivize private property as the basis for a new-style economy based on the Soviet Union's concept of socialist principles: this was problematic for Mongolia's herding economy.

The industrial sector also developed. What had been small-scale nomadic settlements, such as Darkhan, Erdenet and Baganuur were developed as industrial centres. The mining complex at Erdenet became a showpiece and an exemplar of 'Soviet-Mongolian friendship and cooperation'. This was proclaimed on a commemorative plaque fashioned in copper that had been mined both at Erdenet and in the Soviet Union and which was unveiled at the site on 30 March 1981. As the economy grew so did the population.

Between 1921 and 1988 the number of Mongolian citizens had quadrupled to 2 million.

Although development in Mongolia followed models that had been tried in the Soviet Union, especially in its Asiatic regions, it was at least acknowledged that there were differences. One of the most unusual features of the discourse on economic development that persisted into the Tsedenbal years was the assertion that Mongolia had somehow managed to bypass the stage of capitalism and had leapt from its feudal past directly into a socialist present and future, the justification for the rapid collectivization programme. Mobile propaganda units toured the grasslands to spread the word about this miracle and the benefits of collectivization and industrialization; propaganda posters in the style of Soviet socialist realism were deployed to reinforce the message.[11]

Economic development was a major priority of the Tsedenbal administration; its policies focused on the livestock sector, attempts to increase the production of food grains by over 70 per cent and the spread of electrification. Under a Three-Year Plan for 1958–60 agreed at the MPRP congress in March 1958, the priority shifted to the transformation of the Mongolian economy from its existing reliance on stock-rearing to an agricultural-industrial economy, on the conventional Soviet model and with aid from the Soviet Union. In the early 1950s, aid had also been expected from China which had not yet become estranged from Moscow. In the early 1960s the contribution of the industrial sector to gross national product (GNP) rose to 38 per cent, largely as a result of investment from the Council for Mutual Economic Assistance (CMEA, but in the West often called Comecon). By 1979 the official English language newspaper, *Soviet Weekly*, in a feature on its reliable ally, described Mongolia as an 'agrarian-industrial state' although livestock production still amounted to 77 per cent of the agricultural output.[12]

The pride and joy of Mongolia's Soviet-supported industrialization was the new city of Erdenet, the site of the renowned huge copper and molybdenum mining and concentration works. Without the contribution of specialist designers from the USSR's Ministry of Non-ferrous Metallurgy; the technical training of engineers and others in the USSR; and the provision of power lines from a plant near Lake Baikal, the city could not have been built. Soviet contributions to the industrialization of Mongolia also included a programme of road construction throughout the 1950s and 1960s and the Trans-Mongolian Railway that linked Moscow, Ulaanbaatar and Beijing. Naturally this was not purely altruistic as the Mongolian economy was developed in the USSR's interests but this programme of modernization did raise the standard of living in Mongolia. Medical care and education were provided free of charge and the average life expectancy rose from 32 years in 1921 to 65 years in 1979.[13]

A Sino-Mongolian Agreement on Economic and Cultural Cooperation, signed in 1952, was a milestone in creating a new relationship between the traditional adversaries: China supported the building of railway lines and other major construction project with loans and the supply of Chinese labourers. Ulaanbaatar also followed Beijing in its support for the Bandung Conference of 1955 and the concept of the Five Principles of Peaceful Coexistence in international relations.

On the surface the signing on 31 May 1960 of another agreement, the Treaty of Friendship and Mutual Assistance with China, should have been an indication that bilateral relations continued to be warm, but fears of the impact of an increasingly powerful China and memories of historic claims over Mongolian territories created an undercurrent of tension and suspicion.

From 1960 onwards the relationship between China and the Soviet Union grew steadily worse and, after military clashes on their common borders at the end of the decade, they were no longer allies but adversaries. Mongolia sided with the USSR, both for immediate practical reasons and because of the historic fear of an ascendant China. Aid from Beijing was discontinued, and cross-border trade shrank dramatically.

Under a new economic plan endorsed by the MPRP in 1966 there was a further push to transform the traditional nomadic pastoral economy into one closer to the ranching system of the American prairies and to develop the small industrial sector. The intrinsic difficulties of effecting this transformation were exacerbated by blizzards, severe winter conditions including the feared *zud* in which there were large scale deaths of livestock from starvation, followed by drought with the consequent failure of harvests. During the next Five-Year Plan from 1971 to 1975, in spite of poor weather there were improvements, many of them due to aid and joint ventures between Soviet and Mongolian government and business.

Although economic development was based solidly on the pattern of the Soviet Union there were opportunities to express the difference and the 'Mongolness' of Mongolia. In 1962 a set of postage stamps was issued in Ulaanbaatar to commemorate the eight-hundredth anniversary of the birth of Chinggis Khan. A new monument to the great unifier of the Mongols was also erected at Gurvan Nuur in Khentii aimag. This expression of a distinct Mongolian identity was probably directed more against the Chinese than the Soviet Union, but Moscow objected.[14]

The case for Tsedenbal

An article by two Mongolian academics closely linked to the Tsedenbal Study Academy and written to commemorate the centenary of the birth of the political leader on 17 September 1916, is a concise and relentlessly positive assessment of 'Tsedenbal and his Legacy'. Tsedenbal was the longest serving leader of the MPR and held key posts in the party, the government and the army. His admirers point to his success in maintaining the 'uniqueness' of Mongolia during the period of the Cold War, when all the allies of the Soviet Union were under pressure not to stray far from its 'socialist' model. Mongolia's leaders were persuaded that only a 'socialist-type democracy' could preserve them in a divided world. As it has done so often the history of the Mongols provided the inspiration. Tsedenbal argued that,

> As an individual, Chinggis Khan was an exceptionally talented man. With his wars he proved himself to be a talented military commander. He had a progressive role in uniting the Mongolian people. Chinggis Khan was inarguably an important statesman, an able commander and the founder of Mongolian statehood.[15]

The word 'progressive' sits a little uneasily alongside the name of Chinggis Khan but Mongols have always admired his strength and his international prominence, and it is really his diplomatic skills and his ability to unite the diverse and quarrelling Mongol tribes that present-day Mongols like to highlight so that he can be praised as the forerunner of modern Mongol nationalism. A statue to Chinggis Khan was erected during this period and his career was studied although the public acknowledgment of his importance was much lower key than it became after 1990. One of the reasons for this low-key approach was the criticism levelled at Ulaanbaatar by the authorities in Moscow. Commemorations of the eight-hundredth anniversary of the birth of Chinggis Khan were severely criticized by the Soviet authorities and one member of the Mongolian Politbouro, Tömör-Ochir was accused of 'nationalist tendencies' and 'idealizing' the historical role of Chinggis Khan who had subjected Russia to the 'Mongol yoke' and was expelled 'for anti-party activities'.[16]

Less obviously, Tsedenbal was positive about the role of the Bogd Khan and the preservation of his palace as the Bogd Khan Palace Museum, although work on that project had begun during the Choibalsan years. Tsedenbal was also active in the moved to rehabilitate, often posthumously, those Mongolian politicians who had been purged on fabricated charges during the 1930s and 1940s. His name is associated with new legislation that was enacted as early as the 1940s to protect against further persecutions, and with the full meetings of the MPRP Central Committee in 1956 and 1962 which formalized the rehabilitation process. He is also credited with the creation of the People's Control Committee, a nationwide network of groups that in theory provided a check on government and an opportunity to audit its activities, and with opening up debate on major issues of policy.

He was 'personally involved in the drafting, approval and implementation of the Constitutions of the Mongolian People's Republic of 1940 and 1960', both of which drew on constitutions of the USSR and emphasized the 'guiding role' of the MPRP. In spite of the dominant role of the party, in reality as well as in the constitutions, Tsedenbal's admirers insist that work on these constitutions embodied 'democratic principles' which were a solid foundation for the democracy that emerged after the 1990 revolution. This assessment receives some support from the opinion of the eminent legal scholar, George Ginsburgs, who described the 1960 constitution as 'an advanced model of Soviet constitutionalism ... a pioneering document within the Communist bloc' that was mature and articulate and 'formalised Mongolia's transition to full "socialist" status in the form of a people's democracy', and employing an administrative structure that was virtually identical with the model in the 1936 Soviet Constitution.[17] Clearly a constitution is not the same as the reality of government in practice but it did recognize Mongolia's status as a people's democracy and a *de jure* independent state.

Tsedenbal spearheaded the economic development of Mongolia which, by any international norms, was still backward, in considerable financial difficulties and isolated, apart from its ties to the USSR. Tsedenbal had experience in government before the Second World War and afterwards became chairman of Mongolia's State Planning Commission and, eventually, head of the government. He was politically and personally close to the government of the USSR and had to maintain a delicate balance between developments that accorded with the Soviet definition of what was 'modern' and what was needed for the Mongolian economy which differed in so many ways from that of the other republics of the USSR, especially Russia. The nomadic pastoral economy not only had to provide for the needs of the rural and urban population, it also had to supply raw materials derived from the livestock to industry and contribute to the country's exports. Moscow was pressing Ulaanbaatar to guide nomadic herders into a sedentary lifestyle as that was deemed to be both 'modern' and more efficient. Tsedenbal's government pioneered the Soviet-inspired programme for reclaiming 'virgin land', but also attempted to strengthen the existing nomadic economy by improving livestock breeding with new technology.

Industrialization and urbanization, also Soviet priorities, proceeded apace and the rapidly expanding capital city of Ulaanbaatar acquired new housing, hospitals, schools, colleges and cultural centres. Innovations in communications, which were exceptionally important in a country with such a scattered population, included new radio and television stations, radio relays and the beginnings of satellite communications.

As part of the first generation of political leaders with any modern education, in his case like almost all the others derived from study in the Soviet Union, he considered education a high priority and during his tenure thousands more pupils and students gained access to secondary and tertiary education. A modern Soviet-style medical system was also extended throughout Mongolia. Tsedenbal also gave his support and encouragement to the monks of the Gandan monastery, which was the only monastery in operation during his rule, although it did not open fully until 1990. He was also 'personally involved in the restoration of such ancient Buddhist monasteries as Amarbayasgalant and Manjushir'.

On the international stage Tsedenbal was active in pressing the case for Mongolia's entry to the United Nations in 1961. In April 1973 he was responsible for a resolution to the MPRP Central Committee which authorized the beginning of negotiations with the United States on establishing full diplomatic relations, although these were not finally established until 1987.

Tsedenbal was constrained, although not unwillingly, by his close political and personal relationship with the Soviet leadership and his conviction that the Soviet model, and particular the economic model was, with some modifications, the one that Mongolia had to follow. In spite of this it is possible to see that he was able to make concessions to the unusual economy and culture of Mongolia. It is certainly the case that, during his terms of office as premier and president, Mongolia abandoned much of the authoritarianism of the Stalin and Choibalsan era, became far less hidebound ideologically, and moved towards being a more open-minded society. It is unlikely that Tsedenbal could have achieved even those limited improvements if the Soviet Union had not already been paving the way.[18]

Changes at the pinnacle of power

Tsedenbal seemed settled as premier and head of state but there was internal opposition to his rule and concern that his health was failing. The composition of the ruling party was also changing. In spite of the changes that took place during his rule, he was too closely associated with the Stalinist culture of purges and authoritarianism that had flourished under his mentor Choibalsan. The role of his wife, Anastasia Tsedenbal-Filatova, Russian born and close to the Brezhnev family was coming under question and there was a popular feeling that she had accrued far too much personal power.

When the MPRP annual congress met in 1971 to elect the Politburo, the Central Committee and the Secretariat, over 80 per cent of the members were new. Three years later Tsedenbal would step down as premier in favour of Jambyn Batmönkh, although he retained the MPRP general secretaryship and was head of state until 1984. Relations with the USSR remained close, although there had been frequent conflicts when Ulaanbaatar demanded more aid than Moscow was prepared to provide.

After the death in 1982 of the Soviet Communist Party general secretary, Leonid Brezhnev, who had held that office since the ousting of Khrushchev in 1964, and the brief interregnums of his two ailing successors, Yuri Andropov and Konstantin Chernenko, the USSR entered the reform period under Mikhael Gorbachev. The watchwords of this period of challenge and drama were glasnost and perestroika and it became clear that the new regime intended to inaugurate a profound transformation of the economy and society of the Soviet Union. Crucially for Mongolia, Gorbachev's administration also sought an accommodation with the People's Republic of China (PRC). In theory the two Communist states were allies but any real cooperation had broken down as early as 1960 and relations had never recovered from the ideological dispute of the early 1960s, China's Cultural Revolution and the border war of 1969.[19] The attempted Soviet détente with China was a step too far for Tsedenbal and he assiduously removed those forward-thinking officials who advocated closer relations with Beijing and thus threatened his position. He travelled to Moscow in August 1984 for medical treatment and in his absence was unceremoniously dismissed as president. This was engineered by Batmönkh and other opponents in Ulaanbaatar, but it was with the active assistance of the government of the Soviet Union. He was stripped of all his political honours, his membership of the MPRP was rescinded, and he only avoided a trial because of his frail health. His remaining years were spent in a flat in Moscow, where he died in 1991.[20]

Tsedenbal's legacy remains controversial: his detractors blame him for the stagnation of the national economy which grew but conspicuously failed to encompass reform during his reign, and for his despotic style of government. His political associates, who endorse his loyalty to Moscow, have sought to restore his reputation and together with relatives and friends arranged for a statue of him to be erected in Ulaanbaatar; it stands outside the National Academic Drama Theatre close to the city centre. Mongolia is still not willing to reject fully the legacy of the Soviet years, as is shown by the fact that a statue of Tsedenbal's predecessor, the undoubtedly controversial Choibalsan, which was erected in 1946 still stands outside the National University. When the MPP won the Khural elections in June 2016, one of its priorities was tp celebrate the centenary of Tsedenbal's birth.

Batmönkh and the harbingers of reform

Tsedenbal was replaced by the man who had ousted him, Jambyn Batmönkh, an academic economist and university administrator and, in Morris Rossabi's view, a 'stolid apparatchik', who was MPRP general secretary from 1984 to 1990. Batmönkh was willing to allow political and economic reform, and gradually came to accept the need to emulate Gorbachev's Soviet perestroika in Mongolia. He issued directives on economic decentralization and renewal and *Unen* (*Truth*), the official daily newspaper of the MPRP, even published a complete translation of the decisive speech on economic liberalization that Gorbachev had delivered to the Congress of the Soviet Communist Party in 1986. Batmönkh was slower to implement reforms in the structure of the party and government, but the character of the political hierarchy was already evolving; by 1989 it contained a significant number of influential individuals who were committed to greater openness and accountability, if not to full multi-party democracy.[21]

In that year, Batmönkh was also responsible for a commission that officially acknowledged the scale of repression under Choibalsan and also criticized Tsedenbal for having created his own cult of personality. Under Batmönkh, but following the lead of the USSR, relations with China gradually improved. Trade and communications between the two countries at all levels were established on a regular basis after decades of unsatisfactory relations.

Batmönkh will probably be best remembered for his role in Mongolia's transition to democracy as Soviet power unravelled between 1989 and 1991. He is respected for resolutely refusing to use force to preserve the MPRP in power and overseeing the resignation of the Politburo and the government in March 1990, weakened by the withdrawal of support from Moscow. He retired to grow vegetables and died in 1997.

Batmönkh's administration was succeeded by the first post-Soviet government of Mongolia, under Punsalmaagiin Ochirbat, which came to power during the democratic revolution. P. Ochirbat (usually referred to with his initial if not his full matronymic – unusually not a patronymic as he adopted his mother's name after the death of his father when he was 5 years old – to distinguish him from G. Ochirbat who was briefly MPRP general secretary), who served as president from 1990 to 1997, was the first president of Mongolia to be directly elected.[22]

Economy and society on the eve of reform

The management of the Mongolian economy under Tsedenbal had emulated as far as possible the Soviet model. It was a centrally planned economy, a system that is often described by its detractors as a 'command' economy. Economic planning was therefore a high priority and, although Five-year plans were the norm, the most significant plan for Mongolia was a three-year plan that was adopted at the MPRP's 13th Congress in March 1958. Its objective was to transform the country from an economy based primarily on livestock rearing to an agricultural-industrial economy: in order to achieve this transformation, substantial economic aid would be required. In June 1962, after it had been admitted to the United Nations, Mongolia had also become a member of the CMEA (Comecon): this enabled Ulaanbaatar to secure loans and aid and regulated its economic relationships with the USSR and its allies. Mongolia's economy had encountered serious problems in the 1960s, due in part to disastrous weather, and another economic plan that was approved in 1966 concentrated on attempts to transform the nomadic style of herding into a ranch-style system that the government believed would be a more stable method of managing livestock.

Although there was industry and agriculture in Mongolia during this period the basis of the economy remained the raising of livestock and this was organized though collectives, the *negdel*, which literally means 'unity' or a 'union':

> Between 1960 and 1990, practically every Mongolian herding household was a member of a local collective organisation, the *negdel* in which livestock production was managed jointly in line with socialist state planning. The *negdel* implied some specialisation of labour, since all collective livestock was segregated by species and by age, furthermore, a number of technical and administrative posts allowed some members to be partly or fully occupied as non-herders. Essentially the *negdel* was a comprehensive unit meeting every single aspect of the herding household's social and economic needs. It offered free education, health care and pensions. It provided veterinary services, animal shelters, hay and transportation for people and equipment. It marketed all livestock products jointly, and supplied consumer goods in return.[23]

In addition to the collective system, almost all families retained a small private herd. There were restrictions on the number of sheep, cattle and horses that could be held in private ownership, but according to some estimates, this private sector amounted to one-third of the total of the national herd before 1990. Reform of the system began during the Batmönkh years; production agreements between the *negdel* and herders were approved by the government in 1987 and herding families were gradually given greater scope to generate their own income. Full privatization was not introduced until after the fall of the one-party state in 1990.[24]

Mongolia and the outside world

Mongolia's remoteness and isolation until the 1990s has led to its being described as a 'black hole in Central Asia', but it did have relations with other countries, primarily with the USSR for the geographical and historical reasons that have been outlined, but also with other neighbouring states.

Until 1990 the MPR was always described as a 'satellite' of the USSR. It was not a constituent republic of the Soviet Union, as were Kazakhstan or Kyrgyzstan, although Tsedenbal had been in favour of its being fully incorporated into the USSR. In its relationship with Moscow, Mongolia was more independent than the Soviet republics but less autonomous than the Eastern European states which were sometimes also referred to as 'satellites'.

Ulaanbaatar followed Moscow's policy, especially in foreign relations, very closely but it did not always do so slavishly and without complaint. Szalontai Balazs, in an article published in the *Mongolian Journal of International Affairs*, discusses documents in the Hungarian archives which reveal that the leadership of the MPRP resented being dominated by foreigners and attempted to fashion an economic policy independent of Moscow while remaining close enough to continue receiving support and financial aid. Although Soviet diplomats in Mongolia do not appear to have voiced any complaints, representatives of Eastern European diplomatic missions submitted a report complaining about their ill treatment by Mongolian officials. Some of these complaints arose from misunderstandings, the diplomat's unfamiliarity with local customs and the degree of informality with which they were treated. Others were more serious and indicate that Mongolian officials resented the way in which they were treated by diplomats from the Soviet bloc and expressed this antipathy with unhelpfulness and insubordination or even low-level harassment. Between 1960 and 1964, diplomats from 'fraternal' countries complained that their movements were monitored; that there had been attempts to interfere with diplomatic mail; and that they were prevented from employing local staff that had not been vetted by the Mongolian Foreign Ministry. Affronted diplomats interpreted these moves as a way for a country that was disparaged as 'underdeveloped and politically dependent' to assert its sovereignty, if only symbolically.[25]

There were also genuine policy disputes when foreign officials considered Mongolian projects to be unrealistically overambitious, or over rural policies which would have damaged the interests of the USSR by reducing the availability of cheap meat and minerals for Moscow. Aid from Moscow to Mongolia was a fraught topic that frequently led to political wrangles. Tsedenbal was willing to use these disputes to advance Mongolia's interests but he did not attack the 'fraternal' officials directly and neither did he employ cultural nationalism as a weapon in the disputes. He was too wedded to close cooperation with the USSR. Curiously the Sino-Soviet dispute that blew up in the early 1960s had the side-effect of lessening the conflicts between the Mongolians and the rest of Comecon.

Tsedenbal was potentially at risk from changes in Soviet policies after Khrushchev had been forced out of office in 1964. Some opponents in the MPRP Central Committee attempted to use the occasion to accuse Tsedenbal of overreliance on the economic support of the Soviet Union, incompetence and lack of respect for party discipline. He managed to repulse this attempted coup, partly by accusing his accusers of playing into the hands of the Chinese.[26]

The economic development of Mongolia that was modelled so closely on the experience of the Soviet Union differed in one startling respect. Mongolia's progress was described, improbably, as 'leaping from feudalism to socialism' and missing out the capitalist stage that orthodox mechanical Marxism prescribes in its description of historical progression. Russian models and methods were also employed in the media, education, technical training and many other fields. Models employed in China, which might have been considered more appropriate to Mongolia were not publicly approved of, but Chinese trade and labour played an important part in the construction of modern Mongolia.

War memorial at Zaisan

A prominent symbolic representation of the relationship between Mongolia and the USSR is the Zaisan memorial. It is set on a hill to the south of the capital Ulaanbaatar, and just across the Tuul River, and offers a panoramic view of both the city and the river. The memorial commemorates members of the Soviet armed forces killed during the Second World War and the images on its mural are intended to represent the friendship between the peoples of the USSR and Mongolia. These include Soviet support for the revolution of 1921 led by Sükhbaatar; the defeat of the Japanese Guandong Army by the Soviet Red Army in the battle of Khalkhyn Gol on the Mongolian border in 1939; the defeat of Nazi Germany; and post-war successes such as the Soviet space flights. Next to the memorial is a tank that was bought by Mongolian subscription for a Soviet tank brigade in 1943. Previously this stood at a crossroads between the Zaisan monument and the centre of Ulaanbaatar but it was moved to the foot of the monument in 2003. The tank took part in the defeat of German forces in Berlin in 1945 and the route that it took from Moscow to Berlin is set out on a map nearby.

This monument has long been a focus of school and college excursions and for meetings on other patriotic occasions, but the symbolism of dependence on the Soviet Union sits oddly with a post-independence culture. It does not take much imagination to discern the underlying message that the Soviet Union afforded Mongolia protection against the Japanese and German armies, and that this protection was only possible because of the close relationship between the MPRP and Moscow. The relationship was not entirely one-sided: in Moscow's eyes, the defence of Mongolia was essential for the protection of the Soviet Union's eastern flank during the Second World War. The alliance was one of mutual, if unequal, interests.[27]

Relations with China

Relations with Moscow were central to the politics of Mongolia but the great power to the south could not be ignored. Ulaanbaatar's relations with Beijing mirrored those of the Soviet bloc, but traditional suspicions of China's intentions towards Mongolia remained in the background through the Batmönkh transitional period and Mongolia's democratic revolution. These relationships are complicated by the presence in China of a large Mongolian minority – this is considered in more detail in Chapter 9.

When the Chinese Communist Party (CCP) came to power in 1949 it was assumed that there would be a close alliance between Beijing and Moscow. In parallel with agreements signed between the USSR and the PRC, a Sino-Mongolian Agreement on Economic and Cultural Cooperation was signed in 1952: it was intended to last for ten years and provided for significant Chinese aid towards the construction of railways and other projects, and for the sending of Chinese labourers to work in Mongolia. Ulaanbaatar concluded another Treaty of Friendship and Mutual Assistance with China in May 1960 but the radicalization of Chinese policies during the Great Leap Forward period and the estrangement from Stalin of the Chinese leader Mao Zedong made closer relations more difficult. The Mongolians were firmly aligned with the Soviet Union during the Sino-Soviet dispute, which dominated the 1960s and culminated in armed conflict between Chinese and Soviet troops on their common border in 1969. The Soviet Union stationed large numbers of troops in Mongolia during the 1970s and both sides feared that political tensions and border clashes could escalate into a full-scale war. As the dispute deepened, aid from China was discontinued and trade between the two countries was drastically reduced. Economic and political relations did not recover until long after the Cultural Revolution and the death of Mao Zedong in September 1976.

Mongolian association of Sinologists, October 1990

A little-known meeting that took place in Ulaanbaatar in October 1990 sheds an interesting light on the priorities of the Chinese and Mongolian governments and the tentative way in which they approached each other. The Soviet Union was in the process of disintegrating and in Mongolia a wave of demonstrations that had taken place the previous January brought about the resignation of the entire Politburo the following month. Although the political future of the country was uncertain, Ulaanbaatar was calm that October.

A conference billed as the inaugural meeting of the Mongolian Association of Sinologists was held between 16 and 19 October 1990 under the rubric of 'China's Reforms and Open Door Policy'. Many of the participants were not, strictly speaking, academic sinologists but all had a professional interest in China. Although the conference was intended to be international it consisted almost entirely of a Chinese delegation and the Mongolian hosts. Individuals from the United States and the deputy editor of the Russian language journal, *Far Eastern Questions*, had expressed an interest in attending but were unable to do so: one representative of the Soviet Embassy, by the name of Steshov, attended briefly; but the only Western attendee was the present author. The Chinese fielded a strong and well-organized team of six, including two senior staff from the State Commission for Restructuring the Economy, one of whom was its deputy director, Zheng Dingquan, who led the delegation. They were accompanied by economists from the Chinese Institute for Regional Economic Studies at the Chinese Academy of Social Sciences. This delegation was reinforced by the presence of the Chinese ambassador to Mongolia and two of his embassy staff, one of whom spoke excellent Mongolian (I had assumed that he was from Inner Mongolia but, in fact, he was from Shanghai) and was able to interpret far more effectively than the official Mongolian interpreters; they clearly had little experience of conference interpreting between Mongolian and Chinese, which was not surprising in light of Mongolia's long isolation from the PRC.

Foreign delegates were housed in the Ikh Tengger State Guest House, a complex of buildings set in a fold in the mountains just to the southeast of Ulaanbaatar in a closely guarded area which also contained the residences of the president and prime minister. It was a peaceful setting where elk roamed freely and the atmosphere was relaxed in spite of the armed guards patrolling the ridges above the guest house.

The Mongolian Association of Sinologists was established in January 1990 as 'a public organization incorporating sinologists, interpreters and individuals who have professional relationships with China'. Its aim was to 'actively contribute to the consolidation of the traditional friendship and cooperation between the peoples of Mongolia and China ... as well as to act as a mediator in establishing trade and economic contacts and relations of cooperation between individuals, industrial, trade research and cultural organisations and firms'. Although claiming to be independent it had close links with the Mongolian Academy of Sciences and the Ministry of Foreign Affairs. The president of the association, Mr. H. Ayurzana, was on the staff of the ministry, had lived in China and spoke fluent Chinese. In his personal life he was also clearly a Sinophile with an educated taste in Chinese furniture and porcelain.

The conference venue was the headquarters of the Mongolian Association for Friendship with Foreign Countries in the Ministry of Foreign Affairs building, which lay to the south of Peace Avenue and close to Sükhbaatar Square. Meetings with members of the cabinet took place in the government buildings. The papers presented to the conference by the Chinese team concentrated on the reform of China's economy, border trade and the development of special economic zones. The aim of the delegation was to present China as the obvious model for Mongolia's post-Soviet development. Mongolian delegates addressed the relevance of China's experience to Mongolia and the debate that followed covered a range of topics that included the problems of a market economy in a socialist society; land ownership and the role of foreign capital. Mongolian participants were particularly concerned about the impact of economic reform on commodity prices, fearing that these would increase significantly. The conference ended with detailed discussions on Chinese-Mongolian economic relations with two senior members of the Mongolian cabinet, First Deputy Prime Minister Ganbold and Deputy Prime Minister Purevdorj.

The Mongolian Association of Sinologists is apparently no longer active, but it played a useful role in connecting Chinese and Mongolian researchers and diplomats at a time of dramatic change. For the Chinese delegation it provided an opportunity to promote the experience of the PRC as a model for Mongolian economic development and to see for themselves the impact of the democratic revolution on their northern neighbour.[28]

6

Democratic Revolution: Mongolia after the collapse of Soviet power (1991–2019)

'In 1990 Mongolia saw a peaceful revolution that ushered in democratic reforms and transformed Mongolia into a democratic state with a democratic constitution, a multiparty system and a parliament.'[1] This depiction of the 'democratic revolution' by Mongolian scholars at the National Museum in Ulaanbaatar is fundamentally accurate but it makes the process seem far smoother and less troublesome than it really was. During what was a comprehensive transformation of the political system, Mongolians rejected the 'socialist' model of the USSR that the country had adhered to since 1924 and began to embrace a market economy and political pluralism. To underline and encourage Mongolia's emergence from its subservience to the USSR, there was also a campaign to put greater emphasis on Mongolia's pre-Soviet history and traditional culture. For many this was done with the intention of replacing the variant of Soviet culture that the country had accepted for decades.

The Berlin Wall was breached on 9 November 1989 and the Soviet Union finally collapsed on 25 December 1991. In between these momentous events, Mongolia experienced its own political upheavals and a rapid transition from a one-party state to a democratic multiparty system. Protests and demonstrations calling for greater democracy came to a head with a mass hunger strike on 7 March 1990: the Politburo of the ruling Mongolian People's Revolutionary Party (MPRP) resigned en masse on 12 March. The brutal suppression of the Chinese democracy movement in Beijing's Tian'anmen Square on 4 June 1989 was still fresh in the minds of Mongolia's political elite and MPRP general secretary, Jambyn Batmönkh, who was also president, firmly rejected the use of force to maintain its authority. He declared that the party needed to renew itself if it were to be able to deal satisfactorily with the political crisis. Many new political groupings were formed, some of which lasted only a matter of months before merging with others or disbanding: it took some time before a relatively stable political order emerged. Mongolians refer to this period as their democratic revolution, but it was in many ways a counter-revolution; in the process many of the most fundamental political and economic developments of the previous sixty or seventy years were reversed.[2]

Soviet President Mikhail Gorbachev's ideas of glasnost and perestroika had already attracted the attention of the younger generation of aspiring Mongolian leaders. One of these, Tsakhiagiin Elbegdorj, who was later to be elected president of Mongolia, came into contact with Gorbachev's thinking while studying military journalism at the Military Political Institute of the USSR in the Ukrainian capital Lviv. When Elbegdorj and like-minded colleagues returned to Mongolia they found that they were prevented from discussing these radical concepts within the bureaucratic apparatus; senior figures regarded Gorbachev's reforms as a serious threat to their authority. Undaunted they began to meet and organize independently.

The first pro-democracy demonstration was organized by the newly formed Mongolian Democratic Union (*Mongolyn ardchilsan kholboo*, MDU) at the Youth Cultural Centre in Ulaanbaatar on 10 December 1989. This was International Human Rights Day, which the authoritarian regime of the MPRP had planned to mark with banal and formal speeches and ceremonies. Instead, onlookers witnessed a group of some 200 protesters with banners and placards calling for the end to 'bureaucratic oppression' and insisting on a commitment to implement Gorbachev's ideas of perestroika and glasnost, which now had their Mongolian equivalents in *uurchlun baiguulalt* and *il tod*. The demonstrators were young, educated and, like Elbegdorj, had access to publications from the Soviet Union and the West. The MDU, which was a loose coalition of opposition forces, was the first non-Communist political grouping to emerge during the democratic revolution. As its members struggled to define their political positions there were defections and splits but from this group there eventually emerged the Mongolian National Democratic Party (*Mongolyn ündesnii ardchilsam nam*, MNDP) in October 1992.[3]

Zorig

The hero of the movement in 1989, and the moving spirit behind the MDU, was Sanjaasürengiin Zorig whose statue now stands in the centre of Ulaanbaatar. With a mixed family background of Buryat and Russian ancestors as well as Khalkh Mongols, Zorig had been educated in Mongolia and, in the early 1980s, at the elite Moscow State University where he had come into contact with radical student groups. Back in Mongolia he was a postgraduate student at the Mongolian National University, where he also taught. He became increasingly frustrated at the rigidity of the Mongolian elite and its refusal to respond adequately to the changes that were under way in the Soviet Union. He gathered around him sympathetic young people in an informal group that by 1988 had acquired the name of the New Generation. Intellectually and politically they were a mixed group with no consistent or coordinated policy other than the desire to see the removal of the existing one-party state. Zorig was appointed the General Coordinator of the MDU and was the intellectual inspiration behind the first flowering of this new political forum.[4]

Mongolian Democratic Union

During the demonstration of 10 December 1989 in Sükhbaatar Square, as the young reformers proclaimed the birth of their new political movement, the MDU, one of the most popular songs that they sang was 'The Sound of the Bell'. It began with the lines:

Restricted my words to tell
Shielded my eyes to see
Signal of our fortune, the bell sounds
Awakens us from doziness
The bell's ringing awakens us
Let it forever awaken us.[5]

'The Ring of the Bell', *Khonkhnii Duu*, was composed by one of the demonstrators, S. Tsogtsaikhan. It became the anthem of the protesters, was adopted by the democratic movement as a whole and was played and recorded by a dissident rock group. In 2014 on the twenty-fifth anniversary of the revolution, the anthem was awarded a state honour by President Elbegdorj as an important symbol of the democratic revolution.[6]

By 17 December and after many long meetings, the MDU had agreed on a basic programme with which it challenged the government of the MPRP. Support for the party and the movement for democracy mushroomed and by January 1990 it could muster over 1,000 supporters. A demonstration on 14 January in the square outside the Lenin Museum featured banners that called for the rehabilitation of purged politicians and evoked the spirit of Chinggis Khan.

Support for the reformers was concentrated in Ulaanbaatar but they began to attract followers elsewhere, notably among the workers of the Erdenet copper mines, where the miners had unresolved grievances against the government, including the fact that Mongolian members of staff at the mine were paid less than their Soviet counterparts for equivalent work.

The main demand of the MDU was for the creation of a genuinely independent Khural (parliament) on the basis of free elections. Another demonstration in support of this demand took place on 21 January 1990. In spite of the bitter cold of a deep Mongolian winter the protest attracted thousands of participants and was marked by the determination of the MDU leadership to honour the memory of Chinggis Khan as an alternative to the heroes of the Mongolian revolution or their Soviet counterparts. 21 January was the anniversary of the death of Lenin in 1924 and images of Lenin, and especially those of Stalin, became the targets of the reformers.

The demonstrations in Ulaanbaatar became larger and more frequent and were echoed by protests in provincial cities. On 4 March 1990 a mass meeting in Victory Square (later renamed Independence Square) attracted 90–100,000 people. The protesters demanded that the MPRP call a special convention; that the ruling Central Committee be replaced; and that the party be separated from the government. A hunger strike was called by the MDU, recalling the protest by the students and citizens of Beijing's Chinese democracy movement in Tian'anmen Square the previous year. In Ulaanbaatar thousands of Mongolians demonstrated their support on 7 March. Students and schoolchildren flocked to Sükhbaatar Square where they were joined by local people including monks from Gandan, still the only monastery permitted to operate in Mongolia at that time. Sympathy strikes broke out among workers in Erdenet and in the cities of Darkhan and Mörön.

The existence of the MDU as a coalition of reformers obscured the deep confusion and complexity of the political views under its umbrella. Individuals and groups struggled to come to terms with the legacy of the past and the immediate challenges faced by the government and the country. Among the new political parties that declared themselves during the revolution there were the Democratic Socialist Union, New Progressive Union, Mongolian Social Democratic Party, Mongolian National Democratic Party, Free Labour Party and Mongolian Green Party. It is not surprising, in view of the number of different groupings, that it was extremely difficult for the opposition to achieve any level of political consensus. In the event few of the parties survived in their original form as the country struggled to create a multiparty democracy.[7]

Painful transition to multiparty democracy

The more uncompromising and doctrinaire elements of the ruling MPRP leadership called for a robust response to the demonstrations and the suppression of the movement by force. The party general secretary, Batmönkh, however, was resolutely opposed to the use of violence. On 4 June 1989 in Beijing's Tian'anmen Square, force had been used by the Chinese authorities against democracy movement demonstrators with deadly effect; the repercussions have had a deleterious effect on the political culture of China ever since. In spite of resistance from within his party and government, Batmönkh supported Gorbachev's programme of reform and had begun to implement changes in the structure of the bureaucracy to make it less old-fashioned and more transparent. In 1989 he had created a commission to analyse the repression of the 1930s and the responsibility for the thousands who had been killed, and to reverse the political verdicts on those who had been purged.

Within the ruling MPRP there was a growing body of support for the demands of the reformers but the party was divided and the government vacillated. An obdurate faction advocated deploying the army and police to suppress the demonstrations in Ulaanbaatar, using as an excuse the sporadic outbreaks of violence that had occurred in spite of the determined non-violent stance of the leadership of the MDU. Members of the government and the Politburo attempted to negotiate a compromise but the protesters remained adamant in their demands for fundamental changes. Conscious of the disastrous impact of the military suppression of the Tian'anmen protests and pressed by the Soviet government to avoid a violent end to the demonstrations, the MPRP backed down. On 9 March 1990 Batmönkh announced his resignation and that of the entire membership of the Politburo in a statement that was broadcast on radio and television. The hunger strike was ended and the demonstrators left Sükhbaatar Square. It had been a textbook example of a successful civil disobedience campaign. On Monday 12 March, members of the existing parliamentary assembly, the People's Great Khural (*Ardyn Ikh Khural*), which had met only nine times since 1960, converged on Ulaanbaatar and agreed to repeal Article 82 of the Mongolian Constitution. Article 82 was the legal basis for the one-party state and its repeal precipitated the collapse of the MPRP regime. Because the reformers were suspicious of the MPRP's motives, demonstrations continued until they had succeeded in obtaining an assurance that multiparty elections would be held on 27 July 1990, the first ever open elections in Mongolia.[8]

This appeared to be a major victory for the reformers but the outcome of the elections was a severe disappointment. The MPRP retained control of 357 seats; the Mongolian Democratic Party took 16; Ganbold's free-market National Progressive Party had 6; and the Mongolian Social Democratic Party won 4. The reasons for the failure of the reformers to take control of the Khural were many and varied. The MPRP still enjoyed considerable support, especially in the rural areas: it was the incumbent government and therefore a safe bet in the minds of those who were not intellectually committed to the democratic movement. It also had the organizational and financial strength which the embryonic parties lacked. The reformers were divided and they were also inexperienced and naïve about the preparation needed to win a genuinely open election. When the newly elected assembly met in September 1990, the MPRP was firmly in charge but it had new leaders. Punsalmagiin Ochirbat was president and Dashiin Byambasüren, a reformer who had kept closely in touch with the hunger strikers, became prime minister. A further concession to the reformers was the appointment of Ganbold, the leader of the National Progressive Party, as the first deputy prime minister.[9]

Mongolia had reached a crossroads in its political history. The one-party state had been effectively challenged and, although the ruling party remained in power, it recognized that it could not continue as before. The reformers were not in a position to take over: they were weak and divided, struggled to define their political identities and had yet to build the support necessary to replace the MPRP. Mongolia was attempting to create a democratic system under difficult if not desperate circumstances and in a rapidly changing society. In addition to the newly created political parties, new social groups were beginning to make their voices heard and new conflicts were emerging. Increasingly there were concerns about the growing gap between the rich and poor and the emergence of a destitute underclass that gravitated towards the cities as the rural economy collapsed. Inflation rose to 26 per cent and allegations of corruption, especially in connection with the awarding of mining rights, were commonplace.

In spite of these problems, Mongolia's transition from a one-party state to a multiparty system and an open economy was initially peaceful. It was not, however, painless, above all because of the economic and social problems that ensued. The subsequent attempts to achieve a transformation from a planned, although primarily pastoral and agricultural, economy to an entrepreneurial and free-market system were intended to solve the country's problems but they created more difficulties. Mongolia, like many states after the collapse of Soviet power in the USSR, and other developing countries, was subjected to a set of model reform policies – often known as the Washington Consensus. This model had the support of powerful global financial institutions, mainly based in Washington, including the World Bank, the International Monetary Fund and the United States Treasury. Under the Washington Consensus, financial support was offered only to those countries that were prepared to accept the imposition of neoliberal or market-fundamentalist policies. The success or failure of these policies in Mongolia has implications for the wider applicability of these models in other developing countries, in particular those emerging from rigidly planned economies:[10]

> In 1991 Mongolia's Soviet advisers left the country while simultaneously the former CMEA [Comecon] markets vanished overnight. The result was devastating; Mongolia suffered the most serious peacetime economic collapse any nation has faced during this century. In the first four years after independence, crop production was halved and industrial output dropped by one third. Mongolia's per capita gross domestic product also declined by one-third.[11]

Mongolian reformers and the Soviet Union

The attitude of Mongolian reformers to the USSR was ambivalent. The aid and other benefits that had accrued from Mongolia's close relationship with Moscow had to be acknowledged. Although the initial Soviet-style collectivization that had been imposed on Mongolia in the 1930s had been an unmitigated disaster, the more realistic systems introduced later, and the programme of industrialization and urbanization on the Soviet pattern, had led to a stable economy although without substantial growth. Most Mongols only achieved a low standard of living but there was little abject poverty. Aid and trade ceased abruptly immediately after the collapse of the Soviet Union and the extent of Mongolia's previous dependence on the USSR was immediately apparent. In late 1990 there were few goods on the shelves of shops, even the special shops for officials and foreign visitors, and poverty and destitution became widespread.[12]

The Soviet connection had also shielded Mongolia from Chinese influence. Although there had been resentment at the privileged position that Russian advisers occupied in the Mongolian system, there was no fear of mass immigration by Russians, while the prospect of Chinese control or settlement alarmed many Mongols. Most of the reformers had studied in the USSR or Eastern Europe, during the period when ideas of reform were beginning to take root, and many also had family ties either with Russians or with other ethnic groups in the Soviet Union, particularly the Mongolian-speaking Buryats. Soviet influence pervaded the universities and cultural organizations and Russian was the second language of almost all educated Mongols. Nevertheless the resentment at the authoritarian nature of Soviet political attitudes and the way that Mongolians were treated as second-class citizens was deep-seated.[13]

New constitution and new politics: Chinggis Khan's eight-hundredth birthday

A constitutional referendum in 1990 and a vote in 1992 led to the establishment of Mongolia's first fully democratic parliament. Since then elections, mostly peaceful, have been held every four years. Under the constitution that was signed into force by President Ochirbat on 25 January 1992 the single-chamber parliamentary assembly was reduced in size from 430 to 76 seats and was renamed the Mongolian National Great Khural (*Mongol Ulsyn Ikh Khural*) and required to meet every six months for a minimum of seventy-five days. It is often referred to simply as the Khural as the other chamber, the Lesser Khural, resurrected briefly in 1990, was abolished in 1992.

Politics also began to develop outside of the electoral process: new newspapers appeared as the political debate widened. Symbols of the new era include a redesigned national flag and coat of arms and particularly the reappearance of the old golden *soyombo* symbol which had been replaced under the Stalinist regime. A monument was erected to commemorate the seven hundred and fiftieth anniversary of the creation of the *Secret History of the Mongols* and a special edition was printed of what had become almost a sacred book. The re-examination of Mongolia's history, of which this was a part, culminated in 2006 with the opening of a monument to Chinggis Khan as part of celebrations for the eight-hundredth anniversary of the Mongol Empire that he created. It was far more successful than a previous attempt in 1961 to celebrate the eight-hundredth anniversary of Chinggis Khan's birth. That project became mired in controversy and Mongolian and Russian ideological disputes, but a monument was eventually erected close to what was believed to have been Chinggis Khan's birthplace. The new monument created in 2006 stands at the front and to the left of the newly renovated government buildings as viewed from Sükhbaatar Square: this is where the joint mausoleum of Sükhbaatar and Choibalsan stood until it was demolished in 2005 and the symbolism of the replacement is obvious. Banners displayed at the ceremonial opening proclaimed the celebration of '800 years of Mongolian People'.[14]

MPRP resurgent

In the general elections of January 1992, although the pro-liberalization Ganbold was re-elected to the Khural, his influence has been greatly reduced. The old leadership of the MPRP was once again in control, but the return to a form of the old government did not resolve the country's problems. There were some economic achievements but desperate poverty was increasingly widespread and the government was rocked by scandals involving currency speculation and general corruption. Democratic reformers who were critical of the policies of foreign aid donors pointed to their existence as a privileged and isolated elite and criticized their ignorance of the 'strong family, tribal and regional identifications' of Mongolian people' which made nepotism almost inevitable. The government was seen by many Mongolians as corrupt, complacent and ineffectual and there was a general mood of public disillusion.[15]

The first democratic constitution that had been approved by the Khural in 1992 was amended in 2000. Under the original constitution the president was elected for a period four years and that term was renewable. The parliament, the single chamber State Great Khural, which has seventy-six representatives, was also elected for four-year terms, and this body appointed the prime minister and the cabinet. The 2000 amendment gave the president the right to dissolve the legislature in the event of the Khural not being able to come to an agreement on nominating a prime minister, effectively increasing the power of the presidency.

Democrats in power

The MPRP expected to win the elections held in 1996 but on 14 February the two main opposition groupings, the Mongolian National Democratic Party and the Mongolian Social Democratic Party came together in a coalition under the title of Democratic Union (*Ardchilsan kholboo*, DU, also translated as Democratic Alliance, DA). Their campaign was politically and financially supported by government and party organizations in the United States and they won forty-five seats, with three to allied independent parties. This gave them an overall majority, although not of the size necessary to force through any measures that required a two-thirds majority in the Khural as the MPRP still retained twenty-five seats.

The DU consolidated their power by restructuring the government apparatus with a reduced number of ministries and replacing existing officials with bureaucrats sympathetic to their policies. One drawback for the DU was that they were primarily a coalition of the educated urban elite and most of its supporters had little contact with the politics of the rural grass roots where residual loyalty to the MPRP was still strong.

The economic policies of the DU were no more successful than those of their predecessors. Inflation rose; the Mongolian currency, the *tugrik*, fell dramatically against the dollar; there was increasing pressure on the already impoverished lowest sector of the population; and unemployment was around the 20 per cent mark. A disastrous decision to abandon customs tariffs on imported goods led to a dramatic fall in state revenues, to the point where the government was even unable to feed and clothe the army. Corruption was rampant within the party and the government.

Not surprisingly local elections in the autumn of 1996 revealed a swing of support away from the DU and back to the MPRP. This was confirmed on 28 May 1997 when the result of the presidential election was announced. The MPRP candidate, the 'uninspiring Bagabandi' in Rossabi's view, defeated P. Ochirbat of the DU. In 1996 the Democratic Union coalition under Elbegdorj, won the parliamentary elections, ousting the MPRP from its majority in the Khural for the first time. Elbegdorj, one of the founding fathers of the Mongolian democracy movement and a hero of the 1990 demonstrations, became prime minister in 1998 and again in 2004 before being elected president in 2009. In spite of Elbegdorj's electoral successes the opposition lost the 2000 elections for the Khural disastrously when the MPP won seventy-two out of the seventy-six seats but fared better in 2004 as part of the Motherland Democratic Coalition, although the MPP still had a small majority of seats. The president from 2005 to 2009 was Enkhbayar of the MPRP.[16]

From 1997 to 2000 the DU coalition struggled to find its way. It was hampered by the certainty that democracy could not be achieved without an absolute commitment to an economy with minimal state involvement, but at the same time could not avoid the odour of corruption that hung over the processes of privatization and the receipt and distribution of foreign aid. In December 2000 following serious losses in the elections for the Great Khural, the MNDP merged with other groupings in December of that year and the Democratic Party (*Ardchilsan nam*) was born [17]

Death of Zorig

On 2 October 1998, Zorig, a leading actor in the democracy movement and a well-known member of the Khural since 1990, was murdered in his own flat in Ulaanbaatar. Many features of this violent death remain unclear but it is generally accepted that two unknown assailants had tied up his wife, when they discovered that Zorig was not at home, and then stabbed him to death when he walked in. Among the unexplained and bizarre features of the assassination was the theft of bottles of soy sauce and vinegar from the refrigerator.

Sanjaasürengiin Zorig had been a prime mover in the democracy movement since the demonstrations of January 1990 in Sükhbaatar Square and for some he was the real instigator of the movement. He differed from many of the other members of the DU in his attitude to the implementation of market reforms and criticized the pace of privatization and corruption in the government's management of the economy. The DU had come to power in 1996 and in 1998 Zorig was appointed minister of infrastructure. He oversaw the merger of the state-owned Reconstruction Bank with the commercial Golomt Bank which was controlled by supporters of the DU. MPRP members of the Khural walked out to show their disgust at what at best demonstrated a serious conflict of interest. Elbegdorj no longer had a majority and was obliged to resign. Zorig was the main candidate to replace him as prime minister.

The murder has never been solved but Zorig's supporters believe that he was assassinated to prevent him from unmasking corrupt members of the government. Zorig's death plunged the government and indeed the entire Mongolian political world into crisis and it was some weeks before an alternative premier could be appointed. A statue to Zorig, as a martyr for democracy and clean government, has been erected in a small square opposite the Central Post Office and a film has been made of his political career. His sister, Oyun, stepped into his shoes and replaced him in the Khural. In order to pursue Zorig's ideals she formed the Civil Will Party (*Irgnii Zorig Nam*). *Zorig*, the personal name of the martyred Khural member, also means 'will' in Mongolian.[18]

MPRP back in power after 2000 elections

The DU coalition, which was seen by many, especially foreign donors, as the great hope for Mongolia fell into disarray. Senior party members were implicated in major corruption scandals and, as the parliamentary elections of 2000 approached, the coalition collapsed and factional groups formed new parties. Not surprisingly in the July elections, the MPRP was returned to power after taking seventy-two of the seventy-six Khural seats. Nambaryn Enkhbayar was nominated as prime minister. The DU had lost power but the greater damage was to the confidence of the Mongolian electorate in the democratic process; surveys indicated that the public did not judge the Khural or its members fit to govern on their behalf.

In power, the MPRP government was little different from the DU. It was committed to improved wages and welfare payments but was unable to escape from the trap of privatization. In the rural areas the livestock industry was in decline and there was an inevitable migration in search of non-existent jobs in the cities where unemployment remained dangerously high at over 20 per cent. By 2004 the number of Mongolians with an income that kept them below the poverty line was estimated by the World Bank at 36 per cent of the total population, a figure that had been fairly constant for the past decade. In the revolution of 1990 Mongolia had escaped from its dependency on the Soviet Union; now it found itself largely reliant on international aid provided by organizations that all insisted on neo-liberal market reforms which were damaging its economy.

In the 2004 elections the MPRP only managed to retain thirty-six of the seventy-two seats it had previously held. The split opposition did not enjoy great public support and the outcome was an agreement between the MPRP and an opposition grouping with a new name, the Motherland Democratic Coalition, which took two months of horse-trading to put together. Elbegdorj returned as prime minister of what some have termed – following German usage – a grand coalition. This followed an agreement that the post would be filled by a member of the MPRP after two years.[19]

Election of 2008, riots and aftermath

The 2008 election resulted in a clear victory for the Mongolian People's Revolutionary Party (MPRP, *Mongol ardyn khuvsgalt nam*) which gained forty-seven out of the seventy-six seats in the Khural, leaving the Democratic Party with twenty-six seats. The result, however, was controversial because opposition supporters alleged that there had been electoral fraud, although international monitors disagreed and concluded that the elections had been free and fair. There were serious riots in which 5 people died and over 300 were injured in a night of demonstrations and looting. This was a rare occurrence for post-Soviet Mongolia, as previous elections had been free of violence, and a state of emergency was declared. The headquarters of the MPRP was attacked, a nearby art gallery was set on fire and many works of art were stolen or destroyed. By 3 July 2008 the streets were once again quiet but opposition Democratic Party leaders accused the MPRP of having used the riots to crush dissent.[20]

Return of the Mongolian People's Party

For many years the political situation had been extremely confused with various smaller groupings, shifting alliances and changes in personnel and leadership. By the end of the twentieth century, politics in Mongolia had settled into a contest between the two major parties. After prolonged internal debate, the former ruling party, the MPRP rejected its Moscow-orientated Marxist-Leninist heritage and espoused social democracy. To mark this ideological reorientation it changed its name to the Mongolian People's Party (MPP, *Mongol ardyn nam*) in 2010. In fact this was not a new name but a reversion to the original name of the party between 1920 and 1924. To complicate matters even further a new party was formed in 2010 by dissenting members of the former MPRP who continued to use that name for their breakaway organization.

In elections for the legislature in 2012, the renamed MPP received fewer votes than the Democratic Party which however still did not achieve an overall majority; the two parties formed another coalition under Prime Minister Dendeviin Altankhuyag, the leader of the Democratic Party, who had replaced Elbegdorj after his resignation following the controversial elections of 2008. Altankhuyag remained prime minister until 5 November 2014 when he was voted out of office by the Khural, accused of mismanagement, corruption and nepotism, while one of his key assistants was being investigated for embezzlement connected with a scheme to subsidize coal purchases by the poorer residents of Ulaanbaatar.[21] Altankhuyag was succeeded by Terbishdagva on a temporary basis and then on 21 November by Chimediin Saikhanbileg, who had led the Democratic caucus in the parliament from 2008 to 2012.[22]

The Democratic Party and its divisions

Since 1990 the main opposition to the MPRP and its allies has been the Democratic Party and its forerunners. This young political grouping came together under its current name in 2000 from the diverse parties that had emerged from the democratic revolution. These original groups continue to influence the Democratic Party, although they do not correspond precisely with current factions. Party loyalty and solidarity inhibit open discussion of factional differences, but it is accepted that there are six major groupings: Altangadas (Pole Star), Shonkhor (Falcon), MoAH (MDU), MUDN (Mongolian National Democratic Party), North East Asia and Neg Ardchilal (One Democracy). Altangadas, which is led by Altankhuyag is the most powerful and the 'falcon' symbol of Shonkhor alludes to its right-wing orientation. Like factions within other Asian political parties, such as the Liberal Democratic Party in Japan, their differences are more a matter of loyalty to individual political leaders than distinctive ideological or political platforms.[23]

Presidential elections 2017

A Mongolian General Election Commission had been established in 1992 to anticipate and manage concerns about the fairness and credibility of elections. The 2008 elections had resulted in unusually violent demonstrations but reactions to the running of subsequent elections were not as negative: after the introduction of an electronic – biometric – system which attracted some criticism, external monitors found growing confidence in the electoral process.

The tone of the election campaign of June 2017 was distinctly nationalist and populist. Miyeegombyn Enkhbold of the MPP campaigned under the slogan, 'United Mongolia will win'; Khaltmaagiin Battulga of the Democratic Party chose 'Mongolia will win' and Sainkhüügiin Ganbaatar of the MPRP preferred 'Let's choose Mongolia'. The candidates constantly alluded to the Mongolian nation and putting its interests first; referred to historical and events and legends; and appeared in publicity photographs wearing the traditional Mongolian *deel* or riding horses in the grasslands. They also underlined the necessity of preserving Mongolia's territorial integrity, although there were no existing border disputes or any other similar concerns at the time.

After the fall of the Soviet Union, Marxist-Leninist ideology had lost much of its authority and was generally replaced by nationalism in one form or another. In Mongolia this has primarily taken the form of anti-Chinese sentiment, including an obsession with identifying whether individuals were of 'pure blood' or of mixed Chinese-Mongolian ethnicity, and to a lesser extent Russian-Mongolian ancestry although that is not seen as such a negative factor. In the campaign run by the Democratic Party there were frequent references to the background of the MPP candidate, Enkhbold, who they claimed was of partly Chinese origin.

Agence France-Presse reported that:

The waving flags, triumphant songs and rousing speeches of a Mongolian presidential campaign rally were interrupted by a fight that broke out in the crown. A group of men [supporting Enkhbold] had entered the event for Democratic Party candidate Khaltmaa[giin] Battulga on Friday carrying posters denouncing the businessman, prompting his supporters to shove the interlopers and tear up their placards, all the while chanting: 'You're mixed Chinese! You're mixed Chinese!'[24]

Both Enkhbold and the MPRP candidate Ganbaatar had made public their family trees in an attempt to prove their uncontaminated Mongolian lineage. Scurrilous propaganda included videos that circulated on local social media, purporting to show scuffles involving the police and Chinese residents. The voice-over accused the MPP of losing its values and 'running a half-Chinese person' in the election. Anti-Chinese prejudices were shared by protesters, some of whom came from Russian-Mongolian mixed marriages.[25]

Battulga woos Putin

With the election of Khaltmaagiin Battulga on 8 July 2017, the Democratic Party regained control of the presidency that it had held during the Elbegdorj years, although the Khural was still dominated by its opponents, the MPP. Battulga is a colourful character, a wealthy businessman and property tycoon who as a young man achieved great success in traditional Mongolian wrestling. This is a distinctive sport, but not unique as it has some similarity to the Japanese sports of judo and sumo and even to Cumberland wrestling in the United Kingdom. Battulga was a member of the national wrestling team from 1979 to 1990, won the world championship in 1989 and also headed the Mongolian Judo Federation.

Battulga is a staunch Mongolian patriot who was responsible for the construction of a giant statue of Chinggis Khan on the banks of the Tuul River to the east of Ulaanbaatar. It was at this spot, according to legend, that Chinggis found a golden whip that inspired his drive to leadership and conquest. Battulga's success was due in no small part to his antipathy to China; he was fully in tune with the prevailing public mood at this time. Loans to Mongolia and investment in the mining industry increased China's influence and its visible presence in Mongolia. Many Mongolians were affronted by Beijing's threats of retaliation after the visit of the Dalai Lama in 2016, which is considered below. The Dalai Lama duly congratulated Battulga on his victory.[26]

Battulga's policy was to seek increased trade and investment from sources other than China and this approach drew him closer to Putin's Russia. Russia was Mongolia's ally and closest trading partner during the eight decades of the Soviet Union and Battulga had previously transacted business there. In August 2017 Battulga visited Hungary to attend the World Judo Championships. Here he had his first opportunity to meet the Russian President, Vladimir Putin, also a judo aficionado who holds a black belt and is ranked 8th *dan* for his service to the sport. Part of their conversation was published on the Kremlin website:

> President of Russia Vladimir Putin: Mr President, I am very glad to have the opportunity to meet you. We know you both as a politician

and a good athlete. I would like to congratulate you on the excellent performance of Mongolian judokas at the world championships here.

As for bilateral relations, we will have an opportunity to speak about them in more detail in Vladivostok, where I know you are planning to attend the forum as well. But it is already clear that the trend in trade is good. While last year it fell by 20 percent, in the first half year of 2017 it grew by over 34 percent.

Work is being done on the political track, as well as in the economic and cultural areas. Our traditional Russian-Mongolian ventures are working hard and shipments are up. So, we will have plenty to discuss in depth in Vladivostok.

President of Mongolia [Khaltmaagiin Battulga]:

Good evening to you once again. I am very pleased to meet with you at such a remarkable event as the World Judo Championships. It is great that we are meeting at this event because it is something we are both interested in and fond of. I believe it will serve us well in the future. Naturally, we are planning to have a working meeting in Vladivostok in the near future.

The presidential election in Mongolia was less than two months ago. Considering modern realities, I am planning to further expand relations with our northern neighbour.

You have just said that trade has grown. This trade owes something to cross-border regions and I think it is important to pay attention to the relations between border regions because we have a common border of over 4,000 km.

Naturally, we are primarily interested in investment. Our priority is railways. We have a joint venture, Ulan Bator Railways, with fifty-fifty participation.[27]

The China factor

The ancient mistrust of China, Mongolia's powerful neighbour to the south, was resurfacing and pushing Battulga's Mongolia back towards Russia, its rather less powerful neighbour to the north and west, the neighbour that it had rejected in 1990 when it was still the Soviet Union. Mongolia cannot ignore the fact that China has emerged as the major economic power in East Asia, and indeed Eurasia. Although Battulga was emphasizing ties with Russia, his government was still encouraging direct investment from the People's Republic of China (PRC) while engaging in a balancing act between the two powers to protect its political and economic independence. In addition to his business experience with both Russia and China, Battulga was involved in bilateral commercial agreements with the two states.

The rabid anti-Chinese prejudice that appeared in some campaign material is not necessarily shared by the whole of the population although there is a consensus that Mongolia must not become too dependent on its giant neighbour. The Chinese head of state, Xi Jinping, made a state visit to Mongolia in 2014 and President Elbegdorj's return visit to China took place in November 2015. Their discussions centred on Mongolia's declaration that it intended to be a 'permanent neutral state' while simultaneously maintaining a 'comprehensive strategic cooperative partnership with both China and Russia. Official policy was that this was the best way of stabilizing 'Mongolia's peripheral situation' but it illustrates the complex diplomatic manoeuvres necessary for a small country between two giants. This was to be supplemented by reviving the old concept of a 'third neighbour' policy, reaching out to other countries for additional political and economic ties.

Relations with China were also strengthened by the agreement in June 2016 in Tashkent on a China-Mongolia-Russia economic corridor which would operate within the parameters of China's ambitious 'One Belt One Road' project and Russia's Eurasian Economic Union. Mongolia offered to contribute five 'channels' to this corridor: railways, highways, a power grid, an oil pipeline and a gas pipeline. On 1 and 2 October 2016, a Chinese delegation, led by Liu Yunshan, a member of the CCP Politburo Standing Committee made an official visit to Mongolia. They met President Elbegdorj and approved measures to implement bilateral agreements agreed previously by their officials.

A more discordant relationship became apparent later that year when the Dalai Lama began a four-day visit to Mongolia. As the Dalai Lama is revered by Mongolian Buddhists who follow the rituals and traditions of Tibetan Buddhism, he was enthusiastically welcomed by representatives of Mongolian monasteries and India's ambassador to Mongolia. The Dalai Lama spoke at the Gandan monastery in Ulaanbaatar, the country's largest monastery, before travelling to other religious foundations. Both the Dalai Lama and the leaders of Mongolian Buddhism emphasized that the visit was purely spiritual but there was severe criticism from Beijing where the Dalai Lama is regarded as a divisive political figure because of his association with the Tibetan independence movement. Following protests by Beijing and the cancellation of bilateral meetings on loans and development projects, the Mongolian foreign minister, Tsendiin Mönkh-Orgil, announced that the government would not extend any further invitations to the Dalai Lama, although it was not the government that had invited him, and indicated that the Buddhist leader would probably not be 'visiting Mongolia again during this administration'. He acknowledged that such 'misunderstandings' risked damaging links between the two countries. After the ritual protests and apologies, economic realities triumphed over China's political rhetoric, which has become routine whenever the Dalai Lama travels abroad. Sino-Mongolian relations suffered no lasting damage. In February 2017 Beijing agreed on financial aid and loans to Mongolia, said to be on preferential terms, but a bailout from the International Monetary Fund to the value of US$ 5.5 billion was agreed and this would offset the influence of China to some extent.[28]

7

Collapse and recovery of the Mongolian economy

The immediately observable consequence of Mongolia's democratic revolution of 1990–1 was the disappearance of the one-party state and its replacement by a multi-party political system that was far from perfect, but has in general managed to function. The overwhelming majority of Mongolians were not directly involved in the political developments, but none could remain unaffected: while many positively welcomed the change, most were more concerned about the parlous state of the economy and the effect this had on their everyday lives.

After the demise of Soviet power in 1991, the flow of aid and trade from Moscow and its Eastern European allies that had sustained the Mongolian economy for decades suddenly ceased. In the absence of sufficient quantities of convertible currency, barter trade became more common for both internal and foreign trade. Poverty, already a serious problem in Mongolia, became desperate, especially in the rural areas and the smaller towns. Mongolia's response to this crisis was to introduce a comprehensive programme of privatization and reform, measures similar to those adopted in the new, genuinely independent states of Poland and Rumania and what was then still Czechoslovakia. This enterprise was potentially perilous as Mongolia lacked even the most basic financial and marketing infrastructure outside the state system, but it had the enthusiastic support of the World Bank and other international financial organizations. Enthusiasm for the economic policies advocated by the international bodies was not universal: sceptical voices were raised to counsel against unrealistic expectations for such a rapid programme of privatization. The varied, and often incompatible, expectations of leading Mongolians, and their policies for development and economic growth, are reflected in the plethora of political parties that emerged after 1990.[1]

The social consequences of the collapse were complicated but, for many Mongolians, they were disastrous in the short term. Before 1990, urbanization in Mongolia had made significant but unspectacular progress as part of the planned economy: at the time of the creation of the MPR in 1924, very few Mongols lived in towns but by 1990 between 55 and 60 per cent of the population were urban dwellers. This figure was largely due to the expansion of the capital, Ulaanbaatar. The scale of urbanization, which paralleled developments in the Soviet Union, was regarded as a marker of economic and social progress and modernization.

The immediate impact of the adoption of a market economy was a reversal of this process. In the mid-1990s, Rolf Gilberg and Jan-Olof Svantesson observed that, 'Since the demise of the command economy, however, there has been a marked abandonment of the towns as people move back fulltime into the pastoral economy'[2]. It was fortunate that many urban Mongols had continued to maintain links with their extended families living in the countryside; some had continued to own livestock while working in the towns and cities. This made the return to a herding economy on the steppes less of a catastrophe than it might otherwise have been; for many it confirmed the correctness of traditional Mongol attitudes that attached a high value to the ownership of livestock.

Not all unemployed urban dwellers could be accommodated in herding enterprises, especially those in the larger cities who had worked for the government or other state-owned enterprises and suddenly found themselves redundant. Many found alternative work as drivers, traders or in other posts that were mostly less well paid and had lower status than their previous employment. The *ger* settlements on the peripheries of Ulaanbaatar and other cities are sometimes compared with shanty towns in other developing countries but as conglomerations of family *gers* constructed in the traditional style they are more orderly, although lacking in modern facilities. The *ger* communities expanded to accommodate those who could not afford the soaring rents of the inner cities as well as those who had migrated from the grasslands in search of work. Mining and logging became increasingly important as alternative sources of incomes, notwithstanding their potential for causing severe environmental degradation in what was already a fragile ecosystem.

The fate of the herding economy

Collectivization of the herds had begun in 1930. The earliest attempt to reorganize the herding economy ended in failure after what Morris Rossabi describes as 'a poorly planned and brutal effort at collectivisation'. By the end of the 1950s, when compulsion had been replaced by 'economic incentives, persuasion, education and propaganda', the process was virtually complete. Between 1960 and 1990 most livestock-rearing households belonged to one of 255 *negdel*, cooperative production associations that accounted for some 75 per cent of Mongolia's livestock. By the 1990s the livestock herding economy could be characterized as semi-nomadic, rather than fully nomadic as had previously been the norm, but herding was still the typical way of life for approximately one-third of the total population of Mongolia, some 150,000 households.[3]

The *negdel* were eventually merged with the *sum*, the basic organs of local government in the rural areas, and the combination was known as the *sum-negdel*. Like the Soviet models on which it was based, it was more than a political and economic unit as it provided education, healthcare and pensions to its members. It was also responsible for the services required to support the raising and care of animals such as veterinary medicine, animal shelters, fodder and marketing services. The *negdel* was not wholly owned by the collective and by the 1980s, after the implementation of more liberal economic policies, as many as one third of the animals raised in the *negdel* were privately owned by its members.[4]

The process of privatization of the *negdel*, or that part of it that was not already privately owned, began in 1987 before there was any suggestion that the Soviet system or its Mongolian counterpart were under serious threat. The initial arrangements included an agreement between the *negdel* administration and individual herding families on production quotas and the level of wages that should be paid to the herders. In 1989 these agreements were replaced by a leasing system, under which herders became responsible for generating their own income. By the time of the democratic revolution in 1990, the process of privatizing the *negdel* was already underway. In 1990 the administration of the *negdel* was formally separated from that of the *sum*, the local government. Full privatization continued through 1991 and 1992 and left the herders entirely subject to market forces. On the one hand, they were no longer subject to the state regulations that had limited the number of livestock that individual herding families could own. On the other, they had to survive without the security of guaranteed quotas, the quantity of animal products that the state had previously agreed to purchase from them. In spite of the gradual nature of the privatization process it was not entirely smooth and there were many conflicts over the allocation of collective assets to individuals and companies after the dissolution of the *negdel*.

Under pressure from a severe economic recession, herding families found themselves obliged to abandon some of the modern systematic and streamlined practices of the *negdel*, which encouraged specialization, mechanization and the application of scientific techniques. In order to make a living they reverted to the long-established system of mixed herds that were composed of the five domestic animals traditionally raised by Mongols: sheep, goats, cattle, horses and camels. Such systems were superficially less efficient and required more labour but ironically this helped to absorb some of the surplus labour from the cities where the breakdown of the planned economy had left many without employment. Herding families needing extra labour were only too willing to accommodate relatives who had previously migrated to the cities in search of work.[5]

Besides managing the marketing and distribution of goods produced by the herders, the *negdel* had regulated the use of pastures to minimize damage to the environment. After its demise, it was necessary to create new institutions or fall back on older systems to deal with these issues. Some of the newly created bodies were private companies; others were cooperatives and could either be based on an existing *negdel* or be incorporated into one. Public services that had previously been provided by the *negdel*, including the communications infrastructure, healthcare for people and animals, and cultural activities, were drastically reduced and in some cases ceased to exist. The State Fodder Fund, which had kept animals fed in an emergency, collapsed, leaving herding families to their own devices in the event of natural disasters which are far from infrequent in the Mongolian environment. Although the return to a near subsistence style of raising livestock enabled much of the rural population to survive reasonably well, the effect of market forces was uneven and led to a greater degree of poverty and inequality than rural Mongolia had experienced for many decades. The pastoral economy had become subject to the vagaries of market relations and in general herders were not prepared for its implications. Nevertheless, in the transition to a market economy they proved more resilient in the face of the dramatic changes than some of their urban counterparts.[6]

Market experiment and economic crisis

After the disappearance of Soviet trade and aid, the reformers, in power for the first time and in many cases inexperienced in both government and economic affairs, were obliged to search for new partners. The only available alternatives were a closer relationship with China – which many found unacceptable because of prejudice, for historical reasons, or out of genuine apprehension at the power of the rising Chinese economy – or investment from international bodies, mainly from the West. Under the influence of international agencies, including the United Nations Development Programme, the International Monetary Fund, the Asian Development Bank and the World Bank, the new leadership set about liberalizing and privatizing the economy. Mongolia became a laboratory for enthusiastic Western market economists, but inevitably it was the Mongolian people who took the greatest risks. They had, however, very little control over the policies.

Mongolia was lobbied ruthlessly by proselytizing experts in privatization. International donor organizations offered aid and investment in exchange for a commitment to their common ideology of economic liberalization and the abandonment of a planned state sector. One of the most enthusiastic Mongolian proponents of Milton Friedman's style of market economics, in spite of his own limited experience, was D. Ganbold, the first deputy prime minister (who had attended the 'Sinologists' conference in October 1990). Faced with a discredited Soviet system, few realistic alternatives and the superficial attractions of investment on a massive scale, it was not surprising that in Mongolia, as in other states of the post-Soviet world, there were many other disciples of privatization and the neo-liberal ideology. In taking this route, however, Mongolia was out of step with the most successful Asian economies of the post-war period – the Asian Tigers, Japan, South Korea, Hong Kong and Singapore, which have been praised almost universally for their enterprise and economic success – all rely heavily on state investment and intervention.

Other members of the Mongolian democratic opposition were less enthusiastic than Ganbold and argued with some force against the application of one international model to all economies, irrespective of how relevant it might be. Of particular concern was the failure of overseas economists to take into account the specific conditions of the Mongolian economy, especially the predominance of a pastoral economy. Few of the visiting experts had any experience of such an economy which, although apparently individualistic, traditionally relied on a significant degree of cooperation to overcome some of the problems of a harsh geographical environment and had accepted a degree of collectivization during Mongolia's alliance with the Soviet Union.

Largely because of the insistence of international aid agencies, the policies of economic liberalization were adopted in a manner that was described, even by its adherents, as shock therapy. The immediate impact was disastrous. Prices rose dramatically; wages were held at a low level; capital flow from the Central Bank was restricted; and social welfare programmes were severely curtailed. Trade collapsed and the empty shelves in Ulaanbaatar's shops in the autumn of 1990 spoke for themselves. Rationing was introduced and ordinary Mongolian families, whose standard of living was already low, suddenly found themselves dangerously impoverished.[7]

Economy of Democratic Mongolia

In Mongolian political circles, the 1990s were dominated by ideological struggles over the direction of the economy. On the one hand were those who wished to move rapidly to a free-market economy, irrespective of the short-term problems that this would create for the population. Prominent among these, as has been noted, was Ganbold, in spite of his lack of expertise and experience in Western economics, and a range of powerful international sponsors. On the other hand there were those in both the Mongolian People's Revolutionary Party (MPRP) and the Democratic Party who either wished for a slower transformation or who resisted the process altogether. The results have been patchy. There has been a marked increase in the country's GDP and social provisions have improved: the visible and desperate poverty of the 1990s has to a large extent been alleviated but many Mongolians still live on a very restricted income.

In 2013, the Mongolian Embassy in the United States announced that, 'Since 1990, Mongolia has successfully transitioned into a market-oriented economy from [a] centrally-planned economy. Today, Mongolia is one of the world's fastest growing economies'. Impressive high growth rates were possible because of the unusually low starting point. Mongolia's GDP increase of 6.4 per cent in 2010 was followed by a figure of 17.5 per cent for 2011. This was largely the result of international investment in the mining industry and high prices for copper, gold and iron on the world market, but infrastructure development, particularly in transport, to cater for the demands of other sectors also played an important part. A slower growth rate of 12.3 per cent in 2012 reflected lower international prices, but was supported by the recovery of agriculture, forestry and fishing from adverse winter conditions in 2009 and 2010 which had resulted in great loss of livestock, and 'steady growth in construction, transportation and ICT [information and communications technology] industries'.[8]

Mongolia's industrial sector, for decades a relatively insignificant component but now growing rapidly, consists of mining and quarrying; manufacturing; construction; and energy, which includes electricity, gas, steam and air conditioning. Of these, mining is by far the most significant and of greatest interest to foreign investors. In 2013, the government in Ulaanbaatar sold bonds to the value of US$ 1.8 billion on international markets, largely on the basis of the performance of the mining sector; in the future the commercial exploitation of mining is expected to have the greatest impact on the economy of any sector. Known mineral reserves include major deposits of gold, copper, uranium and coal, but the government estimates that only 15 per cent of the country's mineral reserves have been fully mapped.

The two best-known mining projects are Oyu Tolgoi and Tavan Tolgoi (*tolgoi* being a hill or mound). Oyu Tolgoi is located in the South Gobi region, some 550 kilometres due south of Ulaanbaatar and only 80 kilometres from the border with China's Inner Mongolia. Projected annual figures for

2018, when the mine was due to reach its maximum production capacity, were 0.6 million tons of copper, 20.3 tons of gold and 93.8 tons of silver. Tavan Tolgoi is approximately 100 kilometres to the north-west of Oyu Tolgoi: Mongolian sources claim that it has one of the largest deposits of coal in the world with 7.4 billion tons of coking and thermal coal available for extraction. The majority shareholder in the Tavan Tolgoi project is Erdenes MGL, a company owned by the Mongolian government.

Even after making allowances for overoptimistic projections of potential yields, there is no doubt that the mining sector will play a key role in the development of the Mongolian economy. Since the year 2000, the mining sector's contribution to the national GDP has increased from 14 to 25 per cent. Copper, gold and coal are the country's principal exports and Mongolia is one of the most important exporters of coal to China. This has naturally raised concerns about the overdependence of the Mongolian commodity on these exports and the potential risks from unpredictable fluctuations in world market prices.[9]

What had been concerns became realities in 2016. Ulaanbaatar had borrowed on the world financial markets to fund much needed infrastructural development but, with the decline of the world price of minerals and the reduction of demand, notably from China, Mongolia was suddenly faced with a debt crisis and risked defaulting on its financial obligations. Finance Minister Choijilsuren Battogtokh acknowledged that the country was 'in a deep state of economic crisis' and that the government might 'not be able to finance salaries and operational costs of government departments'. As a result of Mongolia's reliance on mineral exports in an unstable international market, its economic growth slowed dramatically to 1 per cent in 2016: the following year an analysis from the World Bank, a major source of investment in Mongolia, argued that 'in the near term, the Mongolian economy continues to wrestle with persistent economic imbalances'. Although there was a recovery in the early part of 2017, again because of growth in the mining sector, the absence of diversification was identified as the main underlying problem facing the economy. The slow pace of poverty alleviation remains a major concern.[10]

Funding Mongolian development

Growth in the Mongolian economy in the early twenty-first century had begun to stall even before the global financial crisis of 2008, and the government in Ulaanbaatar found itself obliged to apply for an International Monetary Fund (IMF) loan in 2009. Since then foreign investment has been viewed as the salvation for Mongolia's economic difficulties, particularly in mining but also in agricultural production and infrastructural development. The forestry sector has always been important, but illegal logging and deforestation have plunged the industry into a crisis. The World Bank has expressed concerns about the way Mongolia has been balancing the competing demands of development and environmental protection, and particular attention has been drawn to the social and environmental impacts of developing the mining industry; air pollution in Ulaanbaatar, which affects residents of the *ger* suburbs disproportionately; and the water network.

In spite of Mongolia's historic wariness about the intentions of China, its great neighbour to the south, trade with the People's Republic of China (PRC) is essential to the country's development and 85 per cent of Mongolia's exports went to China in 2013, principally copper, clothing, livestock, cashmere, wool, skins, fluorspar, metals and coal.

The IMF provided a loan of US$ 242 million to Mongolia in 2009 and the success of this financial transfusion was celebrated the following year at a reception in Ulaanbaatar. Mongolia's economy grew in the following three years, the rate reaching double digits but growth slowed down in the wake of the international financial crisis; in October 2016 the government applied again to the IMF for assistance. The terms on which the IMF was prepared to offer a loan were not clear at the time of writing. There was a change of government following the parliamentary elections of June 2016 when the Mongolian People's Party (MPP, the successor to the communist-era MPRP) under Jargaltulgyn Erdenebat achieved an overwhelming victory over the Democratic Party, winning sixty-five out of the total of seventy-six seats: this made it politically more likely that the incoming government would feel able to accept stringent conditions while blaming the former government, now the opposition, for the economic difficulties that the country faced. Whatever conditions external funders impose, Mongolia is likely to favour financial support from the IMF if the only realistic alternative is China. Since Ulaanbaatar already relies on the PRC to take the majority of its exports it will be reluctant to be in any greater financial or political debt to Beijing.

The economic analyst M. Chimeddorj, assessing the difficulties faced by the Mongolian economy in October 2016, accepted that a 'slight recession' was likely. The nation's economy is heavily oriented towards primary sectors with mining exports forming such a large percentage of the state budget and is highly sensitive to changes in the costs of raw materials which were declining on world markets. He urged strict financial discipline with budget cuts and investment only in essential infrastructure projects – an implicit criticism of the previous Democratic Party government's financial management – while acknowledging the need to maintain current levels of social welfare spending. He encouraged the government to embark on a process of restructuring its international loans and to participate in IMF Standby Arrangements. He was also reluctant to advise reliance on loans from China as this was likely to involve either Chinese or joint-enterprise companies, and there were concerns that they would import foreign labour to work on any projects that they financed, with insufficient benefit to the Mongolian economy or Mongolians looking for work. For similar reasons he supported the existing policy of refusing permission for foreign banks (particularly the Bank of China) to establish branches in Mongolia, arguing that the local banking system was not sufficiently robust to compete with them on an equal basis.[11]

Mongolia may be wary of dependency on China, but it is still willing to cooperate with Beijing on projects deemed beneficial to the national economy. On 13 October 2016 President Elbegdorj played host to Liu Yunshan, a senior member of the Standing Committee of the CCP Politburo, who at that time was formally ranked fifth in the Chinese leadership and who was in Ulaanbaatar to give final approval to major projects in cooperation and regional development strategy that had already been worked through in detail by officials.[12]

Ulaanbaatar: Contemporary economy and society of the capital

Ulaanbaatar in the early twenty-first century is far more prosperous than it was in 1990, the final year before the democratic revolution. That prosperity, however, is unevenly distributed. The centre of the city, around Sükhbaatar Square appears well developed and well planned, incorporating most of the buildings that were constructed in the 'Soviet satellite' era with modern high-rise architecture and dominated by the ultra-modern Blue Sky Tower and Hotel (as will be elaborated on in Chapter 10). It was completed in 2009 and stands just to the south of Ulaanbaatar Square next to the former Lenin Club which had been built in 1929 as part of a programme to train cadres who would transmit modern 'socialist and international culture' – of the Russian variety – to Mongolia.[13] The Blue Sky Tower, which was the tallest building in the city until the record was taken by newer hotels, is a useful landmark which can be seen from many of the outlying districts. In addition to the hotel it provides office and residential accommodation for the wealthiest clients and is marketed as the epitome of exclusive luxury living. Its construction has been tied to the evolution of Mongolia's new political system. The building work started in 2006 but was temporarily brought to a standstill after political wrangling when the Democratic Party lost the disputed 2008 general election.

Further from the centre in the southeast of the city near the Narantuul market or in the northwest close to the extensively expanded and refurbished Gandan monastery there are areas still hardly touched by development and where 1960s apartment buildings and shops and poor low-rise houses or *ger* compounds remain.

Much of the city's population now dresses in a style that would be modern or fashionable in most other cities of Asia and the rest of the world; the *deel* is in general no longer everyday wear on the streets, although some elderly individuals still prefer it, and is reserved for formal occasions. The pickpockets and child beggars who were a feature of the economic collapse of 1990s Mongolia still make their presence felt, although there are far fewer today. Many cafes, bars and shops are equipped with elaborate CCTV systems to combat theft and violence but with limited success.[14]

Gers today

The characteristic Mongol dwelling is the *ger*. *Gers* evolved to suit the lifestyle of the Mongols, which has for centuries been based on nomadic pastoralism and transhumance from winter to summer pastures and back, and are portable and relatively easy to set up, take down and transport. Similar structures can also be found among Kazakh, Kyrgyz, and Turkmen people and other speakers of Turkic languages who also practice nomadic pastoralism. These are of slightly different designs, and are known to these peoples as yurts, a name which is more familiar than *ger* in the West.

The *ger*, a form of housing designed for the nomad lifestyle, would appear to have no place in a modernizing and increasingly urban society but they are still a major feature of life in Mongolia, even in large cities such as the capital Ulaanbaatar. The *ger* has become a national symbol for the Mongols, who are reluctant to see its demise, and its basic structure has been incorporated into larger and more permanent architectural designs. Modern buildings often have a *ger* attached or nearby. There was a *ger* on the roof of one wing of the State Guest House during the Mongolian People's Republic (MPR). In a large room inside the Winter Palace of the Bogd Khan, which was built in what was the most modern up-to-date Russian-style in 1908 as part of a complex of traditional Buddhist temples, there is a *ger* lined with the skins of 150 leopards that could be used in winter or be erected outside the palace in fine weather.

The capital, Ulaanbaatar, has been constantly developed with old Soviet era blocks of flats now complemented or replaced by more modern high-rise buildings. The *ger* districts have existed on the periphery of the city for decades and are still in place. Illustrations in a book on the architecture of Mongolia published in 1988 show clearly the northwestern outskirts of the city against a backdrop of mountains. Newer buildings have sprouted up nearer the city centre but the remainder of the view is filled with *gers*. Some of these have since been demolished to make way for new construction projects but the *ger* districts with rows of *ger* and shacks, many of them separated by wooden or corrugated tin fencing, still remain.

There is a misconception that these *ger* estates are recent developments and are related to the economic changes that resulted from the demise of one-party rule and close ties to the Soviet Union. This is not the case. Although urbanization is a relatively recent phenomenon in a society that was slow to adopt sedentary ways, by 1960 industrial development and construction was already attracting people from the rural areas to Ulaanbaatar in search of work and business opportunities. Owen Lattimore, arriving in the capital in the summer of 1961 observed the industrial growth which appeared to be an 'unplanned consequence of the nearby Nalaikha coal mines' but still felt able to describe it as 'a uniquely beautiful city', a description that would be more difficult to justify today. The contrast between traditional and modern housing was already apparent:

> Because the population has grown too fast for the builders to keep up, there are still many wooden-fenced rectangles in which people live in the old white Mongol tents, which make a striking contrast with the modern buildings ... The sharpest contrast between old and new is in the fact that while many people are still living in tents, heat and hot water are piped underground to the modern buildings from a central heat, power, and lighting plant.[15]

This inequality survived a further thirty years of Soviet-style planned economy and has persisted for another twenty-five years since Mongolia's democratic revolution. In addition to the demand for basic facilities such as water and power, the rapid growth of the number of *ger* residents has placed a strain on social provision, including healthcare facilities and local schools. Roads are poor and there is limited public transport. Inadequate organization by local government and inconsistencies in a system for allocating addresses to the *gers* has exacerbated communications problems and residents were found not to have received important messages from the local government. Studies of these communities have highlighted concerns that the *ger* dwellers are unable to participate fully in social activities and are in danger of being socially excluded on a permanent basis. Infrastructure plans that will include the construction of new private housing complexes for current *ger* residents are under development at the time of writing.

Ger districts are found in all of the nine administrative districts of Ulaanbaatar but their development has been particularly marked in Chingeltei in the north, Songinokhairkhan in the west of the city, Bayanzürkh in the south-east and even the central Sükhbaatar district which is also home to most major government and cultural institutions. These urban districts extend into the mountains that surround the capital (four of them considered holy according to Mongol tradition) and it is in the hollow valleys and foothills in the extremities of these districts that most of the *gers* have been established.

There are wide differences of opinion about the persistence of the *ger* districts. Some Mongols, and many from overseas, defend them as a link with the nomadic past but they stand accused of romanticizing poor accommodation with few facilities that in the worst cases could be described as slum housing. Others deplore the lack of planning that has allowed these shanty towns to grow on the outskirts of the capital and the fact that the inhabitants of the *ger* districts are effectively marginalized. It must be said that, although there are relatively few facilities, the appearance of the *ger* districts is far more orderly and the *gers* belonging to individual families are far better spaced than is the case in many third world shanty towns. Many of the inhabitants of the *gers* are former herders forced out of their old lifestyle by the decline of the pastoral economy. Others are employed in government and other jobs in Ulaanbaatar and maintain that they have chosen this traditional lifestyle and are reluctant to move into high-rise flats. This may be making a virtue out of necessity: the demand for accommodation in Ulaanbaatar is very high, the supply of affordable housing is limited and city centre development is focused on accommodating the growing affluent middle class.

Whatever the practical and economic reasons for the persistence of the *ger* communities, the fact that there is still popular support for them is an indication of the psychological grip that traditional ways of life have on a population experiencing the trials and tribulations of modernization.[16]

8

Mongolia and the new East Asian order

Mongolians are only too conscious of the constraints imposed on them by their country's geographical position, but to what extent does this geography have to dictate the country's future? Mongolia is sandwiched between Russia and China and in the past its foreign policy has focused almost entirely on the balance of its relations between the two states: one until recently a great power, the other fast becoming one of the two major world powers. The main global challenge for any government in Ulaanbaatar is how to connect landlocked Mongolia with the wider world and which countries should be given priority for economic and political reasons. There are regional considerations as well as international ones: Mongolia is located in north-east Asia and many of its current leaders have a vision of making a positive and significant contribution to economic and political relations throughout that region. Russia and China will always be important players but Ulaanbaatar is also looking to Japan, South Korea and even North Korea to counterbalance its relations with the major powers. Many politicians in Mongolia envisage that the country will play an increasingly important role as an honest broker in regional conflicts, not least the one that is among the most dangerous disputes in the world, the conflict on the Korean peninsula.

There is however no unanimity within the Ulaanbaatar political elite. Convinced free-market advocates, such as Ganbold and the prime ministers Enkhsaikhan and Enkhbayar, have looked primarily if not exclusively towards the United States, and the West in general, for political alliances and economic support. Broadly speaking those reformers who are not wedded dogmatically to the free market, or to neo-liberal economic policies, are attempting to achieve a balance in the country's international relations, including links with the developing countries of the Third World. They acknowledge the importance of maintaining Mongolia's traditional relations with Russia and China but insist that these require considerable adjustment to adapt to modern conditions.

Elbegdorj and the Ulaanbaatar dialogue

The presidential elections of 2009 and 2013 were both won by the veteran democracy activist and parliamentarian Elbegdorj of the Democratic Party. Elbegdorj had previously served twice as prime minister and, from the demonstrations of 1989 to the present day, he has arguably been the single most influential political figure in Mongolia, particularly on the international stage.

The Mongolian government's perspective on regional relations, and the part that it proposed to play in managing them, was set out in the Ulaanbaatar Dialogue, an initiative introduced by President Elbegdorj in 2013. Acknowledging that the political situation in northeast Asia was complex, Elbegdorj homed in on the relationship between the two Koreas as Ulaanbaatar's main concern. Although there is no border between Mongolia and the Koreas, and they are separated by the Chinese northeastern provinces formerly known as Manchuria, their governments have been involved in joint economic projects. Mongolia has long been interested in the Greater Tumen Initiative to develop the region around the Tumen River at the border between Russia and North Korea, which could provide an outlet for Mongolian exports. The Mongolians are also as concerned as their other regional near neighbours – China, Russia and Japan – about the impact of nuclear proliferation and potential conflict between North and South Korea.

The Ulaanbaatar Dialogue was Elbegdorj's signature strategy and represents his international outlook. It claims to offer a distinctive Mongolian solution to such conflicts as the confrontation between North and South Korea. Elbegdorj recognized that, as a constituent part of Northeast Asia, Mongolia's best interests are served by a stable political environment. The original concept of a regional security dialogue emerged in the 1980s when Mongolia 'called for an all-Asian convention prohibiting the use of force to prevent conflicts'. This was revived in the new millennium and led to a conference, 'Security Perspective of Central and Northeast Asia: Ulaanbaatar as a new Helsinki' under the auspices of the Mongolian Institute of Strategic Studies in 2008. Elbegdorj took the idea further and, on 29 April 2013, at the Seventh Ministerial Conference of the Community of Democracies in Ulaanbaatar, announced the creation of his Ulaanbaatar Dialogue on Northeast Asia Security Initiative.[1]

Ulaanbaatar, it was argued, was an ideal location for such an initiative. As a declared neutral state, Mongolia had good relations with all the other states of Northeast Asia, had no extant territorial disputes, and had played an active part in international bodies including the United Nations, the

Asia-Europe Meeting and the Organisation for Security and Cooperation in Europe: meetings of the latter two bodies were planned for Ulaanbaatar in 2015 and 2016. While not seeking to compete with the ongoing Six Party Talks on the Korean dispute, Elbegdorj argued that the Ulaanbaatar Dialogue could work for 'active engagement and mutual trust' at times when those talks were in abeyance. In the long term the dialogue should result in the creation of permanent 'institutional mechanisms' for dialogue, 'confidence building measures', the 'reduction of military tension' and the 'promotion of regional cooperation'. International conferences on topics relating to regional security took place with the core participants and delegations from other countries. Participants and observers were said to have commented favourably on the potential for Mongolia's role as a regional honest broker.

A conference in Ulaanbaatar organized by the Ministry of Foreign Affairs and Institute for Strategic Studies on 17 June 2014 illustrated both the possibilities and the limitations of the Ulaanbaatar Dialogue. Although some participants, including those from China and Japan, felt obliged to use the occasion to air their grievances about historic disputes, the presence of a North Korean delegation reinforced claims that the Ulaanbaatar Dialogue could become a mechanism for confidence building. One member of that delegation, Lee Yong Pil, who was part of the North Korean diplomatic presence in Ulaanbaatar and had previously worked in the Institute for Peace and Disarmament in Pyongyang, expressed his support for the Ulaanbaatar process and the opportunity to have private conversations with delegates from the United States. In contrast, delegates from South Korea were pessimistic about the possibility of progress through the process.[2]

Relations with Russia

The collapse of Soviet power in 1991 had immediate and dramatic effects on Mongolia, in addition to the overall impact on the economy which has already been examined. As the Soviet military withdrew from Mongolia it abandoned its facilities; this procedure has since become controversial because of the environmental damage that has resulted. The financial relationship between Mongolia and the USSR has led to bitter and prolonged disagreement with the new government of Russia. Loans by the Soviet Union for construction projects have been assessed at between 10 and 20 billion dollars and the government of the Russian Federation considers this sum to be a debt owed to them as the successor regime. Mongolia has argued that this 'aid' distorted the Mongolian economy in the interests of the USSR. Trade with Russia has decreased as trade with China has increased but this is a measure of the relative speed of China's economic development compared with that of Russia.

Diplomatic relations have also focused on issues of border security and energy supplies. The mining complex at Erdenet was the symbol par excellence of Soviet-Mongolian cooperation. It was established in 1973 as a joint venture, which meant that it was partly owned by the USSR and run in partnership, but Soviet control had always been unpopular and many Mongolians were frustrated by the semi-colonial economic relationship that it seemed to symbolize. After the demise of the USSR the joint-venture contract was revised, giving Mongolia 51 per cent of the ownership to Russia's 49 per cent. In practice Russia was not in a position to exercise control and Mongolia benefited financially, but returning Erdenet to full Mongolian ownership became a high priority for Ulaanbaatar, not least because of the need to keep earning hard currency from the sale of its products.

Negotiations continued well into the twenty-first century. On 28 June 2016 the Prime Minister Chimdeiin Saikhanbileg announced that the transfer of ownership to Mongolia had finally been agreed. When Saikhanbileg lost both his post as prime minister and his parliamentary seat in elections the following day, doubt was cast on the validity of these claims. It appeared that Russia had finally agreed to surrender its ownership of the venture at a meeting of the Shanghai Cooperation Organisation (SCO) in Tashkent in June 2016. The negotiations that led to this agreement are far from clear but they migrated from state-state deliberations to discussions between Russian oligarchs and a new body called the Mongolian Copper Corporation which was backed by the private Trade and Development Bank. The financial scandal that ensued, when what had originally been state money began to flow into private hands, resulted in the nationalization of the Erdenet complex in February 2017 after a parliamentary vote.[3]

Relations with China

Modern Mongolia, between 1924 and 1990, was orientated entirely towards the Soviet Union and as far as possible China was kept at arm's length. This was perhaps inevitable because of the support revolutionary Mongols had received from Bolsheviks in Moscow and Irkutsk at the time of their own revolution and Mongolia's determination to avoid Chinese control from which it had broken free in 1911. A brief period of reoccupation after a Chinese invasion in 1919 had only served to reinforce resistance to Chinese influence. The conventional narrative of the whole Soviet period is that Mongolia clung to Russia to defend itself from its historic enemy China.

Although there is a core of truth in this, the relationship between Chinese and Mongolian communities is more complex than that would suggest. Historically, Chinese dynastic governments regarded frontier tribes such as the Mongols and their regimes as a threat to their own existence. There was considerable justification for this: in the past China has several times been ruled by regimes that originated in the frontier regions. The division between the two was, however, far from clear cut: on the frontiers there was a symbiotic relationship between the settled Chinese and the mainly nomadic Mongols, although that does not mean that is was free from conflict. Trade between the two communities was a constant feature of frontier life and at its core was the sale of horses by the Mongols and tea by the Chinese.[4]

The Mongolian People's Republic (MPR) did not have an independent policy towards China; its approach was subordinate to, and mirrored, Moscow's view of Beijing. In theory the three countries were fraternal socialist states, with close relations that were characterized by mutual support. In practice the great divide between Moscow and Beijing, which became obvious in the mid-1950s, eventually obliged the Communist states to take sides: in the end only Albania sided with China. As the Sino-Soviet dispute escalated to the point of military conflict on the borders in 1969, Mongolia's relationship with China became increasingly tense, primarily because the Soviet Union stationed troops in Mongolia as part of its defences against potential attack from China. Although this was regarded by many as unlikely, the Chinese invasion of Vietnam in 1979 made it clear that the use of force by Beijing on its northern frontiers could not be ruled out.[5]

There were attempts by the government in Ulaanbaatar to establish closer relations with Beijing in the 1980s, but in 1983 the expulsion of at least 1,700 Chinese residents from Mongolia, mainly contract workers, soured relations for several years. Mongolia claimed that it was repatriating ethnic Chinese who had not settled, or who would not comply with local laws, but other reports indicated that those expelled had been involved in agricultural or construction work and had refused to be transferred to state or collective farms in the north of the country.[6]

Since the demise of the Soviet Union, and the realization that Mongolia could no longer rely on Moscow for economic aid, relations with China gradually became closer to the normal relations between contiguous states. As Chinese economic growth soared and capital became available for investment abroad, Mongolia was an obvious place to invest. In view of the history of bilateral relations, it is not surprising that Mongolia's response to Chinese financial overtures was ambivalent. Investment in key projects was welcomed but a watchful eye was kept on any attempt to use this investment for political advantage. Trade between Mongolia and China has increased significantly since 1990; when a new Stock Exchange opened in Ulaanbaatar in 1995 there were fears that it would be swamped by investment from China.

Behind this concern lies the Mongolian conviction that, in spite of the recognition of Mongolian independence by the Chinese Communist Party (CCP) and Mao Zedong during the negotiations for the Sino-Soviet Treaty of Mutual Friendship and Assistance in 1950, Beijing still has designs on Mongolian territory. In a review of Franck Billé's book, *Sinophobia: Anxiety, Violence, and the Making of Mongolian Identity*, Gabriel Bamana put the feeling more strongly:

> Rumours of an imminent Chinese takeover of Mongolia are part of everyday life discourse among Mongolians, particularly among inhabitants of the country's capital, Ulaanbaatar. Indeed Mongolians suspect their southern neighbours of plotting to decimate their population and thus eradicate their country by eventually annexing it to China.[7]

While this is an extreme position, the fear of a residual atavistic Chinese dream of recovering Mongolia is not entirely without foundation, although for decades the government of the PRC has not demonstrated any inclination to implement such an annexation.[8] Despite these underlying concerns good working relations have been established between Mongolia and China, largely based on mutual economic interests. Xi Jinping visited Mongolia in 2014 and Elbegdorj returned the compliment in November 2015 to explain Mongolia's permanent neutral status and non-aligned stance and Ulaanbaatar's determination to maintain 'a comprehensive strategic cooperative partnership with both China and Russia, in which way Mongolia's peripheral situation can be stabilised'. It was acknowledged that China was Mongolia's largest trading partner and that as many as 90 per cent of goods produced in Mongolia were exported to China, highlighting Mongolia's exposure to any changes in the Chinese economy.[9] Practical moves to develop this trade were announced in March 2018 with the launch of a freight service on the rail link between Hebei province and Ulaanbaatar. The Chinese side emphasized the products that they would be selling to Mongolia and also the fact that the rail link would be part of the China-Mongolia-Russia Economic Corridor.[10] At the biennial Mongolia-China exposition in Ulaanbaatar in February 2019 platitudes were exchanged on expanding 'bilateral economic and trade ties' with a 2020 target for trade to be at a level of 10 billion US dollars. The Mongolian representative expressed Ulaanbaatar's willingness to diversify its exports and increase those from the non-mining sector to assist in achieving this target.[11]

Shanghai Cooperation Organisation

The essential framework for Mongolia's international relations relies on a balance between its relations with China and Russia; Ulaanbaatar's attitude towards the SCO is a fine example of this. China has proposed that Mongolia should become a member of the SCO but Ulaanbaatar is not enthusiastic. The Mongolians are concerned that membership of an organization in which China plays the dominant role could damage their ability to operate an independent foreign policy.

On the other hand, proposals for enhanced economic links between China and Russia through Mongolia have elicited a more positive response. The Mongolian news agency, *Montsame*, reported on 12 September 2014 that,

> At a meeting with both Mongolian and Russian Presidents, the Chairman of the People's Republic of China Xi Jinping has proposed to construct an economic corridor linking China, Mongolia and Russia. Mr Xi put forward the proposal on Thursday during the 14th Summit of the Shanghai Cooperation Organization (SCO). Highlighting that the development strategies of the three neighbouring countries are highly compatible, Mr Xi noted that both Russia and Mongolia have positively responded to China's vision on building an economic belt along the Silk Road.[12]

The construction of gas pipelines through Mongolia has also been discussed. These would be used for Russia to supply China with gas and could be particularly important to both Moscow and Beijing in the wake of the Ukraine crisis when control of gas supplies became a significant political lever: Moscow might need new customers and Beijing requires large amounts of energy for its continuing economic development. China under Xi Jinping has invested much political capital in its One Belt, One Road project for linking East Asia with Central Asia and the West and Mongolia has a role to play in this as one of the corridors for communications across this vast territory.[13]

Mongolia and the West

As Russian investment and aid was discontinued, Mongolia inevitably had to look elsewhere for financial support and Western countries with developed economies appeared to be the obvious choice. Although these were naturally the highest priority for free-market enthusiasts, in practice all members of the political elite had to formulate a policy for dealing with the West. Mongolia's relations with Europe were not significant in economic terms and Ulaanbaatar's most important relationships with the developed West were with the United States and with international organizations, principally donor agencies, most of which were based in the United States. The pro-market reformers developed close links with the donor agencies and, although they were able to take some credit for the aid and investment that they attracted to Mongolia, they were also blamed when those relationships did not deliver what had been expected. At times the positive effects of aid were overshadowed by concerns about the speed of privatization and allegations of financial corruption.[14]

Mongolia and Japan

Although relations with Mongolia's near neighbours did not appear to offer immense returns on investment in comparison with other alternatives, they have contributed to the country's economic and political security. Japan was interested in the natural resources that Mongolia could produce, as indeed it had been when it was an expansionist colonial power during the early twentieth century. Japan today is wary of being associated too closely with its colonialist past and is not only willing to buy at internationally agreed commercial rates but is also in a position to offer aid and humanitarian assistance, although it cannot compete with China or Russia in any of these roles.

Japan did not establish diplomatic relations with Mongolia until 1972, following the recognition of China by its ally (and occupying power from 1945 to 1952) the United States, and China's admission to the United Nations in 1971. In the early years of this relationship there was little direct aid, apart from a grant for the construction of the state-owned Gobi Cashmere Factory. As Mongolia moved into the era of privatization in the 1990s, 'Japan started extensive bilateral assistance': the reasons for this aid were primarily diplomatic and political, with the aim of contributing to 'peace and stability in Asia'. The level of Japan's Official Development Assistance to Mongolia has varied from year to year and has included: 'support for institution building and human resource development necessary for promoting a market economy; support for rural development; support for environmental protection; and support for development of infrastructure to promote economic activity'. The more visible elements of this aid included the establishment of a Mongolia-Japan Centre in the Mongolian National University in Ulaanbaatar and the improvement of facilities in primary schools. Japan has also contributed to the development of Mongolia through the work of UNESCO and other international organizations. The Embassy of Japan in Ulaanbaatar is actively involved in cultural and social activities.[15]

Mongolia and Korea

Ulaanbaatar's relations with the two Koreas are complicated because of the historical division of the peninsula and the political position of the great powers during the Cold War. Mongolia did not formally recognize the government of South Korea in Seoul until 1990: it could not do so until it had extricated itself from the foreign policy straitjacket of the Soviet Union, which never recognized Seoul. Trade with South Korea has become increasingly important and many Korean businesses have a presence in Mongolia, including low-key operations such as restaurants and coffee shops. Mongolian migrant workers have been employed in South Korea and their remittances were important during the difficult years immediately after the democratic revolution of 1990.

Until 1990 the regime in Pyongyang was the only one recognized by Ulaanbaatar but as both countries nd were subservient to the USSR in their diplomatic activities, neither side influenced the other to any great extent.

Recognition of South Korea created political tensions between Mongolia and North Korea but Ulaanbaatar has increasingly seen its role as an intermediary between the governments of North and South Korea, deploying its status as a permanently neutral state with no nuclear weapons and its 'small country diplomacy' as its qualifications to be the honest broker in the region. Ulaanbaatar's formal position is to press for the renewal of the 'six party talks' on North-South relations on the peninsula but there is evidence that it has also been acting quietly as a go-between, conveying confidential diplomatic messages between Pyongyang and Washington.

Mongolia is also interested in developing economic ties with North Korea as part of its 'third neighbour policy' by which it seeks to diversify its overseas economic relations and reduce its dependency on either China or Russia. A treaty signed with Pyongyang in 2009 provides for sales of Mongolian coal to North Korea and for the use of the North Korean ice-free port of Rason, an important development for landlocked Mongolia seeking to increase its exports.[16]

Mongolia and Central Asia

Mongolia is classified as an Inner Asian rather than a Central Asian country, although the criteria for this distinction are quite subtle. There are many differences, linguistic, religious and cultural between the countries in these two regions, but all share a nomad tradition and most have experienced domination by Russia and the Soviet Union. The only Central Asian country with which Mongolia has significant relations is Kazakhstan which is the largest and most powerful of the Central Asian successor states to the Soviet Union: since western Mongolia is also home to a significant Kazakh minority with cross-border ties, some relationship is inevitable and essential. Kazakhstan, like Mongolia, experienced serious economic problems after the break-up of the Soviet Union but, in spite of these difficulties, significant numbers of Mongolian Kazakhs migrated to Kazakhstan in search of work. By the late 1990s many had returned after the Mongolian economy began to recover from its initial teething problems.[17]

9

The Mongols and China: Inner Mongolia and Ulaanbaatar's relations with Beijing

Although this book focuses primarily on independent Mongolia, since it is about the Mongols, it would not be complete without a closer look at part of the wider community of Mongols in China's Inner Mongolia. There are more Mongols in China than there are in Mongolia and this is an important factor in Ulaanbaatar's approach to its southern neighbour. Although the two communities have lived under different regimes, which were both nominally 'Communist' – until 1990 in the case of Mongolia – close contact has been difficult and the differences between them have been exaggerated by the policies of the two governments. Nevertheless the existence of these Mongol lands outside Mongolia has had an effect on both Mongolia and China, and it is important to consider the relationship between the two communities.

The society and political structure of Inner Mongolia before the twentieth century was much closer to the imperial Chinese system than was Outer Mongolia. This is partly for reasons of geographical proximity and, because of this, Inner Mongolia was absorbed by the Manchu Qing dynasty long before Outer Mongolia. In Owen Lattimore's words, the 'administrative structure of Inner Mongolia was linked more closely than that of Outer Mongolia to the system that the Manchus set up in China'.[1] The Revolution of 1911 that brought about the downfall of the Manchu Qing dynasty 'delivered the Mongols [of Inner Mongolia] into the hands of Chinese warlords with limited local interests'. This was quite different from Outer Mongolia which 'immediately slipped out of China's control'.[2]

Of course the Inner Mongolia of the Manchu period did not occupy the same territory as the current Inner Mongolian Autonomous Region: Inner Mongolia was divided between several Chinese provinces, underwent considerable political changes, and lost and gained territory between 1911 and the creation of the new Inner Mongolia Autonomous Region by the Chinese Communist Party (CCP) in 1947, two years before the foundation of the People's Republic of China (PRC).

Mongols in Inner Mongolia remained under Chinese rule during the revolutionary period of the 1920s and 1930s when Outer Mongolia was struggling to forge an independent state. They were however not directly under the rule of the National Government of the Republic of China that Chiang Kai-shek had established in Nanjing in 1928. Day to day control was in the hands of Chinese warlords, who might have been formally allied to Nanjing but did not accept its authority in all matters. Under the warlords, Chinese emigration and colonization developed rapidly. Land in Inner Mongolia could be acquired easily, either bought cheaply or simply seized, irrespective of whether local Mongols regarded it as their traditional grazing lands. This encouraged the migration of Han Chinese into the region. In theory the policy of the Chinese Nationalist Party (Guomindang) on minority issues was to promote assimilation but in practice this meant encouraging the use of the Chinese language and discouraging any minority languages, such as Mongol and Tibetan.

Mongols began to resist this colonization, but the traditional Mongol aristocracy was weak and demonstrably unable to defend its feudal subjects against the encroachment by Chinese settlers. Mongols in the Ordos region of Inner Mongolia developed resistance organizations or 'clubs' that took their name from documents known as *duguilang* (based on the Mongolian for 'circle', *dugui*); these were 'round robins' with the names of the club's members radiating from the centre in such a way that no individual could be identified as the ringleader in any political activity. These cells operated independently and without knowledge of each other's membership.

De Wang

Although weak nobles, especially those in Inner Mongolia who were unable to protect their subjects from the effects of Chinese colonization, were among the targets of the Mongol insurgents, some aristocrats did become leaders of the resistance. The most famous – or notorious – of these was the young Prince Demchukdonggrub (1902–66) a Chahar Mongol of the Plain White Banner who was often known by the Chinese version of his name – De Wang (Te Wang or Prince De). De Wang emerged as a leader in 1931 as Japan was poised to invade Manchuria and demanded that Chiang Kai-shek grant autonomy to Inner Mongolia, which at this time was not one political entity; different Mongol areas were attached to various Chinese provinces. De Wang argued that Inner Mongolia would be strategically vulnerable in the event of a Japanese invasion and that Mongol resistance would be stronger if the Mongols had a government of their own. He believed that Mongols would be more willing to defend such a government, whereas they would be less enthusiastic about protecting a Chinese warlord regime from the Japanese.

De Wang was not in a strong position: he relied heavily on the support of the high lamas and the old tribal aristocracy and was not willing to concede the social changes demanded by some of his more radical supporters. Chiang Kai-shek, who headed the National Government in Nanjing, was in no position to force provincial warlords to concede the autonomy that De Wang demanded, and they schemed against the Mongol leader.

The Japanese invasion that had begun with the occupation of Manchuria in 1931 reached Inner Mongolia in 1934. The Japanese,

> made enough moves favourable to the Mongols to prevent unity of action between anti-Japanese Mongols and Chinese, and at the same time prevented unity among the Mongols by subdividing Inner Mongolia, dealing with [De] Wang in only one of the subdivisions. By the end of the war [De] Wang was disliked by the Chinese as a 'Japanese puppet', but deeply respected by most Mongols. In their eyes he was no puppet of the Japanese. Not being strong enough to resist them, he had resorted to evasion.[3]

This is a persuasive rationale for Prince De's actions but the region of Mengjiang, the Mongol Border Autonomous Region which he controlled during the Second World War with its capital at Kalgan (Zhangjiakou), is regarded by most Chinese historians as nothing more than a Japanese puppet regime. A history of allegations of collaboration with the Japanese occupiers have coloured Chinese attitudes towards the region ever since. They have also affected the responses of Beijing to any Inner Mongolian pressure for autonomy from China, which is treated almost as a continuation of the treachery of the Second World War period. After the foundation of the PRC in 1949, De Wang, who had also fought against the forces of the CCP, was declared to have been a 'war criminal'. He had lived in Beijing during the final years of the Guomindang regime but moved swiftly to Mongolia when the CCP took over. The government of the Mongolian People's Republic (MPR) then deported him back to China, where he was tried for treason and imprisoned. After an early release he worked in a historical museum in the Inner Mongolian capital of Hohhot.[4]

Inner Mongolia Autonomous Region

Mongolians living in the PRC are considered by the Chinese government to be just one of the fifty-five official ethnic minorities or 'nationalities' of China. Government officials avoid acknowledging the fact that they are also part of the much wider Mongol nation that stretches far beyond the borders of the PRC. Inner Mongolians are aware that the most important of the Mongolian communities, for both cultural and geopolitical reasons, remains that of the independent nation of Mongolia, with which they have to have dealings, but are not so aware of other groups in the Buryat and Kalmyk republics inside the Russian Federation.[5] Inner Mongolia is not surprisingly the most important region for Mongols living within China but there are also Mongol communities in the north-east (Manchuria) and speakers of minor languages of the Mongol family can be found in other provinces. Supporters of a long established but weak Mongol independence movement reject the term Inner Mongolia, which they consider an expression of a traditional Chinese colonial mentality; they prefer to call the region in which they live Southern Mongolia.

The Inner Mongolia Autonomous Region (*Nei Menggu zizhiqu*) was formally constituted in 1947, which was, as has been noted, two years before the establishment of the PRC. The leading Mongol in the administration of the region was Ulanhu (Ulanfu), who had actively resisted the Japanese, unlike some other Mongols who were prepared to collaborate. Unusually for someone who was not a Han Chinese, he was both party secretary and governor of the region between 1947 and 1967 when he was purged during the Cultural Revolution.

The current population of Inner Mongolia is approximately 25 million. Ethnic Mongols make up less than 20 per cent of this total, but there are 4 million of them and that, ironically, is more than the total population of Mongolia which is just over 3 million. Although the Mongols are overall a minority in Inner Mongolia there are some administrative divisions, banners, in which they are the overwhelming majority. Not only do the Chinese dominate in demographic terms, they also control most economic activity other than herding. In particular they are in charge of the mining and other extractive industries which have been developed under the PRC and contribute most to the modern economy. These enterprises have become the focus of increasingly acrimonious disputes between the Chinese government and developers, who are mostly Han Chinese, and traditional herders who are exclusively Mongols.[6]

The creation of the autonomous region was one of the outcomes of the Second World War and the subsequent civil war. After the unconditional surrender of Japan in 1945, the Japanese forces occupying the Mongol regions were disarmed and there was in effect a power vacuum in the region. Inner Mongolia was reoccupied by a combination of Soviet, Mongolian and finally Chinese Communist forces which were transferred from their bases in

Manchuria, and it was agreed that this territory would be returned to China. The idea of a unified but separate Inner Mongolia was, perhaps surprisingly, more popular with local Mongols than a union with the MPR, a state that was formally independent but had been ideologically and practically close to the USSR since 1924. The MPR, for its part, did not wish to absorb the territory of Inner Mongolia for many reasons; the fact that the latter had such a large Han Chinese population was undoubtedly the most important one. Although this was the view that prevailed, it was not universal and there is residual support for pan-Mongolism and the concept of a Greater Mongolia that would include all those whose language and culture was accepted as Mongolian. The implementation of such pan-Mongol policies is not accepted by those in power.

Ulanfu

Ulanfu (1906–88) was the founding chairman of the Inner Mongolian Autonomous Region. He was a genuine ethnic Mongol and hailed from the Tumed Left Banner, the name of the administrative region close to the city of Hohhot that was formerly known by its Chinese name of Guisui and reverted to its Mongol name when it became the capital of Inner Mongolia in 1952: the administration of De Wang had previously used the name Hohhot. Ulanfu had been a member of the CCP since 1925, although for some time he was also a member of the Guomindang; this was not unusual in the 1920s during the period known as the United Front when the two parties cooperated. He had also been associated with other revolutionary and nationalist organizations in Inner Mongolia. Ulanfu studied in Moscow at Sun Yat-sen University and the University of the Toilers of the East and from 1929 was engaged in underground political work for the CCP in Inner Mongolia. For his military experience in the resistance to the Japanese, and in the subsequent civil war with the Nationalists, he was promoted to the rank of general in 1955.

Ulanfu played a crucial role in the negotiations that led to the creation of the autonomous region in 1947 and he remained chairman of the autonomous region and a loyal supporter of the Communist Party until 1966 when, like many of the old guard of Communist Party leaders, he became the target of political attacks during the Cultural Revolution. He was one of the senior political figures protected by Zhou Enlai and he survived the Cultural Revolution, serving as vice president of China from his rehabilitation in 1983 till his death in 1988.

Mersé

As far as the CCP was concerned, Ulanfu was the most important figure in Inner Mongolia and the genuine loyal and heroic leader of the Mongols. However a comparison with the career of another less well-known activist of that region, Mersé, a contraction of his birth name Mersentei, who was also known by his Chinese name of Guo Daofu, illustrates the complexity of ethnic and political relationships in that region. Mersé, a shadowy figure, was born in 1894 into an aristocratic family of the Daur subgroup of Mongols in Hulunbuir League which is in the eastern part of Inner Mongolia. His early influences included Mongolian youth groups and the father of Chinese nationalism, Sun Yat-sen, and he played a key role in the creation of the Inner Mongolian People's Revolutionary Party (IMPRP) in 1925. This organization was intended to operate as a united front body with the backing of the Chinese Nationalist Guomindang, the CCP and the Comintern. Unlike Ulanfu, Mersé's primary political allegiance was with the MPR and the Comintern and this brought him into conflict with other members of the IMPRP, who saw the future in terms of an alliance with the Guomindang. Mersé led an uprising against the Chinese Nationalists in 1928 but his support for the MPR and the Comintern was not reciprocated and the rising was crushed by the Chinese military. In 1931 Mersé opposed the Japanese occupation of Manchuria and sought sanctuary in the Soviet consulate in Manzhouli. His subsequent fate is unclear but it is most likely that he disappeared into the Soviet gulag and died there. He was later criticized for having been a traitor to both the Mongolian people and the CCP, although there is no reliable evidence to show that he changed his political allegiances during those turbulent years. The contrast between the two leaders illustrates yet again how the relationship with China and the Chinese blighted political movements that involved Mongols.[7]

Language and literature of Inner Mongolia

In Mongolia (the former MPR) the national standard language is Khalkh Mongol and all other varieties of Mongol, like Buryat, Oirat and Kalmuk, are treated either as dialects or separate languages. Khalkh Mongol is not regarded as the standard in Inner Mongolia; the official language of the region is known as Southern Mongolian and is based on a group of Mongolian languages and dialects spoken among southern Mongols that include Chakhar, Ordos, Baarin, Khorchin, Kharchin Oirat, Tumut and Alasha. There is a greater continuum of comprehensibility between these different forms of Mongol than this list of separate languages might suggest and the Inner Mongolian standard pronunciation is based on a dialect that is not too different from that of Ulaanbaatar. There are inevitably differences in vocabulary, and to some extent the grammar, but these variations are not so great as to inhibit communication between educated Mongols from the two regions. The distinctions are however important to the different communities, as ethnic and cultural markers, and they also reflect the fact that there are political differences between Mongolia and China.

According to the eminent twentieth-century Mongolist, Nicholas Poppe, 'These languages do not differ from one another. The difference is mainly in the pronunciations. Therefore mutual understanding among those tribes is easy'. The same cannot be said for communication between Mongols and Chinese. As has been noted in Chapter 1, the Mongol language is close to Manchu, is not related to Chinese in any way and is not written in the Chinese script. Traditionally it was written in the vertical script, derived ultimately from Middle Eastern scripts such as Syriac. This script, which is complicated and often ambiguous, was abandoned in (Outer) Mongolia and, after an experiment with a Latin-based alphabet, it was replaced with the Cyrillic script under the influence of the Russian-dominated Soviet Union. It has however been retained in Inner Mongolia for a variety of reasons, principally the need to differentiate Chinese Mongols from those of Mongolia. There was no established tradition in China of using the Cyrillic script and considerable resistance to any idea of introducing it in the 1950s when the government of the PRC was actively looking at ways of reforming the Chinese script. Instead of Cyrillic, China created the *pinyin* system of romanization based on the Latin alphabet but that never replaced Chinese characters and it was not used to write Mongolian.

Since the Mongolian democratic revolution of 1990-1 the government of independent Mongolia has attempted to revive the old script for reasons of national pride and to stress the continuity of contemporary Mongol culture with that of the pre-Soviet period, but it has not replaced Cyrillic for practical purposes. It has been reintroduced into the school curriculum but is still rarely used other than as ornamentation. By contrast Inner Mongolia has a continuous tradition of its use in publications and in everyday life, although Chinese, as both the language of the majority population of the region and the national language of the PRC is the dominant idiom of the autonomous region.[8]

Religious institutions in the Alxa (Alashan) region of Inner Mongolia

Religious Mongols in Inner Mongolia, in common with independent Mongolia, follow the Lama Buddhist tradition of Tibet. Even in Inner

Mongolia, which has been influenced for centuries by Chinese culture, the Buddhist religion follows a different tradition from the Chinese schools of Buddhism and is based on scriptures in Tibetan and Sanskrit. Some Buddhist temples remain in use for worship in Inner Mongolia but most were closed, and many destroyed during the Cultural Revolution. Since the opening of China in the 1980s, and the revitalization of its economy, there has been a move to restore some of the temples and this can be observed in the city of Bayanhot and the surrounding Alashan region.

The Alxa or Alashan League is the most sparsely populated region of Inner Mongolia but, even in this relatively undeveloped area, the population is predominantly Han and the Mongols only account for just over 20 per cent of the total. The league is divided into three administrative districts which have traditional Mongolian names. They are the Alxa Left and Right Banners and the Ejin Banner.

The Alxa region is over 600 kilometres south-west of the Inner Mongolian capital of Hohhot, from where it can be reached after a long rail journey. It is more easily accessible by road from Yinchuan, the capital of the neighbouring Ningxia Hui Autonomous Region. The road from Yinchuan to Alxa passes through an old and dilapidated section of the Great Wall. Mosques of the local Chinese-speaking Hui Muslim community, who are more usually associated with Ningxia, can be found well inside Inner Mongolian territory in the Alxa League.

The main city and administrative centre of the Alxa League is Bayanhot, which is also known by its Mongolian name of Alxa and is located in the Left Banner of Alxa League. The majority of the city's population are Han Chinese, but remnants of the old Mongol town are still visible around the Lama Buddhist monastery which is also known by its Chinese name of Yanfu Temple. It is preserved almost as if it were a museum but it still functions as a place of worship and Mongols, mainly of the older generation, still use it for prayer. Nearby is a museum that contains photographs of the destruction of the *Alxa Baraghun hiid*, a large Mongol Buddhist monastery in the Alxa (Helanshan) Mountains that separate Inner Mongolia from the Ningxia Hui Autonomous Region. The *Alxa Baraghun Hiid*, which is known in Chinese as the Southern Monastery (*Nansi*) was badly damaged during the Cultural Revolution, but by 2001 it was being restored with financial support from the local and national governments. The extensive rebuilding provided work for many young craftsmen, both Han and Mongolian, who were specially trained in traditional techniques to replace and replicate the damaged structures of the old temple.[9]

Gers and camels

The traditional Mongol *ger* is less in evidence in Inner Mongolia than in Mongolia further north where there are substantial *ger* communities in stockades on the outskirts of towns and cities including the capital Ulaanbaatar. However it remains a symbol of the distinctiveness of Mongol culture. Mongols in contemporary Inner Mongolia are more likely to live in blocks of flats or other accommodation that is similar to their Han neighbours. The *ger* can still be seen and it is so flexible that it can also be used as a temporary structure to house workers on construction projects.

The camel was once an indispensable part of the livestock of Mongol nomads but, as many Mongols have adopted settled lifestyles, camels have become increasingly redundant and abandoned camels that have been left to return to the wild can often be seen roaming the Inner Mongolian countryside. Horsemanship was once seen as an essential component of Mongol culture as horses were the only means of fast and efficient transport in the Gobi and the grasslands. For young urban Mongols the horse is still popular for cultural and sporting reasons but for practical purposes is being replaced by the motorcycle.[10]

Inner Mongolian resistance, nationalism and development

Organizations campaigning for independence have existed in Inner Mongolia since the 1950s; the Chinese prefer to designate such groups as 'separatists'. Compared with similar movements in two other regions under the control of the PRC, Xinjiang and Tibet, there have been far fewer Mongolian activists and they have had a much lower profile. The Chinese authorities have suppressed them whenever they showed signs of gaining support and have been able to neutralize them by arresting a small number of leading members.

The collapse of Soviet power between 1989 and 1991 reawakened interest in secession in Inner Mongolia in a movement that ran in parallel with the democratic revolution in independent Mongolia but was not directly connected with it. In 1990, the year of the popular protests in Ulaanbaatar that eventually brought down the MPR, there were also demonstrations in Inner Mongolia calling for independence for Southern Mongolia. Some secessionist groups with a pan-Mongolian perspective openly demanded the right to join the MPR which was then in its final days, although this was not encouraged by any political figures in Ulaanbaatar. In 1991, leaders of a group based near the Inner Mongolian regional capital, Hohhot, were imprisoned for two years for separatist activities and twenty-six others were placed under house arrest. A second group of activists was also broken up and its leaders arrested in 1995. Its most prominent member, Hada, who does not use a patronymic, was charged with separatist activities and espionage in 1996 after he had taken part in discussions about the possibility of establishing a new Inner Mongolian People's Party (IMPRP) that would campaign for independence. Hada was sentenced to fifteen years imprisonment after which he should have been released by 2011 but he was not finally freed from prison until 2014.[11]

The movement for independence in Inner Mongolia is weak. There is no strong feeling of ethnic consciousness in the region and secession from China does not have a broad base of support. This is partly due to repression by the state which inhibits open political discussion and organization but it also reflects division among the Mongols and the unavoidable fact that they are vastly outnumbered by Han Chinese. In addition, whereas the economy of Mongolia suffered badly after the collapse of the USSR, Inner Mongolia has been relatively successful, although Mongols in the region could argue with some justification that this success benefits the Han majority rather than them. By and large, Inner Mongolia's Mongols accept that their future lies with China, in spite of all the difficulties they have with the Chinese, and not with Mongolia. Post-1990 governments in Ulaanbaatar have been no more enthusiastic about an irredentist movement to incorporate Inner Mongolia than their predecessors. It would unnecessarily antagonize the Chinese and risk inward investment from that quarter. If it were to succeed, integrating over 4 million Mongols from China would create unacceptable economic and social problems for independent Mongolia.[12]

It has been the long-term aim of the CCP to oblige Mongols, and other nomads, to make the transition from a herding economy to modern agriculture and industry; the conflict of interests between their traditional lifestyle and the demands of modernization are at the root of protests in Inner Mongolia. This policy of course derives from the same Soviet model that was imposed on the MPR.

According to the Southern Mongolian Human Rights Information Centre, 640,000 herders were forced to leave the grasslands and relocated in urban centres in 2001. This was described as 'ecological migration' and declared to be essential to reduce overgrazing and avoid sandstorms and the desertification of the region's delicate grasslands. Those Mongols who were displaced had to seek unskilled work in agriculture or find employment in the mushrooming mining industry or in the towns: all of these options would place Mongols, who had formerly been largely independent herders, under the control of Han Chinese businessmen and officials. The ecological case has been rejected by Mongol activists who argue that herding causes far less damage to the environment than extractive industries or even intensive agriculture.[13] Since the 1990s, the landscape of Inner Mongolia has been transformed by the expansion of coal mining and the extraction of iron ore, copper and rare earths. Many Mongols complain that they have been 'marginalised, sidelined, ignored ...' and that their very identity has been threatened as the disappearance of grasslands removes their livelihood and their homes. Some Mongols have responded successfully to these challenges by moving into 'modern' employment but many have been left behind by the rapid development of new economic sectors. Not surprisingly the discontent caused by government policies has led to resistance and even violent disturbances.[14]

May 2011 disturbances in Inner Mongolia

Demonstrations on a large scale drew the complaints of Mongols to the attention of the international community after the death of an ethnic Mongol herdsman, Mergen, in the Xilingol League in the north of Inner Mongolia on 10 May 2011.[15] Xilingol is a region of Inner Mongolia that has managed to retain a thriving nomadic culture and Mergen was the leader of a group of twenty of his fellow herdsmen who were protesting at the level of noise and pollution produced during mining operations, and the impact this was having on their herds. The protestors tried to prevent trucks from carrying coal across traditional grazing lands; Mergen was hit by a truck driven by a Han Chinese and was killed as it dragged him along. Demonstrators surrounded the government offices of the Right Ujumchin Banner and children from a local secondary school protested outside government offices in the regional centre, Xilinhot.[16] As the protests escalated the government ordered parts of nearby counties to be cordoned off. Police descended on schools and colleges and many students were forced to remain in their classrooms until the protests were over.[17]

Riot police moved into the centre of the regional capital, Hohhot, to deal with protests there; surveillance of students in all colleges was increased; and internet access was suspended. People's Armed Police (PAP) units were also brought in from Baotou, Inner Mongolia's main industrial city. The government blamed the crisis on foreign interference in the region and warned of action against anyone taking part in a 'political conspiracy of external hostile forces and a very few internal extremists'. By 4 June 2011, the anniversary of the crushing of the Democracy Movement in Beijing's Tiananmen Square in 1989, Hohhot, Xilinhot and other towns had been placed under martial law. Infantry units of the People's Liberation Army were moved in from Hebei province and protestors and anyone suspected of sympathizing with them were detained. Two universities which teach primarily in the Mongol language, the Inner Mongolia University for Nationalities in Tongliao on the border with Manchuria and the Nationalities University in Hohhot, were closed.[18]

Public response of the Chinese government

The public response of the Chinese authorities towards the Mongol protesters was positive and conciliatory, but the official press insisted that the protests were caused by economic worries and played down any suggestion of ethnic conflict.[19] The Han Chinese truck driver, Li Lindong, was sentenced to death after a hurried trial, and reportedly executed: no Mongols were put on trial, although many had been arrested.[20]

The government of Inner Mongolia promised to 'discipline the mining industry' and compensate herdsmen for damage to the environment caused by coal extraction. Hu Chunhua, who was at the time the Secretary of the Inner Mongolian CCP Committee, recognized the public anger that had been aroused by the death of Mergen and announced the setting up of a programme to inspect mining sites throughout the region.[21] In Beijing there was great alarm in spite of the fact that, unlike protestors in Tibet or Xinjiang, Mongols have no significant international support network.

The Ulaanbaatar government, constrained by its own economic problems and political instability, was not in any position to support an insurgency in Inner Mongolia even if it had wished to do so. Mongolia has become increasingly, if reluctantly, economically dependent on Beijing since the collapse of the USSR in 1991. During the 1990s it had little foreign exchange and relied on barter agreements with China and other neighbours, such as Kazakhstan.[22] In June 2011, the Mongolian government accepted a loan of $US 500 million from Beijing to construct processing plants and for much needed infrastructure improvements, including roads.[23] The Mongolian prime pinister, Sükhbaataryn Batbold, made an official visit to China from 15 to 17 June 2011 at the invitation of his opposite number from China, Wen Jiabao, to discuss economic cooperation 'in mineral development, infrastructure construction and technology sharing on animal husbandry'. Any mention of Inner

Mongolia was avoided after the disturbances but it is worthy of note that the statement mentioned animal husbandry as well as those aspects of development that required the introduction of high technology. It was a public acknowledgment by Ulaanbaatar that the grievances of China's Mongols had been taken seriously by Beijing.[24]

10

Looking back to the future: Mongolia's search for identity and the contemporary cult of Chinggis Khan

When considering Mongolia's likely future direction it is useful to return to some of the most important issues that the country has faced since 1990, and to examine in more depth their significance. Mongolia faced major challenges when it was cut adrift from the Soviet mother ship in 1990. The most urgent, and the most obvious, was the need to restructure the economy after the loss of financial support from Moscow. There were serious casualties in the process of reorganization and, although Mongolia has achieved a degree of economic stability, it is still faced with considerable problems, not least the allegations of widespread corruption and financial irregularities within the governing elite.

In the longer term the challenges are less tangible though no less important in determining the path that Mongolia is following through the twenty-first century. Post-Soviet Mongolia has had to decide on its national and cultural identity and its relationship with both the Soviet era and the pre-Soviet past.

There was an understandable temptation to reject outright the Soviet past, but this risked throwing out the baby with the bathwater. Equally there was a temptation to glamorize the history of the Mongolian nation or the Mongol people, particularly those periods when Mongol power and influence were in the ascendant. These were often periods of authoritarian rule and brutal and bloody warfare: authoritarianism and brutality did not fit the vision of a new and modern Mongolia. Although the status of Chinggis Khan as a world-renowned military and political leader remains high, his legacy is mixed to say the least.

The same can be said of the revival of pre-Soviet religious traditions. The reopening of monasteries and the resumption of Tibetan Buddhist scholarship and teaching by the monks has been welcomed with few reservations. This is important as it redresses the wrongs done to thousands of lamas in the 1930s, but educated Mongols are unlikely to seek a return to the time when the monasteries siphoned off thousands of the most intellectually able young men. This is less likely to happen in a world in which there is a real choice of alternative career paths open to adolescents; the monasteries will still attract those who are inclined towards a life of study and prayer.

The return of shamanism has not been welcomed as enthusiastically although belief in the spirit world remains popular, especially in the rural areas. In the grounds of the Gandan monastery in Ulaanbaatar stands a pole with a box attached to it. The box contains sacred relics and has become a strange and unofficial shrine which is venerated by local people, some of whom appear to be in a highly emotional state. Shamanism in the past provided rituals for dealing with crises and the most intractable problems of life, but some aspects of the belief were associated with cruel sacrifices and that aspect of the religion is not being celebrated.[1]

Other challenges are primarily geopolitical. What place should the new Mongolia occupy in the Asia, and indeed the world, of the twenty-first century? These are new challenges, but reactions to the options open to Mongolians are coloured by Mongolians' historical experiences, none greater than their attitudes to Russia and above all to China. The actual or potential influence of China still dominates the political discourse in Mongolia, even if it is not always explicit, as the government works to negotiate new roles and relationships in its region and more widely.

Reasserting identity

From 1924 to 1990, in what can for the sake of brevity be called the Soviet period, the traditional Mongolian way of life appeared to have been subsumed under a generalized Soviet culture. Photographs from these decades, especially of urban scenes after the Second World War, feature clothes, buildings, transport and other items and scenes that could have been observed just as easily in Moscow, Almaty or Dushanbe as in Ulaanbaatar. Members of the political elite, and those who wished to join or work with them, aspired to dress like Russians; to work and live in Russian-style buildings; and to travel in Russian-made vehicles. Away from the capital these fashions took much longer to become established and traditional ways of life continued, but the influence of Soviet style and models was otherwise ubiquitous. For Mongolians, the Soviet version of modernity was the only one available to them.

This does not mean that Soviet culture had eradicated Mongolian culture. Time-honoured and distinctive Mongolian customs and manners survived, even if they were not appreciated by the regime. The new Mongolian elite that came to power with the democratic revolution in 1991 could fall back on these traditions which were most prevalent in the rural areas. They began the task of reasserting aspects of Mongolian identity that might have been devalued but had never been completely lost. Many urban Mongolian families retained links with their relatives in the grasslands and these contacts were reinforced in the 1990s as economic problems forced many unemployed city dwellers back to the countryside. Crucially, although the best educated Mongols could also function at a fairly high level in Russian, even the sophisticated urban elite never lost their Mongolian language.

An interesting comparison can be made with neighbouring Kazakhstan which, unlike Mongolia, had been a constituent part of the Soviet Union. By the 1980s, Kazakhstan, and particularly its towns and cities, had become so Russified that even the Kazakh language was in decline. In the mid-1990s, although ethnic Kazakhs were rapidly replacing Russians in positions of authority, their working language, and for some the only language in which they were fully competent, was Russian. Academics at the Kazakhstan Academy of Social Sciences in Almaty spoke of having to go back to the Kazakh *aul*, the countryside, if they wanted to rediscover their language and traditions and understand what it meant to be true Kazakhs.[2]

Urga and Ulaanbaatar: Two tales of a city

There are several large urban centres scattered across the vast territory of Mongolia. Among the better known are the mining centre of Erdenet; the northern industrial city of Darkhan with its cluster of higher education institutions; the commercial centre of Choibalsan close to the Chinese border; and the provincial capital of Khovd in the far west of the country. By far the largest is the capital, Ulaanbaatar.

With a population in 2014 of 1.3 million out of a total national population of 2.97 million, it dwarfs them all. Ulaanbaatar dominates all the other cities and the rural areas, both politically and economically, although it is far from typical of the rest of the country. As has been shown, it has only been called Ulaanbaatar (Red Hero) since the revolution of 1924, which was inspired by anti-Chinese nationalism and supported by the fledgling Soviet Union. Before 1924 it had a series of different names, as will be demonstrated , but for simplicity the city before that date will mostly be referred to here as Urga, the form used most frequently in Western accounts. The histories of Urga and Ulaanbaatar are strikingly different and illustrate the profound and sometimes traumatic political and social transformations in the modern history of Mongolia.

Ulaanbaatar, as the political and economic centre of Mongolia, has inevitably attracted the greatest attention of international financial and commercial concerns and this is immediately apparent in the observable changes to the urban landscape. The changes have not been universal or uniform; the overall appearance of the central area around Sükhbaatar Square has remained remarkably unaltered for decades. The functions of some of the buildings, or parts of them, may have altered but the overall impact remains: solid and imposing government buildings with a powerful presence at the head of a wide central square.

Urga: Palace, big temple, Capital Temple

Traditional Mongol society was almost exclusively nomadic so permanent settlements were rare. Even Buddhist temples in mediaeval Mongolia were not originally fixtures; like the ger tents in which the majority of the population lived they could be moved according to the rhythm of the nomadic calendar.

The origins of Urga were religious and what eventually evolved into a major city began life as the seat of the Jebtsundamba Khutukhtu, the head of Tibetan Buddhism in Mongolia, who was later also known as the Bogd Khan when he became the secular ruler. It was initially a palatial *ger* that moved with the Jebstundamba and grew into an imposing complex of tent temples. Urga represents the Russian pronunciation of Örgöö and the word *örgöö* or *ger örgöö* in classical and modern Mongolian means the palace of a khan or other high-ranking individual. The site of Urga changed 'every few years as the surrounding pastures and woods became exhausted'. It 'moved more than twenty times along the banks of the rivers Orkhon, Selenga and Tula, until it settled permanently ... in 1778', on roughly the site of present-day Ulaanbaatar. Travellers in the nineteenth century noted the contrast between the elaborate constructions of the temple complexes and the 'mud huts or felt tents' of the poorer areas and few failed to remark on the squalor or the narrow streets.[3]

The impact of the palatial tents on the herding families in their simple *gers* can only be imagined:

> When the Lamaist tent temples of Urga ... were still movable, they must have been very large and magnificent ... From pictures of the modern gathering, one can imagine earlier scenes when the great khans and their governments travelled from place to place, when the great Jebtsundamba Living Buddha of Outer Mongolia moved his tent temples in nomadic fashion, and when Urga, though not yet settled, still formed the focal point of government among the tribes of Outer Mongolia.[4]

By the late eighteenth century Urga was an urban settlement and it grew over the next hundred years, its construction influenced by Mongolia's Chinese and Russian neighbours. The city was commonly known as Urga, especially in Russian and other Western accounts, but the Mongols usually referred to it as Ikh Khüree 'the big monastery'. Its status increased as it became a centre of political power in addition to its religious authority. After the collapse of the Chinese Empire in 1911 Mongolia enjoyed a degree of autonomy and Urga became known as the Niislel Khüree, the 'capital monastery'.[5] Regional urban administrative centres that had originally been established by Mongolia's Manchu Qing rulers also began to emerge at this time but none developed sufficiently to rival Urga.[6]

Even in settled Urga the degree of urbanization was limited and there were few buildings that could be described as permanent, other than the Tibetan Buddhist temples, the palaces of the Living Buddha and eventually the Russian Consulate. Most of the population still lived in the mobile and eminently practical *ger* structures but residential estates containing large numbers of these tents became established and they continue to exist, mainly on the outskirts of Ulaanbaatar, as living communities well into the twenty-first century.[7]

James Gilmour (1843–91), a Scottish protestant minister of the London Missionary Society, set out to work in Mongolia in 1870 and in the course of an 'evangelical journey' travelled through the country. He studied the Mongol language seriously but was somewhat hampered by his anxiety to avoid impure conversations. In *Among the Mongols*, which was published in 1882 while he was on leave from his Asian mission, he observed that,

> in nearly every establishment is visible from the street the brazen sheen of the brightly-polished Russian samovar. The streets are moderately busy, with Chinese going hither and thither, and with Mongols bent on shopping expeditions … The whole of the Chinese employed in trade at Urga live a life of self-imposed banishment, being prevented by law from bringing their wives and families, and for the most part revisit their native land at intervals of from five to ten years … The most conspicuous objects in the Mongol town are the temples, which from afar look lofty and grand, but lose much of their imposing effect when approached and examined closely. In these temple premises, and on many street corners and busy places, are erected numerous prayer-wheels supposed to be filled inside, many of them decorated outside, and some of them almost literally covered all round, with prayers, the idea being that any devout believer who turns the wheel, by doing so acquires as much merit as if he or she had repeated all the prayers thus set in motion.[8]

Gilmour was also impressed by the Russian trading and consular presence in Urga and when the Danish explorer and writer, Henning Haslund, arrived there in the 1920s, he was similarly struck by the mixed nature of the population:

> No town in the world is like Urga. Upon us newcomers it made an extremely strange impression. The most conservative eastern life and customs and western innovations like the telegraph, the telephone and the motor-car exist side by side in motley combination. The houses of the Russians cluster round the church with Byzantine cupolas; colossal Buddhist temples rise high over thousands of felt-covered Mongol tents. Mounted Mongols, slippered Chinese, long-bearded Russians and smiling Tibetans swarm between pallisaded compounds whose walls are hung with gaily fluttering prayer-flags. At the most eastern end lies the *mai-mai-ch'eng* of the Chinese, a complete fragment of China in whose innumerable shops the sons of Han offer their wares to the Mongols riding by.[9]

This description highlights very effectively the social and ethnic divisions that would in time evolve into major discontents and pitch Mongolia into a revolution. The most profound discontent arose out of resentment against the Chinese merchants, who the Mongols believed were exploiting them, but there was also antipathy towards the traditional aristocracyt and the wealthy and powerful Tibetan Buddhist elite. The resultant revolution was supported by Russians, not the old Russians exemplified by those who lived in the Tsarist consulate, but the class of Russians who had also rebelled, in their case against Tsarism, and were considered by the Mongols to be preferable to the forces of the Republic of China which had attempted to annex Mongolia in 1919. Haslund refers to the town as Urga but, as his expedition approached the city, they heard news of its change of name; on 25 September 1924 it was not Urga but Ulaanbaatar that they entered, a town with 'fewer lamas and more Mongolian soldiers in Soviet uniform' than they had seen on previous visits.[10]

Hero City to Red Hero

Urga had been christened Ulaanbaatar (Red Hero) to indicate its rebirth as a revolutionary state and an ally of the Soviet Union. Initially some Mongolian revolutionaries had proposed that it be called Baatar Hot (Hero City) but in November 1924, at the first meeting of the People's Great Khural (Assembly) and at the suggestion, or probably the insistence, of Turar Ryskulov (1894–1938), the Comintern's representative, who was a Kazakh from what is now the Almaty region of Kazakhstan, the name of Ulaanbaatar (Red Hero) was formally approved.

Once Mongolia had positively aligned itself with the Soviet Union after the proclamation of the Mongolian People's Republic (MPR) in 1924, the physical appearance of Urga was gradually but completely transformed. New buildings and the overall approach of town planning was either Western – primarily Russian – or consciously echoed the architectural styles of Soviet Central Asia. The construction of a branch of the Trans-Siberian Railway to Ulaanbaatar in the 1930s not only strengthened Mongolia's alignment towards the USSR but influenced the capital's economic development. 'Industries based on the national pastoral products of wool, skin, leather and so on, were founded' and these provided essential supplies for the Soviet economy and attracted aid and other finance from the USSR.[11]

The dramatic changes that have taken place in the appearance of Ulaanbaatar since the revolution of 1924 have been strikingly documented in *Ulaanbaatar Then and Now*. In this book, Bayasgalan Bayanbat, a cinematographer and photographer who was born and brought up in Ulaanbaatar, documents the changes, positive and negative, that have taken place in his hometown. He presents almost 400 photographs of buildings and locations, taken at various points from the 1930s to the present day. Most are in the central areas of the city but some record the transformation, and in some cases the degradation, of what were green open spaces on the city's outskirts. The images demonstrate the overwhelming and unmistakable influence of Soviet-style architecture but also the persistence of some traditional buildings which are a reminder of the original Asian heritage of Mongolia.

On the streets of Ulaanbaatar

The appearance of the people on streets of Ulaanbaatar in the early twenty-first century is very different from the 1920s and 1930s but it is noticeably different even from their appearance in 1990. In 1990, as Haslund had also reported earlier in 1924, there were still many men in Soviet-style military uniforms. In 2016 far fewer men and women were in uniform apart from the police and security guards on modern buildings. The business suit and modern Western-style fashions were *de rigueur* for those who could afford them, and the most striking addition was the proliferation of children walking to or from school in British-style uniforms. In 1990, as Mongolia was beginning its transition to a parliamentary democracy, many men and women wore the traditional *deel* and belt costume. That is now much rarer on the streets of the capital, although the occasional *deel* could still be seen, usually worn by someone of the older generation, or visitors from the grasslands. Some citizens of the capital don traditional dress on formal occasions, such as the visit of the speaker of the Canadian parliament in September 2016 which gave parliamentary deputies and others the opportunity to appear for photographs in Sükhbaatar Square dressed in traditional costume and wearing their medals and other badges and sashes of honour. The poorest segment of the population, the beggars and pickpockets, as always wear what they can.[12]

Built environment of the capital

From the opening of the twentieth century, modern buildings in styles previously unknown in Mongolia began to appear in Ulaanbaatar. Initially these were built to house foreign businesses and the residences of their managers. Some of these were eventually converted for use by Mongol institutions. Western architects were brought in to create the new buildings. A German architect, Kavel Maher, designed a State Printing House and a Hungarian, Joseph Gelet, was responsible for the headquarters of the State Electrification Board. Gelet also designed the Central Theatre, Mongolia's first national theatre, which was set in the northern part of the then city square. He had won a competition by producing plans for a theatre in the shape of a traditional *ger*: a cupola with windows was added to the roof and boxes and seats were attached in two tiers and could seat 800 people. The entire construction was of timber, and when there was a fire the building was burned down completely.

Native building firms began to emerge in the 1920s and they were incorporated into the State Building Trust and a Planning Office was created. Among the achievements of this period were modern roads and a brick works to provide the materials for construction. Little attention was paid to Mongolian styles or aesthetics, and buildings such as the State Bank and the Central Broadcasting Authority were representative of entirely European architectural styles. The 1940s was a boom period for building in Ulaanbaatar and the Ministry of Foreign Affairs and State University were designed by Soviet architects in those years. These and other buildings were influenced by classical European building conventions; features such as Ionic and Corinthian capitals and columns were widely used in the architecture of public buildings. The style of these buildings was disliked by many local residents who resented the changes to what had been the quintessentially Mongolian and Asiatic appearance of their city.

In 1953 a group of Soviet and Mongolian architects began work on a comprehensive plan for the development of the capital over the next twenty years. The planners envisaged a system of ring roads with four main interconnecting roads and a division into a series of linked micro regions. The plan took into account environmental factors including the deep winter frosts and the great oscillation of temperatures that affected Ulaanbaatar, and included provision for water supply, central heating, electricity, and radio and telephone networks.

As Soviet aid and influence grew, so did the number of buildings in a European – or more specifically Russian – fashion. Mongolian students travelled to the USSR for their professional and technical education in architecture and construction techniques, among other subjects. When work began on the Ulaanbaatar plan towards the end of the 1950s these new national specialists made a major contribution, but they continued working in the European style. The most influential of this generation of Mongolian architects was B. Chimid who worked on the overall city plan and created the Union of Mongolian Architects. His best-known building designs are for the mausoleum of Sükhbaatar and Choibalsan, the Central Council of Trades Unions, and the Drama Theatre. The Ulaanbaatar Hotel, for many years the most desirable accommodation for visitors to the capital, was built in 1961 according to designs produced by Chimid and his wife: that building did incorporate some traditional Mongolian features.

To the regret of many Mongolians today, Soviet styles of town planning and infrastructure development became the only acceptable models. By the end of the 1950s, the central Sükhbaatar Square in Ulaanbaatar was surrounded by monumental constructions that echoed the styles of contemporary buildings in the Soviet Union. Construction on these lines continued throughout the 1970s and 1980s; there was very little attempt to create buildings that included any elements of traditional Mongolian design.

It should be remembered that Stalinist era constructions were not the only Russian influence on the built environment of Ulaanbaatar. One notable Russian-style building predates both the Soviet Union and Mongolia's 1924 revolution. In July and August 1921 during the revolt of the herdsmen, Sükhbaatar's military headquarters was in a building that had originally been constructed in 1914 for a Russian merchant. It is now the Museum of Ulaanbaatar's History and stands on the south side of Peace Avenue close to the centre of the city.

Most buildings in Ulaanbaatar are of a more modest design and for the majority of its citizens, home is in one of many blocks of flats, built on a

Soviet or Eastern European model and of fairly austere appearance. These blocks are built in brick or concrete and often have a white-tiled facing. Not all the residents of the capital lived in such modern buildings. As has been observed previously, in Ulaanbaatar, even in the second decade of the twenty-first century, it is still possible to come across isolated *gers* in the city centre, usually behind a wall: more obviously, on the outskirts of the capital, there are extensive compounds where rows of *gers* set behind wooden stockades house the poorer, or more old-fashioned section, of the population. These *ger* communities have evolved for practical reasons but they are a symbol of Mongolia's past in its present and a tangible bridge between traditional and modern housing and lifestyles.

Soviet-inspired buildings are not all dull blocks of the 1950s but, since the Mongolian democratic revolution of 1990–1, Ulaanbaatar has consciously abandoned this style and has embraced new architectural models, often from the West but also drawing on modern designs from its Asian neighbours. The most dramatic is the Blue Sky Tower which provides offices, luxury flats and hotel accommodation with 200 rooms and 12 suites. It was designed in cooperation with a South Korean company and was completed in 2009: with 25 stories and at 105 metres high it was the tallest building in the capital, until even taller hotels appeared during the construction boom that began in 2007. The Blue Sky building towers over central Ulaanbaatar and dominates the skyline when viewed from many different parts of the city. It is made of steel and glass in a distinctive shape that is reminiscent of a sail or a fin: the name reflects its curtain wall of blue glass. The colour is supposed to remind Mongols of the characteristic clear blue skies of which they are so proud, but there is nothing typically Mongolian about the shape of the building. If it is a symbol of anything, it is of the international elite and their Mongolian partners. As the development of Ulaanbaatar continues, new hotels, high-rise apartment blocks, shopping arcades and leisure and office complexes combine to give the capital a livelier and more international appearance.[13]

Sükhbaatar Square and the battle of two names

The greatest transformation of Ulaanbaatar resulted from the construction of Sükhbaatar Square which began in 1946; it was designed as the focus of the Mongolian-Soviet vision for the town and the centrepiece of the capital of the MPR. In spite of the political and physical transformation that has taken place in the wake of the democratic revolution of 1990, it remains the central feature of the city. The statue of the revolutionary hero, Sükhbaatar, on horseback still has pride of place in the centre of the square: dignitaries and tourists alike gather round to be photographed alongside it. To the north of the square is the Government Palace complex; it was formerly the seat of the People's Great Khural (*Ardyn Ikh Khural*), the Mongolian equivalent to Moscow's Supreme Soviet, and is now home to the State Great Khural (*Ulsyn Ikh Khural*) Mongolia's reformed single-chamber parliament, and the offices of the president and prime minister. In spite of the innovative and even alien architecture around the square, this development was not a complete break with the area's history. The modern government buildings occupy the site on which previously stood the Ikh Khüree, the Great Palace-Temple that was the source of both secular and religious authority and which gave the city one of its names before 1924. The temple had its own wide open space, surrounded by smaller temples and other buildings for the Buddhist clergy and aristocrats, and this open space is preserved with the present square. The centre of power remains the same, even if those who exercise that power and the physical form in which that power is represented have changed.[14]

The entire temple complex was destroyed during the anti-religious campaigns of the 1930s: photographs of the open space from the 1920s and 1930s show it being used for political demonstrations and by groups of cyclists. It remained unpaved for some time, even after the installation of the Sükhbaatar monument in 1946.

A mausoleum for the remains of Sükhbaatar (transferred from his original resting place in Ulaanbaatar's Altan Olgii cemetery) and his successor Choibalsan was built in 1954, after the death of the latter. It bore an uncanny, but perhaps not surprising, resemblance to the Lenin Mausoleum in Moscow and was added to the front of the main government building. In 2005 the remains of the two former leaders were removed from the mausoleum, their ashes were reburied in the Altan Olgii cemetery and the mausoleum was demolished. It was replaced by a monument to Chinggis Khan which is still in place.

Since the new regime came into power in 1990 there have been arguments – often acrimonious – over the name of the square and these offer a vivid illustration of the predicament faced by the new political elite in coming to terms with Mongolia's modern history and even its mediaeval antecedents. On Monday 15 July 2013 there was a meeting of the Capital City Citizens' Delegates' Khural (the city council and one of the successors to the Khurals of People's Deputies that were replaced by the 1992 constitution). The head of the Ulaanbaatar City Governor's office, Yo. Gerelchuluun, who had a constitutional veto over the Khural, introduced a draft resolution to change the names of several streets and squares in Ulaanbaatar city. The majority of members of the Khural agreed that Sükhbaatar Square should be renamed after Chinggis Khan 'whose name has travelled 800 years from the founding of the Great Mongol Empire and is now every Mongolian's pride and idol'. In support of this measure there had been representations from 'scientific institutes, researchers, civilians and NGOs', and a decision was made that the name of the square should be changed but that the statue of the hero of the Mongolian People's Revolution, Sükhbaatar, should remain. Although the name was officially changed, the decision was not popular. In September 2016, after a legal action by descendants of Sükhbaatar, the decision was reversed and it reverted to its former name of Sükhbaatar Square, which in any case most of the inhabitants of Ulaanbaatar had continued to use.[15]

The mausoleum of Sükhbaatar and Choibalsan may have gone from the front of the government buildings to be replaced by a statue of Chinggis Khan, but Sükhbaatar on horseback still dominates the centre of the square. On the eastern side the National Academic Theatre of Opera and Ballet, built in 1963 in a neoclassical style still stands out with its salmon pink walls and white columns. The style and the colour scheme of the National Academic Drama Theatre, which is some distance from the square to the south of Peace Avenue, are similar but the outside walls are in a striking darker pink or red.

In the past Sükhbaatar Square was usually free from crowds and traffic, apart from ceremonial state occasions when it could be filled with uniformed troops or schoolchildren doing gymnastics or displays of marching in front of the presiding leadership and admiring crowds. Today, although the square is still used for ceremonial occasions, for most of the time the atmosphere is less formal. Visitors, both foreign and local, gather casually in the square and Sükhbaatar's statue has become a popular meeting place. The southern part of the square is also used as a market for food, drinks, watches, clothes and a variety of other products that are sold from stalls housed in rows of small white tents with Mongolian style pointed tops. Taxis can park at this end of the square, although officially registered vehicles are few and far between which leaves opportunities for enterprising private car owners to earn extra money.

The buildings on the western side of the square have a relatively modern appearance, although all were built during the period of greatest Soviet influence. The building which is now occupied by the National Museum of Mongolian History was built in 1971: it houses an important collection of artefacts which is now the basis of an ongoing reassessment of Mongolian history and ethnographic studies. Banks and office buildings to the south of the museum maintain an austere facade, but the ground floors and basements of some of the buildings have been turned into cafés or bar-restaurants which serve the growing Mongolian middle class and international business people and tourists. The Mongolian Stock Exchange was once a children's cinema and was completely refurbished when the stock exchange was created at the beginning of 1991. Originally painted in pink and white, it was later redecorated in a more sedate grey. The distinctly Soviet-style main post office is just around the corner.

Ulaanbaatar: A tale of two monasteries

The Soviet influence on Ulaanbaatar was entirely secular, in line with the atheism of Stalinist Russia. In the early years it was consciously, and militantly, anti-religious and emphasized projects sponsored by the state and ideas considered by Moscow to be progressive. These views were embraced enthusiastically by the most radical elements in the Mongolian People's Revolutionary Party (MPRP) and during the Choibalsan era, which coincided closely with Stalin's rule in the Soviet Union, this enthusiasm led to political excesses and human rights abuses on an appalling scale. The most brutal of the campaigns were those against religious institutions and personages. Most monasteries and temples were closed during the anti-religious campaigns of the 1930s, even if they were not demolished, but some remained and there was an immediate revival of interest in Tibetan Buddhism after the democratic revolution of 1990. The fate of two of these monasteries in Ulaanbaatar offers an insight into changing attitudes towards religion in Mongolia.

Gandan monastery

The Gandan monastery in the north-west of Ulaanbaatar was built between 1834 and 1838 and was named Gandan after the Dga'ldan monastery outside Lhasa in Tibet that had been founded in 1409 by the monk Tsongkhapa, the originator of the Gelugpa tradition of Tibetan Buddhism which most Mongolians follow. Its full name is Gandantegchinling, although the abbreviated form of Gandan is more commonly used. It survived the religious destruction of the 1930s although it was closed in 1938. It reopened in 1944, partly so that it could be visited by Vice President Henry Wallace of the United States; cynics viewed it as simply a token Buddhist institution, retained to persuade foreigners that the government was not entirely anti-religious. In his 1968 handbook on Mongolia, Alan Sanders listed it under 'places of architectural interest' and noted that 'the last lamas in the country [were] concentrated in Gandan in Ulaanbaatar (82 in 1966)' where they were able to observe limited rituals but also preserved and maintained a library of precious Buddhist manuscripts.[16] Other religious buildings could be found throughout Mongolia but many were either in ruins or needed comprehensive restoration. Gandan remained the only functioning Buddhist monastery in Mongolia until 1990 when the end of the old regime saw a sudden and unprecedented enthusiasm for the revival of Buddhist rituals.

In 1990, following the relaxation of restrictions on spiritual activity, the Gandan monastery was the initial focus of anyone who wanted to exercise their new religious liberties. Older men and women wearing *deel* robes with coloured sashes queued to turn the rows of prayer wheels outside one of the temples, accompanied by a small group of boys in the robes of novice monks. Inside the temples it could be seen that almost all the lamas were elderly and many of them appeared to be ailing or undernourished; there were a few trainees of between the ages of 10 and 14. A photograph of the Dalai Lama hung on the wall and there was a pervasive smell of the butter used for offerings. During breaks in the service the monks were fed a simple meal of rice which was ladled into their bowls from a large metal pan. Other food was distributed by teenage lamas who did not hesitate to use their elbows to clear away any onlookers who might hinder their progress.

By the autumn of 2016 the Gandan complex was almost unrecognizable to anyone who had visited it in 1990. The existing temples were still in place, although they had been renovated, but the monastic estate had been greatly extended with new study and office buildings. More significantly the temples were being used actively for prayer and other ceremonies which embraced the full range of rituals, including chanting from the Tibetan scriptures to the accompaniment of the beating of gongs, cymbals and drums and the blowing of conch-shell trumpets. Three temples are available for worship and are used on a regular basis. Offerings of food and drink are brought in from outside the temple and distributed to the monks, of whom there are more than four hundred: the ceremonies, which are popular with foreign tourists, are regularly attended by local people who sit in benches provided along the walls of the temples.

The most important symbol of the Gandan temple is the 25-metre-tall Magjid Janraisig statue which was in the temple of the same name: it was damaged and moved away to the Soviet Union during the religious suppression of the 1930s. Janraisig is the Mongolian name for the Bodhisattva of Compassion, who is called Chenrezig in Tibetan, Guanyin in Chinese and Avalokitesvara in Sanskrit. The statue was erected in 1912 on the instructions of the Bogd Khan, the Jebtsundamba Khutukhtu, to celebrate Mongolia's freedom from Chinese control. A programme to restore the statue and a fundraising drive were launched in 1991, with the support of the Mongolian president, and its restoration began in 1996. The statue is now completely enclosed in the restored Magjid Janraisig building at the northern end of the

Gandan complex. The rest of the complex consists of the Zanabazar Buddhist University which attracts foreign as well as Mongolian students: it comprises six colleges for the education and training of Buddhist monks; a great assembly hall; and the Gandan Library, which collects, preserves and studies a major collection of Buddhist texts written and compiled in Mongolia, Tibet and India.[17]

Choijin Lama Temple

Another Buddhist place of worship, the Choijin Lama Temple is close to the centre of Ulaanbaatar. It lies to the south of Sükhbaatar Square and the main road that is now called Peace Avenue. It is one of the few remaining traditionally styled buildings in the capital and it sits incongruously just below the most modern, the Blue Sky Tower, and across the road from a smart contemporary café favoured by overseas business people and diplomats. In 1990 it was still surrounded by open fields and, although the site has been preserved and developed, the buildings are still in need of attention and the grounds are not well kept. It attracts fewer visitors than the Winter Palace of the Bogd Khan

The buildings on the Choijin Lama site are not of any great antiquity as they were built for the State Oracle Lama, Luvsankhaidav and his wife by his older brother, the eighth incarnation of the Jebtsundamba Khutkhtu, the Bogd Khan who was last traditional ruler of Mongolia. It is a complex of six temples and was built between 1904 and 1908. It functioned as a monastery until 1937 when it was closed at the high point of the campaign against religion but, instead of being destroyed which was the fate of most monasteries and temples, it was preserved as a museum of religion, the justification for the leadership of the MPRP being that it would serve to educate people about the iniquities of Mongolia's feudal past. The temples were used for prayer and other Buddhist ceremonies and Luvsankhaidav used the open central space between them for his oracular rituals which were carried out in a trance.

Today the monastery retains the atmosphere of a set of temples around a sacred space, but it is now a museum which preserves and displays an extraordinary collection of art works, mainly bronze sculptures which date from the nineteenth century. However, among this collection are, in the words of the director of the museum, D. Otgonuren, 'seventeen unique and inimitable holy objects, jewels among the marvellous artworks produced by Undur Gegeen Zanabazar or his school'. As has been noted in Chapter 1, the seventeenth-century master sculptor, Zanabazar (1635–1723), was also the first incarnation of the Jedtsundamba Khutukhtu; the museum's catalogue of these seventeen sculptures was produced in 2015 to commemorate the three hundred and eightieth anniversary of his birth. The sculptures, exquisite pieces of great technical achievement, are all representative of Buddhist themes or were used for religious rituals. They illustrate the influence of Indian and Tibetan Buddhist art on the Mongolians and also the overlap between shamanic and Buddhist practices. For many Mongolians there is an unbroken link, through the principle of reincarnation, between Zanabazar and the last pre-Communist regime of the Eight Jebtsundamba, the Bogd Khan; this historical connection assumed even greater importance with the revival of Buddhist practice after 1990. In the Palace of the Bogd Khan in the southwest of the city there is also a parallel, more secular link with the pre-Communist past of Ulaanbaatar.[18]

Ulaanbaatar in transition

Many of the blocks of flats built in the Soviet period remain in use; even by 1990 they appeared in attractive whites and browns rather than the uniform grey that is sometimes imagined. Newer living accommodation in a variety of colours has created a more varied skyline but viewed from the top floor of the old State Department Store it is still possible to see *ger*-like structures on the flat roofs of several recent buildings. Developers, especially of hotels, have competed to construct the tallest structure in the capital but, although it is no longer the tallest, the Blue Sky Hotel and Tower just to the south of Sükhbaatar Square still commands more attention than any of its competitors both for its location and its distinctive style.

The Somang Plaza, a Korean-backed enterprise on Peace Avenue and close to the Blue Sky Tower, is a fashionable retail and restaurant complex. It is a rectangular construction of brick and glass and makes no concession to Mongolian artistic styles. Korean investment in Mongolia is growing: the popular Seoul Restaurant, which advertises on billboards across the city, is one of many Korean eating places. On a more modest level, there is a small shopping complex close to the Bogd Khan Winter Palace in the south of the city that has been built with Korean money and looks exactly like shopping complexes the world over. Among other shops, this modern grey and glass construction is home to a branch of the Korean coffee house chain, 'Tom n Toms': the interior is immediately familiar to anyone who has frequented similar coffee houses anywhere in the developed world. A short distance down the road is the local Hyundai concession where those who wish to buy Korean cars can contribute to the ever-growing traffic jams in the city. In striking contrast, just outside the car showroom, stands a set of sculptures;

a dozen or so larger than life figures. They depict one of the camel caravans that would have crossed the Gobi to and from Ulaanbaatar in years gone by, complete with camels loaded with packs, traders on horseback and their dogs.

Development continues in Ulaanbaatar and buildings in some zones are being demolished to make way for new construction. At the time of writing the sprawling Narantuul Market in the southeast of the city still supplied household essentials and an impressive range of second-hand items to thousands of Ulaanbaatar's citizens. Much of that area is scheduled for redevelopment and on the road from the city centre to the market there are already modern shopping centres, not to mention the ubiquitous Irish pub.

Contemporary Chinggis cult

Although Sükhbaatar Square has successfully shrugged off the attempt to rename it Chinggis Khan Square, the statue of the great khan still dominates the front of the government buildings at the north end of the square. Mongolians have long honoured Chinggis Khan as a founding ancestor, even during the period when the government was run by the MPRP and the country was a satellite of the Soviet Union. In 1962, for example, Mongol Post issued a set of stamps to commemorate the eight-hundredth anniversary of his birth in 1162. The four stamps depict Chinggis Khan and artefacts associated with his military campaigns. Unusually for Mongolian stamps of that period, the inscriptions are in traditional Mongol script in addition to Cyrillic which was the only script normally used. This commemoration provoked splenetic criticism from Moscow for its emphasis on Mongolian nationalism rather than socialist internationalism, but the point was made.

Since the fall of the Soviet Union the spirit of Chinggis Khan has been more actively recruited to play a new role as a symbol of unification and Mongolness; celebrating his legacy conveys a sense of belonging to *Mongolchuud* the Mongols. National Pride day, the birthday of Chinggis Khan, is celebrated on the first day of winter in the traditional Mongolian calendar. In 2016 this fell on Monday, 31 October. For the holiday period there was a ban on the sale of alcoholic beverages (although there is no evidence to indicate that either Chinggis Khan or most contemporary Mongols would have considered this to be appropriate) and most markets remained closed. Although railway stations and airports operated according to their normal schedules, checkpoints at the border with China were closed but normal restrictions on driving according to the number plate of the car were temporarily lifted.

More in a holiday mood was the national wrestling tournament held at the Palace of Wrestling at the Bayanzurkh end of Peace Avenue next door to the Ulaanbaatar City Museum. This brought together over a hundred champion wrestlers at province and state level to compete for the national championship in a sport that is recognized as an important symbol of traditional Mongolian culture. Mongolian wrestling is one of the regular features of traditional *naadam* festivals, together with horse racing and archery.

During the same celebrations a tour company organized a Chinggis Festival at the Chinggis Khan Statue Complex on the banks of the Tuul River some 30 miles to the east of the capital. Participants were offered a tour of the complex; visits to the Mongolian Empire Museum; an exhibition of traditional Mongolian calligraphy in the 'script of the eternal sky' that was replaced in the 1940s by the Cyrillic script, but which nationalists and traditionalists are trying to revive; and performances of historical dramas on the life of Chinggis Khan. Anyone named Chinggis or Temujin (Chinggis Khan's original name) was entitled to free entry into these tours and exhibitions.[19]

Negotiating new regional and international roles

Mongolia's 'satellite' status ended abruptly in 1990. For decades, even though Ulaanbaatar did not slavishly copy every aspect of Soviet life and there were many conflicts, the Mongolian leadership was by and large prepared to synchronize its thinking and actions with the prevailing political trends in Moscow. That could be judged as either a straitjacket or a comfort blanket, but when the relationship came to an end it was by no means obvious what direction Mongolia would follow. The traditional conundrum of how the country was to achieve a balance between the conflicting demands of relations with Russia and China re-emerged, although the governments of Russia and China that Ulaanbaatar had to deal with after 1990 were very different than their previous manifestations.

Russia was still of considerable consequence in international terms, but its economy and political authority were at least temporarily in decline and it had withdrawn from many of its previous commitments beyond the borders of the new Russian Federation. China was Mongolia's principal historical antagonist and was still perceived as a potential threat to its sovereignty. By contrast with Russia, however, China was unquestionably in the ascendant. The 'reform and opening' policies of Deng Xiaoping were bearing fruit and the Chinese state was beginning to amass the quantity of capital that would eventually allow it to invest heavily in other countries. Mongolia after 1990 desperately needed capital: China was the obvious source, but financial support naturally came with political strings attached and Mongolians found it difficult to trust the intentions of the Chinese Communist Party (CCP). This relationship was not made any easier by the increased authoritarianism and nationalism of the People's Republic of China (PRC) government under Xi Jinping following his accession to power in 2012. The Mongolian solution was to accept the need for investment and other economic benefits from China while adopting a 'third neighbour' approach to broaden its commercial and financial links with other countries in the region, in particular Japan and South Korea.

International and pan-Asian influences

Diplomatic and economic connections with other countries are not saddled with quite the same historical and political baggage as those with either Russia or China. However even these less intimidating relationships come at some cost to the essential 'Mongolness' that is so important to Mongolians. The Mongolian characteristics of dress, urban construction and many other features of everyday life were under pressure from the Soviet Union for decades. Many Mongolian national and ethnic symbols were discouraged during the period of Soviet domination but , although they may have been overlaid with symbols of a universal 'socialist' culture, they were never completely erased. These traditional symbols, drawn from the history and legends of the Mongols and the life of Chinggis Khan – the only Mongol whose name is known over almost the entire world – were still available in both memory and material objects and could be revived.

One of Mongolia's fundamental challenges in the twenty-first century is to retain or rediscover national styles while embracing modernity, but resisting the seductive modernisms of the West or, more immediately, of its near Asian neighbours, Korea and Japan. The modern, clean lines of Korean restaurants and cafés are attractive, especially to young professional Mongols, just as they are in China and other neighbouring countries. It remains to be seen whether the international coffee and fast food culture poses a genuine threat to traditional cuisines. Western-style clothing, especially of the casual variety, has effectively replaced the *deel* gown for everyday wear, especially for the younger generation in the cities, but that merely continues a process that began during the Soviet period. The *deel* with sash and other accoutrements is still favoured for ceremonial and other formal occasions, but to wear it in everyday life is normally a sign of poverty or rural backwardness.

The one feature of Mongolian life and culture that does not appear to be at all threatened by these dramatic changes is the language. Spoken Mongolian thrives and most Mongols, even in the capital, are monoglot speakers of Mongolian. The language is no more threatened by English in the twenty-first century than it was by Chinese in the early twentieth. Mongols of the older generation retain the Russian that they learned in school, or when studying in the USSR, but English is gradually becoming the preferred foreign language, although there is a strong case for young Mongols to learn Japanese or Korean for commercial and cultural reasons. These new linguistic realities suggest how Mongolia's distinctive culture is likely to survive in a future of intricate regional and international relationships.

Mongolia must necessarily maintain relationships with both Russia and China. Although in economic terms this relationship will be heavily weighted towards China for the foreseeable future, it will become more balanced if the Russian economy improves. Mongolia must also cement relationships with its neighbours, Japan and South Korea, relations which currently work well in terms of trade and investment but will have to be deepened politically and diplomatically. Relationships with North Korea are more problematic, but if Pyongyang ever agrees to open its economy more fully, Mongolia is in a position to take advantage of its existing links with South Korea and its position as a former 'socialist' country to contribute to that opening. The Mongolians aspire to a new role as a permanently neutral country that can act as an intermediary and an honest broker in a complex and troubled region. While they have not yet achieved this ambition, it is surely within their grasp.

Notes

Preface and Acknowledgements

1 The most comprehensive account of Lattimore's life and career is Robert P. Newman, *Owen Lattimore and the 'Loss' of China* (Berkeley: University of California Press, 1992).

Introduction

1 E. D. Phillips, *The Mongols* (London: Thames and Hudson, 1969), pp. 139–44 and *passim*; David Morgan, *The Mongols* (London: Blackwell, 1986), pp. 199–206 and *passim*.
2 J. Boldbaatar. 'The State and Trends of Mongolian Historical Studies', *The Newsletter*, No. 70 (Spring 2015), International Institute for Asian Studies https://iias.asia/sites/default/files/IIAS_NL70_28.pdf.
3 Data from Mongolian Office of National Statistics http://1212.mn/stat.aspx?LIST_ID=976_L03, accessed 21/2/2019.
4 *Montsame Mongolian News Agency*, 29 December 2015; Urgungge Onon (translator and with an introduction), *Chinggis Khan: The Golden History of the Mongols* (London: Folio Society, 1993), p.1.
5 Owen Lattimore, *Nomads and Commissars: Mongolia Revisited* (New York: Oxford University Press, 1962), p. 7; Lattimore recorded interviews, University of Leeds April 1976; Baabar (Bat-Erdeniin Batbayar – edited by C. Kaplonski) *History of Mongolia: From World Power to Soviet Satellite* (Cambridge: White Horse Press, 1999), pp. 399–402.
6 Lattimore, *Nomads and Commissars*, p. iv; *Mongol Journeys* (London: Travel Book Club, 1942); *The Mongols of Manchuria* (London: Allen and Unwin, 1935).
7 Royal Institute of International Affairs, Chatham House, London, 3 May 2015.

1 Mongolia and the Mongols: Land, people and traditions

1 Nicholas N. Poppe, *Buryat Grammar* (Bloomington, Indiana: Mouton and Co, 1960), pp. 1–3.
2 Lattimore, *Nomads and Commissars*, pp. 9–10.

3 Norman Howard-Jones, 'On the Diagnostic Term "Down's Disease"', *Medical History*, Vol. 23, No. 1 (1979): 102-4.
4 Charles R. Bawden, *The Modern History of Mongolia* (London: Weidenfeld and Nicolson 1968), p. xiii.
5 Nicholas Poppe, *Grammar of Written Mongolian* (Wiesbaden: Harrassowitz, 1991), pp. 1-7; Nicholas Poppe, *Buryat Grammar*, pp. 1-3; Jacques Legrand, *Parlons Mongol* (Paris: L'Harmattan, 1997), pp. 29-30; interviews by author with Mongol language specialists, Göttingen, September 2014. Poppe had an extraordinary career, having fled the Soviet Union at the start of the Second World War, he worked with German army units and then in a research institute closely associated with the SS, before settling at the University of Washington. Although his associations with the Nazis raised eyebrows, there is no doubt about his status as the outstanding Western Mongol linguist of his generation.
6 Morgan, *The Mongols*, pp. 16-23.
7 Morgan, *The Mongols*, pp. 55-83.
8 John D. Langlois, Jr (ed.), *China under Mongol Rule* (Princeton: Princeton University Press, 1981).
9 Lattimore, *Mongol Journeys*, pp. 34-8, 39-60; Ferdinand D. Lessing, *Mongolian-English Dictionary* (London: Routledge, 2015), p. 336; Sechin Jagchid and Paul Hyer, *Mongolia's Culture and Society* (Boulder, CO: Westview Press, 1979), pp. 108-9, 118, 170; Shaman Byampadorj Dondog, *Reflections of a Mongolian Shaman* (Kathmandu: Vajra Books, 2014), pp. 22-3.
10 Bawden, *Modern History of Mongolia*, p. xiii.
11 Owen Lattimore, *Nationalism and Revolution in Mongolia* (Leiden: E. J. Brill, 1955), pp. 6-21.
12 Jagchid and Hyer, *Mongolia's Culture and Society*, pp. 19-72, 73-162, 297-310; Lattimore, *Nomads and Commissars*, pp. 16-17.
13 Jagchid and Hyer, *Mongolia's Culture and Society*, pp. 19-72.
14 Jagchid and Hyer, *Mongolia's Culture and Society* 979, pp. 22-3; Ayalagu 'Preliminary survey of keiymori in Ordos' in Johannes Reckel (ed.) *Central Asian Sources and Central Asian Research*. Göttinger Bibliotheksschriften, Band 39 (Göttingen: Universitätsverlag, 2016). pp. 17-41.
15 Observations by the author in Ulaanbaatar, 1990.
16 Lattimore, *Nomads and Commissars*, pp. 4-6.
17 Christopher Kaplonski, *The Lama Question: Violence Sovereignty and Exception in Early Socialist Mongolia* (Honolulu: University of Hawai'i Press, 2014), p. 4 and *passim*.
18 Jagchid and Hyer, *Mongolia's Culture and Society*, p. 299.
19 Jagchid and Hyer, *Mongolia's Culture and Society*, pp. 175-88; Lattimore *Nomads and Commissars*, p. 5.
20 Bawden, *Modern History of Mongolia*, p. xiii.
21 Lattimore, *Nomads and Commissars*, p. 5; *Mongol Journeys*, pp. 270-1, 277-8.

22 Lattimore, *Mongol Journeys*, p. 271.
23 Lattimore, *Nomads and Commissars*, p. 65.
24 Observations by author, September 2016.
25 Giuseppe Tucci, *The Religions of Tibet* (Bombay: Allied Publishers, 1970), p. 241.
26 Gombojab Hangin with John R. Krueger and Paul D. Buell, William V. Rozycki, Robert G. Service, *A Modern Mongolian Dictionary* (Bloomington: Indian University Research Institute for Inner Asian Studies, 1986), p. 75.
27 Jagchid and Hyer, *Mongolia's Culture and Society*, pp. 163–75; Jan Fontein, *The Dancing Demons of Mongolia* (Amsterdam: V&K, 1999), pp. 24–31; Dondog, *Reflections of a Mongolian Shaman*, pp. 1–23; Otgony Purev and Gurbadaryn Purvee, *Mongolian Shamanism* (Ulaanbaatar: Munkhiin Useg, 2006), pp. 64–8, 134–47 and *passim*; Tucci *The Religions of Tibet*, pp. 241–2 and *passim*; Matthew T. Kapstein, *The Tibetans* (Oxford: Blackwell, 2006), pp. 45–50; Jagchid and Hyer, *Mongolia's Culture and Society*, pp. 163–75.
28 Tarab Tulku, *A Brief History of Academic Degrees in Buddhist Philosophy* (Copenhagen: NIAS, 2000), pp. 18–24; Li Yao, 'Lamas Dance with the "Devil" at Beijing Temple', *China Daily*, 12 March 2013; Jagchid and Hyer, *Mongolia's Culture and Society*, pp. 126–30, 242, 378.
29 Paul Hyer and Sechin Jagchid, *A Mongolian Living Buddha: Biography of the Kanjurwa Khutughtu* (New York: State University of New York Press, 1984), pp. 58–9.
30 Morgan, *The Mongols*, pp. 16–23.
31 Jutta Frings (ed.), *Dschingis Khan und Seine Erben: Das Weltreich der Mongolen* (Munich: Hirmer Verlag, 2005), pp. 108–21.
32 Jagchid and Hyer, *Mongolia's Culture and Society*, pp. 219, 238; Craig Clunas, 'The Preface to Nigen Dabqur Asar and Their Chinese Antecedents', *Zentralasiatische Studien*, Vol. 14, No 1, (1981): 139–94.
33 Sonomin Lochin, *Tsendiin Damdinsüren* (Ulaanbaatar: Nepko Publishing, 2015), pp. 28–33, 317–38, 339–41 and *passim*; A. Munkhzul, 'Scholars share views on works of Ts. Damdinsuren', *Montsame Mongolian News Agency*, 22 October 2018.
34 Frings *Dschingis Khan*, pp. 411–12.
35 N. Tsultem, *Mongolian Architecture* (Ulaanbaatar: State Publishing House, 1988) (pages not numbered); Frings, *Dschingis Khan*, pp. 126–95.
36 Tsultem, *Mongolian Architecture* (pages not numbered).
37 Frings, *Dschingis Khan*, pp. 357–79.
38 Baabar (B. Batbayar – edited by C. Kaplonski), *History of Mongolia: From World Power to Soviet Satellite* (Cambridge: White Horse Press, 1999), pp. 72, 82–3.
39 Fontein, *The Dancing Demons of Mongolia*, p. 70.
40 D. Otgonsuren, *Öndör Gegeen Zanabazarin Khostui Unet Byytelyyd* (*Masterpieces of Undur Gegeen Zanabazar*) (Ulaanbaatar: Chojin Lama

Museum, 2015; J. Saruulbuyan (ed.), *National Museum of Mongolia* (Ulaanbaaar: National Museum of Mongolia, 2009), pp. 140–51; Frings, *Dschingis Khan*, pp. 359–79.
41 Baabar, *History of Mongolia*, pp. 72, 82–3; Jagchid and Hyer, pp. 184–5, 232; Otgonsuren, *Masterpieces of Undur Gegeen Zanabazar*; Bayasgalan Bayanbat, *Ulaanbaatar Then and Now: Amazing Images of Ulaanbaatar's History* (Ulaanbaatar: Monosound and Vision, 2013), p. 97; Fontein, *The Dancing Demons of Mongolia*, pp. 70–89. Some works of Zanzabar and his school were included in 'De Dansende Demonen van Mongolie (The Dancing Demons of Mongolia)', an exhibition at De Nieuwe Kerk, Dam, Amsterdam between June and October, 1999, which the present author was fortunate to be able to attend.

2 Revolutionary Mongolia in the early twentieth century

1 Christopher Kaplonski, 'Introduction', in David Sneath and Christopher Kaplonski (eds), *The History of Mongolia*, Vol. III (Folkestone: Global Oriental, 2010), pp. 851–59.
2 Thomas E. Ewing, *Between the Hammer and the Anvil? Chinese and Russian Policies in Outer Mongolia 1911–1921* (Bloomington: Indiana University, 1980), p. 32.
3 A. M. Pozdneyev, 'Mongolia and the Mongols, Presenting the Results of a Trip Taken in 1892 and 1893', excerpts from chapter 2, reprinted in Sneath and Kaplonski *The History of Mongolia*, Volume III, pp. 794–824.
4 Frans August Larson, 'The Lamas of Mongolia', *Atlantic Monthly*, No. 145 (1930): 368–78, reprinted in Sneath and Kaplonski, *The History of Mongolia* Volume III, pp. 878–88.
5 Lattimore, *Nomads and Commissars*, p. 53
6 Lattimore, *Nomads and Commissars*, p. 93; Ewing, *Between the Hammer and the Anvil*, pp. 34–43.
7 Ewing, *Between the Hammer and the Anvil*, p. 37.
8 Batsaikhan Emgent Ookhnoi, *The Bogdo Jebtsundamba Khutuktu: The Last Emperor of Mongolia, the Life and Legends* (Ulaanbaatar: Munkhiin Useg Publishing, 2016), pp. 2–54; Lkhamsurengiin Dendev, *Mongolyn tobch tyyh* (A Brief History of Mongolia) (Ulaanbaatar: Monsudar, 2012), p. 12.
9 Lattimore, *Nationalism and Revolution*, p. 49.
10 Ookhnoi, *The Bogdo Jebtsundamba Khutuktu*, pp. 2–54; Lattimore, *Nationalism and Revolution*, pp. 53–4.
11 The painting is reproduced in Frings, *Dschingis Khan*, pp. 396–7.
12 D. Altannavch, *Bogd Khan Palace Museum: A Brief Guide* (Ulaanbaatar: Interpress, 2001); D. Myagmardorj, *The Guide Book of Bogd Khan Palace Museum* [in Mongolian, Russian and English]

(Ulaanbaatar, n.p., n.d.); Ookhnoi, *The Bogdo Jebtsundamba Khutuktu*. Other observations by the author in 2016.
13 Sir Charles Bell, *Tibet: Past and Present* 2nd edn. (London: Oxford University Press, 1927), pp. 65, 68.
14 Melvyn C. Goldstein, *The Snow Lion and the Dragon: China, Tibet and the Dalai Lama* (Berkeley: University of California Press, 1991), p. 27.
15 Bell, *Tibet: Past and Present*, pp. 64–72; Goldstein, *The Snow Lion and the Dragon*, pp. 27, 24–9; Hugh M. Richardson, *Tibet and Its History* (Boulder, CO: Shambala, 1984), pp. 82–90; Ookhnoi, *The Bogdo Jebtsundamba Khutuktu*, pp. 62–8; Kaplonski, 'Introduction', p. 851.
16 Lattimore, *Nationalism and Revolution* pp. 3–90; Ewing, *Between the Hammer and the Anvil*, p. 37.
17 Lattimore, *Nomads and Commissars*, pp. 75–91.
18 Lattimore, *Nomads and Commissars*, p. 79.
19 Owen Lattimore, 'Introduction', in Urgunge Onon (ed.), *Mongolian Heroes of the Twentieth Century* (New York: AMS Press, 1976), p. xviii.
20 Kh. Choibalsan, 'A Brief History of the People's Indomitable Hero Magsarjav', in Urgunge Onon (ed.), *Mongolian Heroes of the Twentieth Century* (New York: AMS Press, 1976), pp. 113–14.
21 Kh. Choibalsan, 'A Brief History of the People's Indomitable Hero Magsarjav', pp. 105–14.
22 Kh. Choibalsan 'A Brief History of the People's Indomitable Hero Magsarjav', pp. 105–14; Bawden, *The Modern History of Mongolia*, pp. 195–8, 204–5.

3 Establishing the Mongolian People's Republic: Sükhbaatar and Choibalsan (1921–4)

1 L. Bat-Ochir and D. Dashjamts, 'The Life of Sükhbaatar', in Urgunge Onon (ed.), *Mongolian Heroes of the Twentieth Century* (New York: AMS Press, 1976), pp. 143–92.
2 Baabar, *History of Mongolia*, pp. 101–3; Ochir and Dashjamts, 'The Life of Sükhbaatar', pp. 143–92; Bawden, *Modern History*, pp. 187–201.
3 Ochir and Dashjamts, 'The Life of Sükhbaatar', pp. 143–92.
4 Bawden, *Modern History*, p. 188; Fujiko Isono, 'The Mongolian Revolution of 1921', *Modern Asian Studies*, Vol. 10, No. 3 (1976): 375–94; Ewing *Between the Hammer and the Anvil*, pp. 160–71.
5 Fujiko Isono, 'Soviet Russia and the Mongolian Revolution of 1921', *Past and Present*, Vol. 83, No. 1 (May 1979): 375–94.
6 Isono, 'The Mongolian Revolution of 1921', p. 383.
7 Hiroshi Futaki, 'A Reexamination of the Establishment of the Mongolian People's Party, Centring on Dogsom's Memoir', *Inner Asia*, Vol. 2, No. 1

(2000): 37–61, reprinted in Sneath and Kaplonski, *The History of Mongolia* Volume III, p. 930–50.
8 Alan J. K. Sanders, *Historical Dictionary of Mongolia* (Lanham: Scarecrow Press, 1996), p. 114.
9 Isono, 'The Mongolian Revolution of 1921', pp. 382–6.
10 Isono, 'The Mongolian Revolution of 1921', p. 131.
11 Isono, 'The Mongolian Revolution of 1921', pp. 375–94; Isono, 'Soviet Russia and the Mongolian Revolution of 1921', pp. 116–40; Futaki, 'A Reexamination of the Establishment of the Mongolian People's Party', pp. 37–61, reprinted in Sneath and Kaplonski *The History of Mongolia* Volume III, pp. 930–50.
12 Isono, 'The Mongolian Revolution of 1921', p. 389.
13 Sh. Nachukdorji, *Life of Sukebatur* in Lattimore *Nationalism and Revolution* pp. 91–181.
14 Isono, 'The Mongolian Revolution of 1921', pp. 389–92.
15 Sh. Nachukdorji, *Life of Sukebatur* which was published in 1943, translated from the Mongol by Owen Lattimore and Urgunge Onon and included in Lattimore's *Nationalism and Revolution*, pp. 91–181, remains a key source for the life of Sükhbaatar. As Lattimore points out in his introduction, this was a 'political document', an official publication of the Mongolian state it emphasizes Sükhbaatar's role in the revolution and since 1991 Mongolian historians have attempted to redress the balance by publishing material on other revolutionary leaders; Lattimore, *Nomads and Commissars*, pp. 82–4, 86–91, 104–5; Onon, *Mongolian Heroes of the Twentieth Century*; Bawden, *Modern History*, pp. 201–37; Ewing, *Between the Hammer and the Anvil*, pp. 160–71.
16 Isono, 'The Mongolian Revolution of 1921', pp. 392–4.
17 Lattimore, *Nomads and Commissars*, pp. 84–91.

4 Mongolian People's Revolutionary Party in power: The Choibalsan years (1924–52)

1 Sanders, *Historical Dictionary*, p. 50.
2 Bawden, *Modern History*, pp. 328–80.
3 Baabar, *History of Mongolia*, pp. 326–7, 364–5; Bawden, *Modern History*, pp. 328–80, p. 338; Robert A. Rupen, 'The Buriat Intelligentsia', *Far Eastern Quarterly*, Vol. 15, No. 3 (1956): 383–98, reprinted in Sneath and Kaplonski, *History of Mongolia*.
4 Baabar, *History of Mongolia*, p. 227.
5 Baabar, *History of Mongolia*, p. 285.
6 Baabar, *History of Mongolia*, p. 285–8; Sanders, *Historical Dictionary*, p. 48.
7 Baabar, *History of Mongolia*, pp. 337–48, 349–56.
8 Baabar, *History of Mongolia*, pp. 353, 371–5.

Notes

9 Baabar, *History of Mongolia*, pp. 356–75, 375–82.
10 Saruulbuyan (ed.), *National Museum of Mongolia*, p. 170.
11 Saruulbuyan, p. 172; Baabar, *History of Mongolia*, pp. 201–5.
12 Saruulbuyan, p. 173.
13 Lattimore, *Nomads and Commissars*, pp. 114, 117.
14 Lattimore, *Nomads and Commissars*, pp. 84–91, 97–121.
15 Lattimore, *Nomads and Commissars*, pp. 102–3.
16 Lattimore, *Nomads and Commissars*, pp. 99–105.
17 Lattimore, *Nomads and Commissars*, p. 146.
18 G. R. Elton, *England under the Tudors* (London: Methuen, 1956), pp. 149–50.
19 Kaplonski, *The Lama Question*, pp. 3–4.
20 Kaplonski, *The Lama Question*, p. 5.
21 Kaplonski, *The Lama Question*, p. 5.
22 Onon, *Mongolian Heroes of the Twentieth Century*, pp. 200–16.
23 Baabar, *History of Mongolia*, pp. 285–8; Bawden, *Modern History*, pp. 288–301.
24 Bawden, *Modern History*, p. 308.
25 Baabar, *History of Mongolia*, pp. 285–8; Bawden, *Modern History*, p. 308.
26 Baabar, *History of Mongolia*, pp. 292–4; Bawden, *Modern History*, p. 290.
27 Saruulbuyan (ed.), *National Museum of Mongolia*, p. 176.
28 Bawden, *Modern History*, pp. 301–3, 304–15; Baabar, *History of Mongolia*, pp. 296–7, 304–9.
29 Bawden, *Modern History*, pp. 304–5.
30 Lattimore, *Nomads and Commissars*, p. 123.
31 Baabar, *History of Mongolia*, pp. 306–7.
32 L. Dügersüren 'The Policy of the New Turn Followed by the Mongolian People's Revolutionary Party and Its First Results (1932–4)', in *Forty Years of the Mongolian People's Party and the People's Revolution* Ulaanbaatar 1961, cited in Lattimore *Nomads and Commissars* p. 124.
33 Baabar, *History of Mongolia*, pp. 309–17.
34 Lattimore, *Nomads and Commissars*, pp. 122–47; Dügersüren, 'The Policy of the New Turn Followed by the Mongolian People's Revolutionary Party', p. 124; Bawden, *Modern History*, pp. 346–59, 304–15; Baabar, *History of Mongolia*, pp. 317–25.
35 Onon, *Mongolian Heroes of the Twentieth Century*, pp. 200–16.
36 Lattimore, *Nomads and Commissars*, pp. 122–47.
37 Bawden, *Modern History*, pp. 304–15; Baabar, *History of Mongolia*, pp. 296–7.
38 Svetlana Mironyuk (ed.), *Khalkyn-Gol 1939–2009* (Moscow: RIA Novosti, 2009), pp. 5–22; Bawden, *Modern History of Mongolia*, pp. 323, 339; Baabar, *History of Mongolia*, pp. 382–90.
39 Baabar, *History of Mongolia*, pp. 375–82; Bawden, *Modern History*, pp. 328–46 and *passim*.

40 Lattimore, *Nomads and Commissars*, pp. 148–69; Baabar, *History of Mongolia*, pp. 349–82; Bawden, pp. 328–46. The most comprehensive analysis of this can be found in Kaplonski, *The Lama Question*.
41 Baabar, *History of Mongolia*, pp. 349–82; Bawden, *Modern History*, pp. 328–46.
42 Kaplonski, *The Lama Question*, p. 231.
43 Morris Rossabi, *Modern Mongolia: From Khans to Communists to Capitalists* (Berkeley: University of California Press, 2005), p. 6.
44 Lattimore, *Nomads and Commissars*, pp. 148–69; Baabar, *History of Mongolia*, pp. 349–82; Bawden, *Modern History*, pp. 328–46.
45 Bawden, *Modern History*, p. 328.
46 Lattimore, *Nomads and Commissars*, p. 149.
47 Lattimore, *Nomads and Commissars*, pp. 148–69.
48 Baabar, *History of Mongolia*, pp. 349–56, 357–75, 375–82; Bawden, *Modern History*, pp. 187–201; Lattimore, *Nomads and Commissars*, pp. 328–80.

5 Post-War Mongolia: The Tsedenbal (1952–84) and Batmönkh (1984–90) years

1 Saruulbuyan, *National Museum of Mongolia*, p. 183.
2 Saruulbuyan, *National Museum of Mongolia*, p. 194; Baabar, *Yumjaagiin Tsedenbal* (Ulaanbaatar: Nepko, 2016), pp. 85–7.
3 Saruulbuyan, *National Museum of Mongolia*, p. 188; Baabar, *History of Mongolia*, pp. 410–13.
4 Baabar, *History of Mongolia*, pp. 410–13; Saruulbuyan, *National Museum of Mongolia*, p. 188.
5 Baabar, *History of Mongolia*, pp. 410–13.
6 Baabar, *Yumjaagiin Tsedenbal*, pp. 85–7.
7 Bawden, *Modern History*, pp. 325, 333, 375, 400; Baabar, *History of Mongolia*, pp. 375–8; Baabar, *Yumzhagiin Tsedenbal*, pp. 3–42, 111–70.
8 Baabar, *Yumzhagiin Tsedenbal*, pp. 101–5.
9 Saruulbuyan, *National Museum of Mongolia*, pp. 190–5.
10 'Mongolia's Progress', *Soviet Weekly*, 30 June 1979, pp. 6–7.
11 'Mongolia's Progress', *Soviet Weekly*, 30 June 1979, pp. 6–7.
12 'Mongolia's Progress', *Soviet Weekly*, 30 June 1979, pp. 6–7.
13 'Mongolia's Progress', *Soviet Weekly*, 30 June 1979, pp. 6–7; Ole Bruun and Ole Odgaard (eds), *Mongolia in Transition: Old Patterns, New Challenges* (London: Curzon Press, 1996), pp. 168, 206, 239.
14 Observations by the author, September 2016, and *Mongolian Observer* 26 April 2017, https://mongolianobserver.mn.
15 Lodon Tüdev and Tseyen-Norov Jambalsüren, 'Tsedenbal and His Legacy', *The Mongolian Observer*, No. 18, 7 September 2016.
16 Sanders, *Historical Dictionary*, p. xxxvii.

17 George Ginsburgs, 'Mongolia's "Socialist" Constitution', *Pacific Affairs*, Vol. 34, No. 2 (Summer 1961): 141–56.
18 Tüdev and Jambalsüren, 'Tsedenbal and his Legacy'; Baabar, *Yumjaagiin Tsdenbal*.
19 Robert A. Rupen, 'Mongolia in the Sino-Soviet Dispute', *China Quarterly*, No. 16 (Oct.–Dec. 1963): 75–85; Michael Dillon, *China: A Modern History* (London: I.B. Tauris, 2010), pp. 322–3, 342–4.
20 Rossabi, *Modern Mongolia*, pp. 6–7; Sanders, *Historical Dictionary*, pp. 197–9.
21 Sanders, *Historical Dictionary*, p. 20.
22 Rossabi, *Modern Mongolia*, pp. 6–10.
23 Ole Bruun, 'The Herding Household: Economy and Organisation', in Ole Bruun and Ole Odgaard (eds), *Mongolia in Transition: Old Patterns, New Challenges* (London: Curzon Press, 1996), pp. 66–7.
24 Bruun, 'The Herding Household: Economy and Organisation', pp. 66–7.
25 Sergey S. Radchenko, 'Mongolian Politics in the Shadow of the Cold War', *Journal of Cold War Studies*, Vol. 8, No. 1 (Winter, 2006): pp. 95–119; Szalontai Balazs, Tsedenbal's Mongolia and Communist Aid Donors: A Reappraisal', *Mongolian Journal of International Affairs*, No. 12 (2005): pp. 91–5.
26 Radchenko, 'Mongolian Politics in the Shadow of the Cold War', 95–119; Balazs, 'Tsedenbal's Mongolia and Communist Aid Donors', 91–5.
27 Observations by the author, 1990 and 2016.
28 Michael Dillon, 'Sinology in Mongolia', *Bulletin of the British Association of Chinese Studies*, (1991): 71–4.

6 Democratic Revolution: Mongolia after the collapse of Soviet power (1991–2019)

1 Saruulbuyan, *National Museum of Mongolia*, p. 200.
2 Rossabi, *Modern Mongolia*; Christopher Kaplonski, 'Democracy Comes to Mongolia', in Sneath and Kaplonski (eds), *History of Mongolia*, Vol. III (Folkestone: Global Oriental, 2010), pp. 1039–59.
3 Saruulbuyan, p. 203; Rossabi, *Modern Mongolia*; Kaplonski, 'Democracy Comes to Mongolia', pp. 1039–59.
4 Rossabi, *Modern Mongolia*, pp. 4–6; Kaplonski, 'Democracy Comes to Mongolia', pp. 1039–59.
5 Saruulbuyan, *National Museum of Mongolia*, p. 203.
6 Office of the President of Mongolia, 10 December 2014 http://eng.president.mn/newsCenter/viewNews.php?newsId=1382.
7 Saruulbuyan, *National Museum of Mongolia*, pp. 200–14; Rossabi, *Modern Mongolia*, pp. 4–6; Kaplonski, 'Democracy Comes to Mongolia', pp. 1039–59.
8 Saruulbuyan, *National Museum of Mongolia*, pp. 200–14; Rossabi, *Modern Mongolia*, pp. 4–6; Kaplonski, 'Democracy Comes to Mongolia', pp. 1039–59.

9. Rossabi, *Modern Mongolia*, pp. 4–6; Kaplonski, 'Democracy Comes to Mongolia', pp. 1039–59.
10. Rossabi, *Modern Mongolia*, pp. 1–29. Bruun and Odgaard, *Mongolia in Transition*, p. 23.
11. Ole Bruun and Ole Odgaard 'A Society and Economy in Transition', in Ole Bruun and Ole Odgaard (eds), *Mongolia in Transition: Old Patterns, New Challenges* (London: Curzon Press, 1996), p. 23.
12. Observations by the author, Ulaanbaatar, 1990.
13. Rossabi, *Modern Mongolia*, pp. 30–42.
14. BBC News, 11 July 2006.
15. Rossabi, *Modern Mongolia*, pp. 24–7, 49–50.
16. Rossabi, *Modern Mongolia*, pp. 67–79.
17. Rossabi, *Modern Mongolia*, pp. 88–96.
18. Rossabi, *Modern Mongolia*, pp. 90–1.
19. Rossabi, *Modern Mongolia*, pp. 80–114.
20. BBC News, 3 July 2008; *New York Times*, 8 July 2008.
21. BBC News, 6 November 2014.
22. Julian Dierkes 'Saikhanbileg Elected Prime Minister', *Mongolia Focus*, 20 November 2014.
23. D. Byambajav 'Speculation on a New Government and Factions in the Democratic Party', *Mongolia Focus*, 16 July 2012.
24. *South China Morning Post*, 24 June 2017.
25. BBC News, 8 July 2017; Lucy Hornby, 'Khaltmaa Battulga Wins Mongolian Presidency', *Financial Times*, 8 July 2017; Julian Dierkes, 'Battulga, What Kind of President?' *Mongolia Focus*, 27 July 2017; Marissa J. Smith, 'New PM and Cabinet, New Start with the IMF?' *Mongolia Focus*, 17 September 2017; Jessica Keegan, 'Beyond the Ballot – Mongolia's General Election Commission', *Mongolia Focus*, 16 August 2017.
26. http://www.phayul.com/news/article.aspx?id=39260.
27. http://en.kremlin.ru/events/president/news/55446 Bolor Lkhaajav, 'Previewing Mongolia's Presidential Election', *The Diplomat*, 26 May 2017; Julian Dierkes and Mendee Jargalsaikhan, 'Election 2017: Making Mongolia Great Again?' *The Diplomat*, 20 June 2017; AFP, Ulaanbaatar 'Anti-China Sentiment and Centuries-old Hostilities Take Centre Stage in Mongolian Election Campaign', *South China Morning Post*, 24 June 2017; 'S. Ganbaatar's Election Platform', *Mongolia Focus*, 9 June 2017.
28. Lkhaajav, 'Previewing Mongolia's Presidential Election',; Dierkes and Jargalsaikhan, 'Election 2017: Making Mongolia Great Again?'; AFP, Ulaanbaatar 'Anti-China Sentiment and Centuries-old Hostilities Take Centre Stage in Mongolian Election Campaign'; 'S. Ganbaatar's Election Platform',; 'Mongolia Welcomes Dalai Lama Over China's Objections', *Radio Free Asia*, 18 November 2016; *South China Morning Post*, 26 November and 22 December 2016; 'Neutral Mongolia Looks to Be Economic Link', *Global Times*, 8 November 2015.

7 Collapse and recovery of the Mongolian economy

1. Bruun and Odgaard, 'A Society and Economy in Transition', pp. 23–41.
2. Rolf Gilberg and Jan-Olof Svantesson, 'The Mongols, Their Land and History', in Ole Bruun and Ole Odgaard (eds), *Mongolia in Transition: Old Patterns, New Challenges* (London: Curzon Press, 1996), p. 20.
3. Rossabi, *Modern Mongolia*, p. 115 and pp. 30–42.
4. Rossabi, *Modern Mongolia*, p. 115 and pp. 30–42.
5. David Sneath 'Producer Groups and the Decollectivisation of the Mongolian Pastoral Economy', in Sneath and Kaplonski (eds), *History of Mongolia*, Vol. III (Folkestone: Global Oriental, 2010), pp. 1067–88.
6. Bruun, 'The Herding Household: Economy and Organisation', pp. 65–89; Rossabi, *Modern Mongolia*, pp. 114–31; Sneath, 'Producer Groups and the Decollectivisation of the Mongolian Pastoral Economy', pp. 1067–88.
7. Rossabi, *Modern Mongolia*, pp. 30–42, 43–80; author's observations in Ulaanbaatar, October 1990; Punsalmagiin Ochirbat, *The Time of Heaven*, Mongolia Society Occasional Papers, Historical Series, No. 28 (Bloomington: Mongolia Society, 2018), pp. 201–39.
8. Mongolian Embassy website www.mongolianembassy.us 21 May 2013; *CNN* website, 23 August 2016.
9. Neil Hume, 'Beneath the Mongolian Desert', *Financial Times*, 13 August 2018, p. 9; 'PM: Oyu Tolgoi Project Should Use Mongolian-produced Energy', *Mongol Messenger*, 2 September 2016, p. 2.
10. Bruun and Odgaard, 'A Society and Economy in Transition', pp. 23–41; Mongolian Embassy website www.mongolianembassy.us 21 May 2013; *CNN* website, 23 August 2016; Tuvshintugs Batdelger, 'Mongolia's economic prospects and challenges', *East Asia Foruum*, www.eastasiaforum.org, 23 March 2014; World Bank www.worldbank.org, 28 September 2017.
11. M.Chimeddorj, 'Practicing Stricter Financial Discipline Is Important to Beat Economic Troubles', *Montsame Mongolian News Agency*, 28 October 2016.
12. Chimeddorj, 'Practicing Stricter Financial Discipline Is Important to Beat Economic Troubles'; 'Bailing out Mongolia: A Wrong Direction in the Steppe', *The Economist*, 29 October 2016, p. 56.
13. Carole Pegg, *Mongolian Music, Dance, & Oral Narrative: Performing Diverse Identities*, Volume 1 (Seattle: University of Washington Press, 2001), pp. 253–5.
14. Interviews by author, Ulaanbaatar September 2016.
15. Lattimore, *Nomads and Commissars*, p. 174.
16. Tsultem, *Mongolian Architecture*, illustrations 180, 181; visit by author to the ger district in October 1990; Peter Geoghegan, 'Tens of Thousands of Rural Migrants Live in "Ger" Tents on the Edge of Ulaanbaatar', *Guardian*, 3 September 2014; Terbish Bayartsetseg, 'Social Exclusion in the Ger Districts of Ulaanbatar' https://blogs.ucl.ac.uk/mongolian-economy/2015/06/24/social-exclusion-in-the-ger-districts-of-ulaanbaatar;

David Lawrence, 'Mongolia's growing shantytowns: the cold and toxic ger districts' http://blogs.worldbank.org/eastasiapacific/mongolia's-growing-shantytowns-the-cold-and-toxic-ger-districts'; Lattimore, *Nomads and Commissars*, pp. 173–4.

8 Mongolia and the new East Asian order

1 Permanent Mission of Mongolia to the United Nations website, https://www.un.int/mongolia/mongolia/ulaanbaatar-dialogue.
2 Alicia J. Campi, 'Ulaanbaatar Dialogue on Northeast Asian Security', *Eurasia Daily Monitor*, 11 July 2014, www.jamestown.org; Permanent Mission of Mongolia to the United Nations, https://www.un.int/mongolia/mongolia/ulaanbaatar-dialogue.
3 Rossabi, *Modern Mongolia*, pp. 199—203; Lkhagva Erdene and Sergey Radchenko, 'The Mysterious Sale of Mongolia's Erdenet Mine', *The Diplomat*, 9 July 2016.; Ochirbat, *The Time of Heaven*, pp. 241–276.
4 Owen Lattimore, *Inner Asian Frontiers of China* (Boston: Beacon Press, 1962), pp. 167–8.
5 Bruun and Odgaard, 'A Society and Economy in Transition', pp. 37–41.
6 'Mongolia Reportedly Ousts Thousands of Chinese', *New York Times*, 26 May 1983; 'Moscow Defends Mongolia on Repatriation of Chinese', *New York Times*, 3 June 1983.
7 Gabriel Banama, Review of *Sinophobia, Anxiety, Violence and the Making of Mongolian Identity* by Franck Billé, *Mongolian Studies*, Vol. XXXVI, 2014, pp. 80–2.
8 'Mongolia Reportedly Ousts Thousands of Chinese'; 'Moscow Defends Mongolia on Repatriation of Chinese'.
9 Tsedenjav Sükhbaatar, 'Neutral Mongolia Looks to Be Economic Link', *Global Times*, 8 November 2015.
10 'Freight Train Service Linking N. China, Mongolia Launched', *Xinhua*, 27 March 2018.
11 'Mongolia-China Expo Great Opportunity for Mongolia to Diversify Exports to China: Official', *Xinhua*, 12 February 2019.
12 *Montsame Mongolian News Agency*, 12 September 2014.
13 Michael Lelyveld, 'China and Russia Eye Mongolian Gas Route', *Radio Free Asia*, 1 October 2018.
14 Rossabi, *Modern Mongolia*, pp. 207–14.
15 'Japan's Assistance to Mongolia', Embassy of Japan in Mongolia website, http://www.mn.emb-japan.go.jp/news/ODAenglish.PDF. Undated but data cited for 2007.
16 Rossabi, *Modern Mongolia*, pp. 214–19; Bolor Lkhaajav, 'Mongolia's Small Country Diplomacy and North Korea', *The Diplomat*, 29 September 2016.
17 Rossabi, *Modern Mongolia*, pp. 219–20.

9 The Mongols and China: Inner Mongolia and Ulaanbaatar's relations with Beijing

1 Lattimore, *Nomads and Commissars*, p xiii.
2 Lattimore, *Nationalism and Revolution*, p. 22.
3 Lattimore, *Nationalism and Revolution*, p. 29.
4 Interviews with Owen Lattimore, Leeds University, 1976.
5 Bawden, *Modern History*, pp. 1–39 and *passim*; Baabar, *History of Mongolia*, p. 9.
6 Colin Mackerras, *China's Minorities: Integration and Modernisation in the 20th Century* (Oxford: Oxford University Press, 1994), pp. 76–7, 121–2.
7 Uradyn E. Bulag, *The Mongols at China's Edge: History and the Politics of National Unity* (Lanham: Rowman and Littlefield 2002), pp. 141–8 and *passim*.
8 Poppe, *Grammar of Written Mongolian*, pp. 1–7; Legrand, *Parlons Mongol*, pp. 29–30, 47–53; Author's interview with Mongol language specialists, Göttingen, September 2014.
9 Observations by author during visit to Alxa, October 2001; www.alsm.gov.cn/main/.
10 Observations by author during visit to Alxa, October 2001.
11 Michael Dillon, 'Unrest in Inner Mongolia May 2011: Implications for Central Government Policy on Ethnic Minority Areas and the Career of Hu Chunhua', briefing paper commissioned by Europe China Research and Advice Network (ECRAN) for European External Action Service, June 2011.
12 Mackerras, *China's Minorities*, pp. 163–4; *China's Ethnic Minorities and Globalisation* (London: Routledge Curzon, 2003), pp. 46–7.
13 *South China Morning Post* (SCMP), 2 April 2005. The Southern Mongolian Human Rights Information Centre is an émigré organization based in the United States.
14 SCMP, 7 June 2011; personal observations in Inner Mongolia in October and November 2001 confirm this analysis.
15 Dillon, 'Unrest in Inner Mongolia'.
16 SCMP, 26 May 2011.
17 SCMP, 29 May 2011.
18 Southern Mongolian Human Rights Information Centre, website, 30 May 2011, 4 June 2011.
19 SCMP, 31 May 2011; BBC News, 30 May 2011; *Global Times*, 4 June 2011.
20 SCMP, 9 June 2011; *Global Times*, 9 June 2011.
21 SCMP, 31 May 2011; Xinhua (New China News Agency), 2 June 2011; 3 June 2011.
22 Interviews by the author in Mongolia and Kazakhstan, 1990 and 1994.
23 *Ulan Bator Post*, 9 June 2011.
24 Xinhua, 9 June 2011; *Peoples' Daily*, 16 June, 2011.

10 Looking back to the future: Mongolia's search for identity and the contemporary cult of Chinggis Khan

1. Author's observations, Gandan monastery, Ulaanbaatar September 2016.
2. Interviews with members of the Kazakh Academy of Sciences, Almaty, 1994.
3. Charles R. Bawden, *The Jebtsundamba Khutukhtus of Urga: Text, Translation and Notes* (Wiesbaden: Otto Harrassowitz, 1961), pp. 1–4; Baabar, *History of Mongolia*, pp. 71–3; Bawden, *Modern History*, pp. 9, 11–13; Gilberg and Svantesson, 'The Mongols, Their Land and History', pp. 21–2.
4. Jagchid and Hyer, *Mongolia's Culture and Society*, p. 67.
5. The Mongolian word *khüree* originally meant a 'compound' or 'enclosure', but by extension the enclosure that protected a monastery and then the monastery itself.
6. Gilberg and Svantesson, 'The Mongols, Their Land and History', pp. 21–2.
7. Pozdneyev, 'Mongolia and the Mongols, Presenting the Results of a Trip Taken in 1892 and 1893', , pp. 794–824.
8. James Gilmour, *Among the Mongols* (London: The Religious Tract Society, 1888), pp. 150–8 and *passim*.
9. Henning Haslund, *Tents in Mongolia* (London: Kegan Paul, Trench, Trubner, 1934), pp. 68–9, 154 and *passim*.
10. Haslund, *Tents in Mongolia*, p. 154.
11. Gilberg and Svantesson, 'The Mongols, Their Land and History', pp. 21–2.
12. Comparisons based on photographs taken by the author in 1990 and 2016.
13. Baabar, *History of Mongolia*, pp. 262–71; Bayanbat , *Ulaanbaatar Then and Now*, pp. 5–7 and *passim*; Bawden, *Modern History*, pp. 10–11; Tsultem, *Mongolian Architecture*, illustrations 161–200 (text not paginated).
14. Alan J. K. Sanders, *The People's Republic of Mongolia: A General Reference Guide* (London: Oxford University Press, 1968), pp. 16–31; Sanders, *Historical Dictionary*, pp. 99–103.
15. B. Amarsaikhan, 'Central Square Re-named after D. Sükhbaatar', *Montsame Mongolian News Agency*, 16 September 2016.
16. Sanders, *The People's Republic of Mongolia*, pp. 54, 67.
17. Observation by author during visits to Gandan monastery in 1990 and 2016.
18. Otgonsüren, D. Öndör gegeen Zanabazaryn khosgui ünet büteelüüd (An edition of this volume was published by Admon in 2015.); observations by author during visits to Chojin Lama Temple museum in 1990 and 2016.
19. Dulguun Bayarsaikhan, 'What's Happening on Chinggis Khan's Birthday?' *UB Post*, 29 October 2016.

Bibliography

Altannavch, D. *Bogd Khan Palace Museum: A Brief Guide*. Ulaanbaatar: Interpress, 2001.
Amarsaikhan, B. 'Central Square Re-named after D. Sükhbaatar', *Montsame Mongolian News Agency*, 16 September 2016.
Austin, William M., Gombojab Hangin and Urgunge Onon. *A Mongol Reader*. Washington, DC: American Council of Learned Societies, 1956.
Avery, Martha. *The Tea Road: China and Russia Meet Across the Steppe*. Beijing: China Intercontinental, 2004.
Baabar (B. Batbayar – edited by C. Kaplonski), *History of Mongolia: From World Power to Soviet Satellite*. Cambridge: White Horse Press, 1999.
Baabar, *Yumzhagiin Tsendenbal*. Ulaanbaatar: Nepko, 2016.
Balazs, Szalontai. 'Tsedenbal's Mongolia and Communist Aid Donors: A Reappraisal', *Mongolian Journal of International Affairs*, No. 12 (2005): 91–5.
Banama, Gabriel. Review of *Sinophobia, Anxiety, Violence and the Making of Mongolian Identity* by Franck Billé, *Mongolian Studies*, Vol. XXXVI (2014): 80–2.
Bat-Ochir, L. and D. Dashjamts. 'The Life of Sükhbaatar', in Urgunge Onon (ed.), *Mongolian Heroes of the Twentieth Century*. New York: AMS Press, 1976.
Bawden, Charles R. *The Modern History of Mongolia*. London: Weidenfeld and Nicolson, 1968.
Bawden, Charles R. *The Jebtsundamba Khutukhtus of Urga: Text, Translation and Notes*. Wiesbaden: Otto Harrassowitz, 1961.
Bayanbat, Bayasgalan. *Ulaanbaatar Then and Now: Amazing Images of Ulaanbaatar's History*. Ulaanbaatar: Monosound and Vision, 2013.
Bayarsaikhan, Dulguun. 'What's Happening on Chinggis Khan's Birthday?' *UB Post*, 29 October 2016.
Bell, Sir Charles. *Tibet: Past and Present*. London: Oxford University Press, 1927.
Bisch, Jørgen. *Mongolia: Unknown Land*. London: George Allen and Unwin, 1963.
Boldbaatar, J. 'The Eight-hundredth Anniversary of Chinggis Khan: The Revival and Suppression of Mongolian National Consciousness', in Sneath and Kaplonski (eds), *History of Mongolia*, pp. 1019–27.
Boldbaatar, J. 'The State and Trends of Mongolian Historical Studies', *The Newsletter* No.70, Spring 2015, International Institute for Asian Studies https://iias.asia/sites/default/files/IIAS_NL70_28.pdf.
Bruun, Ole, 'The Herding Household: Economy and Organisation', in Ole Bruun and Ole Odgaard (eds), *Mongolia in Transition: Old Patterns, New Challenges*. London: Curzon Press, 1996, pp. 66–7.

.Bruun, Ole, and Ole Odgaard (eds). *Mongolia in Transition: Old Patterns, New Challenges*. London: Curzon Press, 1996.
Bulag, Uradyn E. *The Mongols at China's Edge: History and the Politics of National Unity*. Lanham: Rowman and Littlefield, 2002.
Byambajav, D. 'Speculation on a New Government and Factions in the Democratic Party', *Mongolia Focus*, 16 July 2012.
Campbell, C. W. *Travels in Mongolia*, 1902: A Journey by C. W. Campbell, the .British Consul in China . London: The Stationery Office, 2000.
Campi, Alicia J. 'Ulaanbaatar Dialogue on Northeast Asian Security', *Eurasia Daily Monitor*, 11 July 2014.
Chimeddorj, M. 'Practicing Stricter Financial Discipline Is Important to Beat Economic Troubles', *Montsame Mongolian News Agency*, 28 October 2016.
Choibalsan, Kh., 'A Brief History of the People's Indomitable Hero Magsarjav', in Urgunge Onon (ed.), *Mongolian Heroes of the Twentieth Century*. New York: AMS Press, 1976.
Clunas, Craig. 'The Preface to Nigen Dabqur Asar and Their Chinese Antecedents', *Zentralasiatische Studien*, Vol. 14, No. 1 (1981): 139–94.
Dendev, L. *Mongolyn tobch tyyh* (*A Brief History of Mongolia*). Ulaanbaatar: Monsudar, 2012.
Dierkes, Julian. 'Saikhanbileg Elected Prime Minister', *Mongolia Focus*, 20 November 2014.
Dierkes, Julian, and Mendee Jargalsaikhan. 'Election 2017: Making Mongolia Great Again?' *The Diplomat* 20 June 2017.
Dillon, Michael. 'Sinology in Mongolia' *Bulletin of the British Association of Chinese Studies*, (1991): 71–4.
Dillon, Michael. *China: A Modern History*. London: I.B. Tauris, 2010.
Dillon, Michael. 'Unrest in Inner Mongolia May 2011: Implications for Central Government Policy on Ethnic Minority Areas and the Career of Hu Chunhua', Europe China Research and Advice Network (ECRAN) for European External Action Service, June 2011.
Dillon, Michael. *Lesser Dragons: Minority Peoples of China*. London: Reaktion Books, 2018.
Dondog, Shaman Byampadorj. *Reflections of a Mongolian Shaman*. Kathmandu: Vajra Books, 2014.
Dendev, Lkhamsurengiin. *Mongolyn tobch tyyh* (A Brief History of Mongolia). Ulaanbaatar: Monsudar, 2012.
Erdene, Lkhagva, and Sergey Radchenko. 'The Mysterious Sale of Mongolia's Erdenet Mine', *The Diplomat*, 9 July 2016.
Ewing, Thomas E. *Between the Hammer and the Anvil? Chinese and Russian Policies in Outer Mongolia 1911–1921*. Bloomington: Indiana University, 1980.
Fontein, Jan. *The Dancing Demons of Mongolia*. Amsterdam: V&K, 1999.
Frings, Jutta (ed.). *Dschingis Khan und Seine Erben: Das Weltreich der Mongolen*. Munich: Hirmer Verlag, 2005.

Friters, Gerard M. *Outer Mongolia andIits International Position*. London: Allen and Unwin, 1951.
Futaki, Hiroshi. 'A Re-Examination of the Establishment of the Mongolian People's Party Centring on Dogsom's Memoir', in Sneath and Kaplonski (eds), *History of Mongolia*, pp. 930–50.
Geoghegan, Peter. 'Tens of Thousands of Rural Migrants Live in "ger" Tents on the Edge of Ulaanbaatar', *Guardian*, 3 September 2014.
Gilberg, Rolf and Jan-Olof Svantesson, 'The Mongols, Their Land and History', in Ole Bruun and Ole Odgaard (eds), *Mongolia in Transition: Old Patterns, New Challenges*. London: Curzon Press, 1996.
Gilmour, James. *Among the Mongols*. London: The Religious Tract Society, 1888.
Ginsburgs, George. 'Mongolia's "Socialist" Constitution', *Pacific Affairs*, Vol. 34 No. 2 (Summer 1961): 141–56.
Goldstein, Melvyn C. *The Snow Lion and the Dragon: China, Tibet and the Dalai Lama*. Berkeley: University of California Press, 1991.
Grønbech, Kaare, and John R. Krueger. *An Introduction to Classical (Literary) Mongolian*. Wiesdbaden: Otto Harrassowitz, 1955.
Hangin, Gombojab, with John R. Krueger and Paul D. Buell, William V. Rozycki, Robert G. Service. *A Modern Mongolian Dictionary*. Bloomington: Indiana University Research Institute for Inner Asian Studies, 1986.
Haslund, Henning. *Tents in Mongolia*. London: Kegan Paul, Trench, Trubner & Co, 1934.
Haslund, Henning. *Mongolian Journey*. London: Routledge and Kegan Paul, 1949.
Howard-Jones, Norman. 'On the Diagnostic Term "Down's Disease"', *Medical History*, Vol. 23, No. 1 (1979): 102–4.
Hume, Neil. 'Beneath the Mongolian Desert', *Financial Times*, 13 August 2018.
Hyer, Paul, and Sechin Jagchid, *A Mongolian Living Buddha: Biography of the Kanjurwa Khutughtu*. New York: State University of New York Press, 1984.
Isono, Fujiko. 'The Mongolian Revolution of 1921', *Modern Asian Studies*, Vol. 10, No, 3 (1976): 375–94.
Isono, Fujiko. 'Soviet Russian and the Mongolian Revolution of 1921', in Sneath and Kaplonski (eds), *History of Mongolia*, pp. 910–29.
Jagchid, Sechin, and Paul Hyer. *Mongolia's Culture and Society*. Boulder: Westview Press, 1979.
Kaplonski, Christopher. 'Democracy Comes to Mongolia', in Sneath and Kaplonski (eds), *History of Mongolia*, pp. 1039–59.
Kaplonski, Christopher. *The Lama Question: Violence sovereignty and Exception in Early Socialist Mongolia*. Honolulu: University of Hawai'i Press, 2014.
Kapstein, Matthew T. *The Tibetans*. Oxford: Blackwell, 2006.
Langlois, John D., Jr (ed.). *China under Mongol Rule*. Princeton: Princeton University Press, 1981.
Larson, Frans August. 'The Lamas of Mongolia', *Atlantic Monthly*, No. 145 (1930): 368–78, reprinted in Sneath and Kaplonski, *The History of Mongolia*, Volume III, pp. 878–88.

Lattimore, Owen. *The Mongols of Manchuria*. London: Allen and Unwin, 1935.
Lattimore, Owen. *Mongol Journeys*. London: Travel Book Club, 1942.
Lattimore, Owen. *Nationalism and Revolution in Mongolia*. Leiden: E. J. Brill, 1955.
Lattimore, Owen. *Nomads and Commissars: Mongolia Revisited*. New York: Oxford University Press, 1962.
Lattimore, Owen. *Inner Asian Frontiers of China*. Boston: Beacon Press, 1962.
Lattimore, Owen, 'Introduction', in Urgunge Onon (ed.), *Mongolian Heroes of the Twentieth Century*. New York: AMS Press, 1976, p. xviii.
Legrand, Jacques. *Parlons Mongol*. Paris: L'Harmattan, 1997.
Lelyveld, Michael. 'China and Russia Eye Mongolian Gas Route', *Radio Free Asia*, 1 October 2018.
Lessing, Ferdinand D. *Mongolian English Dictionary*. London: Routledge, 2015.
Li, Yao. 'Lamas Dance with the "Devil" at Beijing Temple', *China Daily*, 12 March 2013.
Lkhaajav, Bolor. 'Mongolia's Small Country Diplomacy and North Korea', *The Diplomat*, 29 September 2016.
Lkhaajav, Bolor. 'Previewing Mongolia's Presidential Election', *The Diplomat*, 26 May 2017.
Lochin, Sonomin. *Tsendiin Damdinsurin*. Ulaanbaatar: Nepko Publishing, 2015.
MacColl, René. *The Land of Genghis Khan: A Journey in Outer Mongolia*. London: Oldbourne Book Co. 1963.
Mackerras, Colin. *China's Minorities: Integration and Modernisation in the 20th Century*. Oxford: Oxford University Press, 1994.
Mackerras, Colin. *China's Ethnic Minorities and Globalisation*. London: Routledge Curzon, 2003.
Magsarjav, N. *Mongol ulsin shine tyyh* (*A New History of Mongolian*). Ulaanbaatar: Monsudar, 2010.
Mironyuk, Svetlana (ed.). *Khalkyn-Gol 1939–2009*. Moscow: RIA Novosti, 2009.
'Mongolia's Progress' *Soviet Weekly*, 30 June 1979.
Morgan, David. *The Mongols*. London: Blackwell, 1986.
Munkhzul. A.'Scholars Share Views on Works of Ts. Damdinsuren', *Montsame Mongolian News Agency*, 22 October 2018.
Myagmardorj, D. *The Guide Book of Bogd Khan Palace Museum* (in Mongolian, Russian and English). Ulaanbaatar: n.p., n.d.
Newman, Robert P. *Owen Lattimore and the "Loss" of China*. Berkeley: University of California Press, 1992.
Nordby, Judith. 'The Mongolian People's Republic 1924–1928 and the Right Deviation'. PhD. Dissertation, University of Leeds, May 1988.
Ochirbat, Punsalmagiin. *The Time of Heaven*, Mongolia Society Occasional Papers, Historical Series, No. 28, Bloomington: Mongolia Society, 2018.
Onon, Urgunge (ed.). *Mongolian Heroes of the Twentieth Century*. New York: AMS Press, 1976.
Onon, Urgungge (translator and introduction). *Chinggis Khan: The Golden History of the Mongols*. London: Folio Society, 1993.

Ookhnoi, Batsaikhan Emgent. *The Bogdo Jebtsundamba Khutuktu: The Last Emperor of Mongolia, the Life and Legends*. Ulaanbaatar: Munkhiin Useg Publishing, 2016.

Otgonsuren, D. *Öndör Gegeen Zanabazarin Khostui Unet Byytelyyd (Masterpieces of Undur Gegeen Zanabazar)*. Ulaanbaatar: Chojin Lama Museum, 2015.

Parkes, Harry. 'Report on the Russian Caravan Trade with China', *Journal of the Royal Geographical Society of London*, Vol. 24 (1854): 306–12.

Pegg, Carole. *Mongolian Music, Dance, & Oral Narrative: Performing Diverse Identities*, Vol. 1. Seattle and London: University of Washington Press, 2001.

Phillips, E. D. *The Mongols*. London: Thames and Hudson, 1969.

Poppe, Nicholas N. *Buryat Grammar*. Bloomington, Indiana and The Hague: Mouton, 1960.

Poppe, Nicholas N. *Grammar of Written Mongolian*. Wiesbaden: Harrassowitz, 1991.

Pozdneyev, A. M. 'Mongolia and the Mongols, Presenting the Results of a Trip Taken in 1892 and 1893', excerpts from chapter 2, reprinted in Sneath and Kaplonski (eds), *The History of Mongolia*, Volume III, pp. 794–824.

Prawdin, Michael. *The Mongol Empire: Its Rise and Legacy*. London: Allen and Unwin, 1961.

Purev, Otgony, and Gurbadaryn Purvee. *Mongolian Shamanism*. Ulaanbaatar: Munkhiin Useg, 2006.

Radchenko, Sergey S. 'Mongolian Politics in the Shadow of the Cold War', *Journal of Cold War Studies*, Vol. 8, No. 1 (Winter 2006): 95–119.

Reckel Johannes (ed.). *Central Asian Sources and Central Asian Research*. Göttinger Bibliotheksschriften, Band 39, Göttingen: Universitätsverlag, 2016.

Richardson, Hugh M. *Tibet and Its History*. Boulder, CO: Shambala, 1984.

Rossabi, Morris. *Modern Mongolia: From Khans to Communists to Capitalists*. Berkeley: University of California Press, 2005.

Rupen, Robert A. 'Mongolia in the Sino-Soviet Dispute', *China Quarterly*, No. 16 (Oct.–Dec. 1963): 75–85.

Rupen, Robert A. 'The Buriat Intelligentsia', *Far Eastern Quarterly*, Vol. 15, No. 3 (1956): 383–98, reprinted in Sneath and Kaplonski (eds), *History of Mongolia*, pp. 950–65.

Sanders, Alan J. K. *Historical Dictionary of Mongolia*. Lanham, Maryland and London: Scarecrow Press, 1996.

Sanders, Alan J. K. *Historical Dictionary of Mongolia*, 4th edn. Lanham: Rowman and Littlefield, 2017.

Sanders, Alan J. K. *The Peoples' Republic of Mongolia: A General Reference Guide*. London: Oxford University press, 1968.

Saruulbuyan, J. (ed.). *National Museum of Mongolia*. Ulaanbaaar: National Museum of Mongolia, 2009.

Sneath, David. 'Producer Groups and the Decollectivisation of the Mongolian Pastoral Economy', in Sneath and Kaplonski (eds), *History of Mongolia*, pp. 1067–88.

Sneath, David, and Christopher Kaplonski. *The History of Mongolia.*
Vol. III, Folkestone: Global Oriental, 2010.
Sükhbaatar, Tsedebdav. 'Neutral Mongolia Looks to Be Economic Link', *Global Times*, 8 November 2015.
Tang, Peter S. H. *Russian and Soviet Policy in Manchuria and Outer Mongolia.* Durham, NC: Duke University Press, 1959.
Tsultem, N. *Mongolian Architecture.* Ulaanbaatar: State Publishing House, 1988.
Tucci, Giuseppe. *The Religions of Tibet.* Bombay: Allied Publishers, 1970.
Tüdev, Lodon. and Tseyen-Norov Jambalsüren. 'Tsedenbal and His Legacy', *The Mongolian Observer*, Edition No.18, 7 September 2016.
Tulku, Tarab. *A Brief History of Academic Degrees in Buddhist Philosophy.* Copenhagen: NIAS, 2000.
Vietze, Hans-Peter. *Lehrbuch der Mongolischen Sprache.* Leipzig: VEB Verlag Enzyklopädie, 1969.

The following newpapers and periodicals have also been consulted:

Economist
Financial Times
Global Times
Mongol Messenger
Mongolia Focus
Radio Free Asia
South China Morning Post
The Diplomat

Index

Abbasid Caliphate 14
aimag, 'province' 58
Alasha dialect 13
Alashan 167–8
Altangadas 133
Altan Khan 23
altruism 59
Amarbayasgalant 112
ambans,' Manchu officials' 50
Amdo 51
Anglo-Tibetan (Lhasa) Convention 50
annexe 6
anti-Bolshevik military intervention 63
anti-Chinese nationalism 61, 63
anti-Chinese sentiments 60, 62, 134
anti-clericalism 87, 90
anti-Manchu sentiments 59
Anti-Rightist Movement in China 107
Aramaic 13
architecture among Mongols 35–7
argal, 'dried animal dung' 21
Asian Development Bank 142
authoritarianism 112

Baabar,(B. Batbayar) 56, 74
Baarin 13
Baasanjav, Banzarjavyn 106
barbaric warrior 53–6
Barga 12
Batmönkh, Jambyn 113, 114, 121, 125
Battle of Khalkhyn Gol 92–3
Battulga, Khaltmaagiin 135
  and Putin 135–6
Bawden, Charles 11
Bayan Tumen. *see* Choibalsan
Bell, Charles 50
Berlin Wall 121

Blue History (Köke sudar) (Injanasi) 32
Blue Sky Tower 147
Blyukher, Vasily Konstantinovich 92
Bogd Khan 44–7, 56, 62, 68, 81, 110
  born in Tibet 45
  death of 46, 68
  head of state 52
  idiosyncrasies 47
  khutukhtu (khutagt) 45
  private idiosyncrasies 47
  Winter Palace (museum) 44, 46
Boldbaatar, J. 1
Boxer movement in China 19
Buddhist lamas 77
Buddhist ornamentation 48
bureaucratic oppression 122
Burkhan Khaldun 29
Buryatia 3, 9
Buryat Mongols 10, 12, 50, 74–5, 84
  migration 10
  and Mongols of Mongolia 10
Buryat Mongol Autonomous Soviet Socialist Republic 10
Buryat Republic 10
Byambasüren, Dashiin 126
bypassing capitalism 86

camels 169
  caravans 19–20
  travelling by 51
Capital City faction 84, 85
Capital Monastery 48
CCP Politburo Standing Committee 137
Central Asia 159–60
Central Committee's Department of Propaganda 54

centrally-planned economy 144
Chagatai Khan 13
Chahar 12, 13
Chahar Mongol 162
Chamber of Red Tears (Injanasi) 32
Chimeddorj, M. 146
China-Mongolia-Russia Economic Corridor 137, 156
Chinese commercial settlement 58
Chinese Communist Party (CCP) 3, 118
Chinese economy 18–19
Chinese Empire
  collapse of 43
Chinese farmers 19
Chinese-Mongolian ethnicity 134
Chinese Nationalist Party (Guomindang) 162
Chinese suzerainty 60, 63
Chinggisid Empire 2
Chinggis Khan 1, 13, 15–16, 110, 124
  eight-hundredth birthday 128
  Ejen Horo 16
Chinggis Khan Square 6, 57
Choibalsan 25, 48, 54, 57, 61, 62, 76, 90, 106
  canonization 73
  childhood 68–9
  dictatorship 94–6
  images of 100–1
  legacy 78–9
  Mongolia's Stalin 57
  succession to Sükhbaatar 70–1
  and Sükhbaatar 69–70
Choijin Lama Temple 18, 39–41
Civil Servants' Group 64
Civil Will Party 131
collectivization 86, 87, 91, 108, 140
collectivization of livestock 68
Comintern Special Commission 86
commercialization 6
Communist Party of the Soviet Union (CPSU) 85, 96
confidence building measures 153

Confucianism 29
Consular Terrace *(Konsulyn Denj)* 62
continental climate 20–1
Council for Mutual Economic Assistance (CMEA) 108, 115
counter-revolution 5, 121
counter-revolutionaries 97, 107
Cultural Revolution 3, 83, 119, 164
Cyrillic alphabet 13, 35
Czechoslovakia 139

Dalai Lama 23, 50, 52, 135
  in Mongolia 137
  Potala Palace in Lhasa 51
Dambadorj, Tseren-Ochiryn 73, 75
Damdinsüren, Tsendiin 33
Danzan, Ajvaagijn 73
Daoism in China 28
Dari 14
Demchukdonggrub 162
Demid, Gelegdorjiin 76
Democratic Alliance (DA) 128
democratic multiparty system 121
Democratic Party and its divisions 133
democratic revolution 5, 121–2, 147
  Battulga woos Putin 135–6
  China factor 136–7
  Chinggis Khan's eight-hundredth birthday 128
  Democratic Party and its divisions 133
  democrats in power 129–30
  elections 2008 131
  Mongolian Democratic Union 123–4
  Mongolian People's Party 132–3
  Mongolian reformers 127
  MPRP, back in power 131–2
  MPRP resurgent 128–9
  multiparty democracy 124–7
  Presidential elections 2017 134–5
  Zorig, Sanjaasürengiin 122–3, 130–1

Democratic Socialist Union 124
de-Stalinization 74, 106
De Wang 162-3
Dogsom, Dansrangiin 64
Dolonor 30
domestic stability 90
Dondogdulam 48
Dorjiev 50
Down's syndrome 10
duguilang, 'round robin' 162

East Asian order 151
  China, relations with 154-6
  Elbegdorj and Ulaanbaatar
    dialogue 152-3
  Russia, relations with 153-4
  Shanghai Cooperation
    Organisation 157
East Khüree 62
East Urga *(Züün Hüree)* 62
economic crisis 142-3, 145
Ejen Horo 15, 16
Elbegdorj, Tsakhiagiin 2, 122, 147
  Ulaanbaatar dialogue 152-3
electoral system 5
enemy classes 87
environmental degradation 140
Erdenebat, Jargaltulgyn 146
Erdene Zuu Monastery 36, 51
erroneous intellectuals 107
ethnic Mongols 9
Ewing, Thomas 43-4

Far Eastern Republic 65
feudal obligation 59
forced collectivization 75
Free Labour Party 124
Frinovsky, Mikhail 77
Futaki, Hiroshi 64

Ganbaatar, Sainkhüügiin 134
Gandan monastery 27, 49, 51, 112,
  137, 148, 176, 187-9
Gandantegchinling (Gandan) 27, 90

Gekker, Anatoliy Ilyich 92
Gelug. *see* Yellow Hat Sect
Gelugpa 23
Genghis. *see* Chinggis Khan
Gers 148-50
  and camels 169
Gobi Cashmere Factory 158
Gobi Desert 19
Golden Chronicle *(Altan tobchi)* 32
Goldstein, Melvyn 50
Gorbachev, Mikhael 113, 114
Great Leap Forward 3
Great Monastery 44
Great Wall network 15
Guangxu emperor 48, 49
Guomindang 3, 162
Gyatso, Sonam 23
Gyatso, Tenzin 23

Han Chinese 12
Hidden Imam 16
Highland Games of 1922 61
Horse nomads 21-2

Ikh Khüree (Urga) 44, 50
Independence Square 124
indomitable hero 53-6
industrialization 108, 111, 127
Injanasi 32
Inner Mongolia 3, 9, 161-2
  De Wang 162-3
  Gers and camels 169
  Inner Mongolia Autonomous
    Region 163-5
  language and literature 166-7
  May 2011 disturbances 171-2
  Mersé 166
  public response of Chinese
    government to protests 172-3
  religious institutions in the Alxa
    (Alashan) 167-8
  resistance, nationalism and
    development 169-71
  Ulanfu 165

Inner Mongolian Autonomous Region 9, 12, 161, 163–5
Inner Mongolian People's Revolutionary Party (IMPRP) 166, 170
Institute of Scripture and Manuscripts 59
institutional mechanisms for dialogue 153
Internal Affairs Committee 95
international financial crisis 146
International Human Rights Day 122
International Monetary Fund (IMF) 142, 145
Irkutsk 105

Jamsrano, Tsyben 73
Japan 4, 158, 163
Japanese invasion of China 77

Kalmyks 12
Kangxi emperor 30–1
Kanjur/Kangyur 32
Kaplonski, Christopher 83
Karakorum 11, 36
Kazakhs 12
Kazakhstan 116
Khalkh 12
  aristocrats 51
  Mongols 10, 18, 122
Khalkh Regular Service 54, 55
Khalkhyn Gol 93
khamjlaga, 'vassals' 81
Khanbalig 14
khans Batu and Orda 13
Kharchin 13
Kharkhorin 36
khar zud 'black disaster' 20
Khorchin 13
khoshuu 22
Khubilai Khan 14
Khujiburlan 60
Khural, Great 104
Khural, Lesser 98, 127

Khutkhtu, Dilowa 47
Khutukhtu, Jebtsundamba 45, 47, 51
khutukhtu (khutagt) 'high lama' 23–4, 45
Korea 159
Kyakhta 64–5

Lama Buddhism 17, 23–7
Lama Buddhists 11, 73
Larson, Frans August 45
Lattimore, Owen 4–5, 10, 15, 45, 47, 52, 54, 83, 87
leftist deviation 87
Lenin 124
Lenin Club 147
Letter 2452 86
Lhasa 50
Liberal Democratic Party, Japan 133
literary culture 31–4
livestock industry 131
Living Buddha of Urga. *see* Bogd Khan
loans by Soviet Union 153
Lundeg, Purevsuren 5
Luvsandorj, Khas-Ochiryn 106

Mad Baron. *see* Ungern-Sternberg, Baron
Magsarjav (1877–1927) 53–6, 60
magtaal, 'eulogy' 48
Manchu authority 45
Manchu Empire 59
Manchu Qing court 51
Manchu Qing dynasty 49, 161
Manchu Qing empire
  Mongols in 16–17
Manchuria 9, 104, 152
Manchu suzerainty 17
Manchu viceroy 55
Manjushir monastery 112
Mao Zedong 3, 83, 89, 118–19
market-fundamentalist policies 126
Marxist-Leninist ideology 134
Marxist terminology in Mongolian 67

mausoleum 73
May 2011 disturbances 171–2
Mersé 166
migration 22
Ming dynasty 15
Ministry of Non-ferrous Metallurgy 108
Molotov, Vyacheslav 93
monastic authority 82–3
monastic bureaucracy 82
Mongolchuud 11
Mongol Empire 13
Mongol 'hordes' 1
Mongolia 151
　anti-Soviet feeling 77
　built environment of capital 182–4
　Central Asia 159–60
　China, relations with 3–4, 154–6
　China reoccupies Mongolia in 1919 61–2
　Choijin Lama Temple 189–90
　climate and seasons 20–1
　contemporary Chinggis cult 191–2
　democratic revolution (1990–1) 43, 139, 149
　economic development 117
　Elbegdorj and Ulaanbaatar dialogue 152–3
　Gandan monastery 27, 49, 51, 112, 137, 148, 176, 187–9
　geography 3
　horse 21–2
　independent of Chinese control 44
　international and pan-Asian influences 193–4
　and Japan 158
　and Korea 159
　languages 12–13
　literary culture 31–4
　Magsarjav (1877–1927) 53–6
　modern economy and society 5–7, 12, 18, 19
　movement of herds 22
　nationalism 56
　party and partisans 66–8
　pastoral economy 22
　pastoral nomadism 19
　population 3, 9, 11, 12
　poverty in 139
　princely residence to Red hero 44
　reasserting identity 176–7
　regional power brokers 4–5
　Russia, relations with 153–4
　and Russia 3–4
　Shanghai Cooperation Organisation 157
　Sükhbaatar Square 184–7
　thirteenth Dalai Lama in 49–52
　and Tibetan Buddhism 25–7
　trade 20
　Ulaanbaatar 180–2, 187
　Ulaanbaatar in transition 190–1
　Ungern-Sternberg, Baron 65–6
　Urga 177–80
　and the West 157–8
Mongolian Academy of Social Sciences 59
Mongolian Affairs Commission 75
Mongolian Association of Sinologists 119–20
Mongolian Autonomous Government 60, 61
Mongolian Autonomous Republic 67
Mongolian Committee of Scientists 61
Mongolian Democratic Revolution (1990–1) 57
Mongolian Democratic Union (MDU) 122, 123–4
Mongolian development, funding 145–7
Mongolian economy 139–40, 153
　democratic Mongolia 143–5
　economic crisis 142–3
　funding Mongolian development 145–7
　Gers 148–50
　herding economy 140–2
　Ulaanbaatar 147–8

Mongolian General Election
  Commission 134
Mongolian Green Party 124
Mongolian Judo Federation 135
Mongolian Lamaism 12, 23–7
Mongolian National Democratic Party
  122, 124
Mongolian National Great
  Khural 127
Mongolian National University 78
Mongolian People's Party (MPP) 33,
  63, 128, 132–3
  Russian revolutionaries and 63–5
Mongolian People's Republic (MPR)
  2, 4, 9, 43, 57, 73–4, 79–82
  allied with Soviet Union 43
  anti-government demonstrations
    88–9
  Battle of Khalkhyn Gol 92–3
  Buryats 74–5
  Choibalsan, images of 100–1
  Choibalsan dictatorship 94–6
  Choibalsan's legacy 78–9
  class struggle, chaos and civil war
    87–8
  independence of 105
  Japan, threat from 91–2
  lamas 83–4
  member of WHO 11
  monastic authority 82–3
  Mongolian purges 77–8, 96–100
  national Mongolian army 59–61
  right deviationist 84
  rural opposition 84–5
  Seventh Party Congress 1928 85–6
  Soviet intervention 75–6
  Stalin's choice 76
  Sükhbaatar 58–9
Mongolian People's Revolutionary
  Party (MPRP) 4–5, 25, 53, 70,
    121, 144
  Central Committee 76, 103
Mongolian purges 77–8, 96–100
Mongolian reformers 127

Mongolian revolution (1921) 10, 46,
  52, 80–1
Mongolian revolutionary movement 61
Mongolian Revolutionary Youth
  League 73, 105
Mongolian shamanism 11–12, 17,
  27–30
Mongolian Social Democratic Party
  124
Mongoljin 2
Mongol Journeys (Lattimore) 15
Mongol lands 11–12
Mongols (Mongolians) 11
  aristocrats 18
  in Chinese Empire of Manchu Qing
    16–17
  inter-tribal rivalry 18
  Manchu banner system 17–19
  martial tribes 17
  nomads and warriors 14
'Mongolness' of Mongolia 109
Mongols, The (Morgan) 1
Mongols, The (Phillips) 1
Mongols and China 161–2
  De Wang 162–3
  Gers and camels 169
  Inner Mongolia Autonomous
    Region 163–5
  Inner Mongolian resistance,
    nationalism and development
    169–71
  language and literature of Inner
    Mongolia 166–7
  May 2011 disturbances 171–2
  Mersé 166
  public response of Chinese
    government 172–3
  religious institutions in the Alxa
    (Alashan) 167–8
  Ulanfu 165
Mongol xel, 'Mongolian language' 10
Mönkh-Orgil, Tsendiin 137
monks 25. *see also* Lama Buddhism
Morgan, David 1

Moscow-orientated Marxist-Leninist heritage 133
Motherland Democratic Coalition 128, 132
multiparty democracy 124–7
multi-party political system 139

National Academic Drama Theatre 113
nationalist revolutionaries 60
nationalist tendencies 110
national Mongolian army 59
National Museum of Mongolia in Ulaanbaatar 68, 88, 92, 121
National Progressive Party 126
Natsagdorj 33
negdel, 'cooperative' 141
　administration 141
　privatization 141
neo-liberal economic policies 151
New Progressive Union 124
Niislel Khüree (Urga) 44, 48, 55, 69
Ninth Incarnation of Bogd Khan 82
Nomads and Commissars: Mongolia Revisited (Lattimore) 5
non-Communist political grouping 122
Northwest Frontier Defence Army 62

Ochirbat, Punsalmaagiin 114, 126
October Revolution of 1917 63, 69, 74
Ögödei Khan 13, 36
Oirats 12, 105
One Storey Pavilion (Injanasi) 32
ongon 29
Ookhnoi, Batsaikhan 47
Opera and ballet 34
Ordos 13
Örgöö 44
Outer Mongolia 9, 11
ovoo, 'cairn shrines' 29
Oyu Tolgoi 144

pan-Mongolian independence 91
parliamentary structure 5
pastoral nomadism 19

People's Commissariat for Internal Affairs 76
People's Control Committee 110
People's Great Khural (*Ardyn Ikh Khural*) 125
People's Liberation Army 172
People's Republic of China (PRC) 3, 9, 52, 146, 161
People's Revolutionary Army 67, 89
Persian 14
Phillips, E. D. 1
pinyin, Chinese system of romanization 167
Poland 139
political authority 51
post-Stalin policies of the Soviet Union 103
post-war Mongolia 103
　Batmönkh 114
　China, relations with 118–19
　economy under Tsedenbal 114–15
　Mongolian association of Sinologists 119–20
　outside world 116–17
　pinnacle of power, changes 112–13
　referendum of 1945 103–5
　socialist construction in Tsedenbal era 107–10
　Tsedenbal 105–7, 109–12
　war memorial at Zaisan 117–18
poverty 139
Presidential elections 2017 134–5
Progressive Buryats 64
province of Qinghai 9
Putin, Vladimir 135–6

Qing court 44
Qing dynasty 1, 16, 17
Qing emperor 63
Qinghai province 52

referendum of 1945 103–5
religious institutions in the Alxa (Alashan) 167–8

Republic of Buryatia 12
Republic of China 61
revolution of 1921 9
right deviationist 84
rightists 107
right-wing opportunism 75, 86
Rossabi, Morris 114, 140
Rumania 139
rural opposition 84, 85, 86
Russian Federation 105, 153
Russian Red Army 56, 62, 65, 70
Russian Revolution 80
Russo-Chinese Joint Declaration of 1913 63

Saikhanbileg, Chimdeiin 153
secular aristocracy 87
Security Perspective of Central and Northeast Asia, conference 152
semi-autonomous Japanese Guandong 93
Seoul Street 6
Seventh Party Congress 1928 85–6
Shamanic rituals 30
shamanism 11–12, 17, 27–30
Shanghai Cooperation Organisation (SCO) 153, 157
Shigenori, Tōgō 93
Shumyatsky, Boris 65
'Sinologists' conference 143
Sino-Mongolian Agreement 109
Sino-Mongolian Agreement on Economic and Cultural Cooperation 118
Sino-Russian Accord of 1913 60
socialist and international culture 147
socialist construction in Tsedenbal era 107–10
socialist fiasco 87
socialist-type democracy 110
Sorokovikov, Innokenty 80
Southern Mongolian languages 12–13, 166

Southern Mongolian Human Rights Information Centre 170
Soviet Communist Party 74, 106, 114
Soviet cultural legacy 34–5
Soviet culture 7
Soviet-Mongolian friendship and cooperation 107
Soviet Red Army 76, 89, 95
Soviet satellite 147
Soviet-style collectivization 127
Soviet-style medical system 112
Soviet trade and aid 142
Soviet Union 3, 57
spiritual authority 24
Stalin, Joseph 69, 92
state-owned enterprises 140
State Planning Commission 111
stolid apparatchik 114
Sükhbaatar 46, 53, 58–9
  canonization 73
  and Choibalsan 69–70
  early years 58
  hero of Mongolia's battle 57
  succession to 70–1
Sükhbaatar Square 6, 128
sum-negdel 141
Szalontai, Balazs 116

tal 19
Tannu Tuva 105
tavan mal, 'five animals' 19
Tavan Tolgoi 145
taxation 73
Third Great Khural (National Assembly) 82
Tibet 172
Tibetan Buddhism 12, 23–7, 45, 51, 68, 82, 84
  scriptures of 31
  on writing in Mongolian 32
Timur 14
Tolui Khan 13
trading town 58
Trans-Siberian Railway 92, 96

Treaty of Friendship and Mutual Assistance with China 109, 118
Treaty of Friendship of 1921 67–8
Treaty of Kyakhta of 1915 60
Tripartite Agreement 63
tsagaan büree, 'conch-white trumpet' 80
tsagaan zud 'white disaster' 20
Tsam dances 30–1
Tsarist Joint Declaration of 1913 63
Tsarist Russia 3, 50
Tsedenbal, Yumjaagiin 77, 105–7, 109–12, 110
Tsedenbal-Filatova, Anastasia 112
Tsetsen Khan 58
Tsogtsaikhan, S. 122
Turkic Chagatai language 13
Tüshet Khan Gombodorj 38
Tuul River 46, 58

Ulaanbaatar 53, 57, 83, 119, 140, 147–8
  Sükhbaatar Square 73
Ulaanbaatar (Red Hero) 2, 5–6, 37, 44, 46, 48
Ulanfu 165
Ulan Ude 12
Ungern-Sternberg, Baron 46, 62, 65–7
  anti-Bolshevik White Guards 52
United Front 165
United Nations Development Programme 142
United States Treasury 126
unity 115
urbanization 111, 127, 140
Urga 44, 58
Uriankhai. *see* Tannu Tuva

Verkhneudinsk 65
Volga River 11

Voroshilov, Kliment 74

war memorial at Zaisan 117–18
Washington Consensus 126
Western market economists 142
Western-style government 46
Winter Palace of Bogd Khan 18
World Bank 126, 142
world conqueror. *see* Chinggis Khan
World Judo Championships 135

Xi Jinping 137, 156
Xilingol League 14
Xinjiang Uyghur Autonomous Region 9
Xu Shuzheng 61, 62

Yangjmaa 60
'yellow feudal' system 82
Yellow Hat Sect 23, 30
Yezhov, Nikolai 97
Younghusband, Francis 50
Younghusband expedition 52
Youth Cultural Centre in Ulaanbaatar 122
Yuan dynasty 15
Yunshan, Liu 137

zairan, 'high-ranking shaman' 29
Zaisan
  war memorial at 117–18
Zanabazar 37–9, 45
zasag, 'banner prince' 58
Zhangjiakou 19–20
Zhao Erfeng 52
Zheng Dingquan 119
Zhou Enlai 165
Zhukov, Georgy 93, 101
Zorig, Sanjaasürengiin 122–3
  death of 130–1

CPSIA information can be obtained
at www.ICGtesting.com
Printed in the USA
LVHW082127240521
688410LV00002B/15

9 781784 535490